Learning Less.js

Develop attractive CSS styles efficiently, using the Less CSS preprocessor

Alex Libby

[PACKT] open source✻
PUBLISHING   community experience distilled

BIRMINGHAM - MUMBAI

Learning Less.js

First published: October 2014

Production reference: 1201014

Published by Packt Publishing Ltd.
Livery Place
35 Livery Street
Birmingham B3 2PB, UK.

ISBN 978-1-78216-066-3

www.packtpub.com

Credits

Author
Alex Libby

Reviewers
JD Isaacks

Max Mikhailov

Mathias Paumgarten

Johan Sörlin

Commissioning Editor
Jonathan Titmus

Acquisition Editor
Neha Nagwekar

Content Development Editor
Arvind Koul

Technical Editor
Pratik More

Copy Editors
Dipti Kapadia

Deepa Nambiar

Stuti Srivastava

Project Coordinator
Neha Bhatnagar

Proofreaders
Ting Baker

Maria Gould

Joanna McMahon

Indexers
Mariammal Chettiyar

Rekha Nair

Priya Sane

Production Coordinators
Komal Ramchandani

Alwin Roy

Shantanu N. Zagade

Cover Work
Alwin Roy

About the Author

Alex Libby is from an IT support background. He has been involved in supporting end users for the last 18 years in a variety of different environments, and he currently works as a technical analyst, supporting a medium-sized SharePoint estate for an international parts distributor based in the UK. Although he gets to play with different technologies in his day job, his first true love has always been with the open source movement, and in particular, experimenting with CSS/CSS3 and HTML5. To date, Alex has written several books for Packt Publishing, including a video on HTML5 and books on jQuery UI. This is his seventh book with Packt Publishing.

I'd like to thank family and friends for their help and encouragement, Arvind for his help and guidance in writing the book, and the reviewers for providing lots of constructive comments with the reviewing—without them, I am sure I wouldn't have been able to produce this book!

About the Reviewers

JD Isaacks has been a software developer for the past 8 years. Before that, he was an information systems analyst in the U.S. Army. He is a devoted husband and father, and when he isn't spending time with his family, he loves to work on all things open source. He has published several projects including a very popular Sublime Text package titled *GitGutter*. You can view his work at `https://github.com/jisaacks`.

> I would like to thank my wife, Christina, for sacrificing many evenings to allow me to work on this book and all my other projects. I would also like to thank my son, Talan, just for being so awesome.

Mathias Paumgarten is a creative developer from Austria. He is currently living and working in Santa Monica, California.

Starting with a background in Flash development, Mathias found his passion for code-driven animation at a very young age. Over the years, while working for and at several agencies, he broadened his skillsets, leaving the web platform and working on installations, using low-level languages such as C and C++.

After graduating with a Bachelor's degree from the University of Applied Sciences, Salzburg, Austria, he decided to leave Austria. While focusing on modern web technologies such as HTML5 and JavaScript, he is currently working as a frontend JavaScript developer.

He has worked for several renowned agencies such as B-Reel, Soap Creative, and Firstborn, working on projects for Sony, Fox Entertainment, PepsiCo Inc., Google, HP, and many more.

As well as receiving recognition such as FWA and other awards, Mathias has also contributed to books such as *HTML5 Games Most Wanted, friendsofED*, and *Mastering openFrameworks: Creative Coding Demystified, Packt Publishing*.

Johan Sörlin is a senior application developer with 15 years of experience in web development. He cofounded Moxiecode Systems and has been the CTO of this company for the past 11 years. Here, he mainly works on open source projects such as TinyMCE, a rich text editor component used by thousands of systems.

www.PacktPub.com

Support files, eBooks, discount offers, and more

You might want to visit www.PacktPub.com for support files and downloads related to your book.

Did you know that Packt offers eBook versions of every book published, with PDF and ePub files available? You can upgrade to the eBook version at www.PacktPub.com and as a print book customer, you are entitled to a discount on the eBook copy. Get in touch with us at service@packtpub.com for more details.

At www.PacktPub.com, you can also read a collection of free technical articles, sign up for a range of free newsletters and receive exclusive discounts and offers on Packt books and eBooks.

http://PacktLib.PacktPub.com

Do you need instant solutions to your IT questions? PacktLib is Packt's online digital book library. Here, you can access, read and search across Packt's entire library of books.

Why subscribe?

- Fully searchable across every book published by Packt
- Copy and paste, print and bookmark content
- On demand and accessible via web browser

Free access for Packt account holders

If you have an account with Packt at www.PacktPub.com, you can use this to access PacktLib today and view nine entirely free books. Simply use your login credentials for immediate access.

Table of Contents

Preface

Imagine the scene if you will – it's 5 pm, late in the day, and your client wants the impossible…

You know the scene – you've created a kick-ass website, but the client isn't happy with the color of the buttons you've used on the site. They say the color shades used aren't quite there and need tweaking. A reasonable request, right? Except that there are dozens of buttons throughout the site, with most of them using different colors… Oh heck… no chance of an early finish then…

Or, is there? There is – what if we could change a handful of values and it automatically changes each button for you? Sounds crazy, right?

Wrong, it is absolutely possible. Welcome to the world of CSS preprocessors and Less! The power of Less means that we can set a couple of values that can be applied to any number of elements (such as buttons). Rather than having to change all of the buttons manually, we change the values and hit a button to recompile our code. Voilà! The code is instantly updated, and the buttons show the new color.

Throughout this book, we'll meet the Less library, learn how to use it, and apply its power to a number of real-world scenarios, such as updating buttons to build a complete theme for CMS systems, such as WordPress. We'll take a look at the subjects such as animating, color management, abstracting frameworks, and creating media queries for responsive sites.

It's going to be a great journey, full of twists and turns – the question is, are you ready? If so, let's make a start…

What this book covers

Chapter 1, Introducing Less, takes us through the roles that both HTML and CSS play, and examines the inherent limitations of using CSS as a technology. We begin our journey by taking a look at the role CSS preprocessors play and how using Less can act as a solution for some of these limiting issues.

Chapter 2, Building a Less Development Toolkit, is where we get to know Less for the first time, with a look at how we can incorporate it in our code, explore its syntax, and create some basic styles. We'll take a look at the different ways of compiling Less into valid CSS and why it is best to precompile code rather than use it dynamically in the browser.

Chapter 3, Getting Started with Less, delves into the wide range of tools and applications that are available and can be useful for working with Less; the chapter will provide some hints and tips on how to build an effective toolkit for working with Less, which you can integrate into your own development workflow.

Chapter 4, Working with Variables, Mixins, and Functions, continues from where we left off in *Chapter 2, Building a Less Development Toolkit,* with a look at one of the key concepts of Less, in the form of mixins. We'll take a look at this incredibly powerful tool, which will help you to save a lot of time when developing Less; we will also cover how we can create variables and functions to create our CSS styling when working with Less.

Chapter 5, Inheritance, Overriding, and Nesting in Less, examines how, with a little forethought and careful design, we can use the power of Less to create new styles based on existing ones, but without the need to duplicate the existing code. We'll also see how Less allows us to split style sheets into smaller, more manageable files, where we can group common styles together, making it easier to manage our development.

Chapter 6, Migrating Your Site to Less, contains the answer to the question asked by many developers when starting with Less: how can I incorporate it into existing sites? We'll take a look at some of the tips and tricks that we can use to gradually transition a site to use Less while still maintaining the existing CSS until it has been converted to its Less equivalent.

Chapter 7, Manipulating Fonts with Less, examines how, with some simple tricks, we can easily maintain any font style used within our site with the help of Less; we'll see how, with a little care and planning, we can make minimal changes that will quickly update font styles throughout the whole site.

Chapter 8, Media Queries with Less, takes a look at how we can use Less to quickly and effectively construct responsive sites using the power of media queries. We'll take a brief look at how media queries work and then move on to take a look at how we need to set expectations with clients and decide what should be supported, before using Less to build our queries.

Chapter 9, Working with Less in a CMS, takes us through how Less can be used to great effect when managing styles for any content management system available today. In this chapter, we'll use WordPress as our example to see how Less can first be incorporated directly in code or by using plugins. We'll then move on to the conversion process, with a look at how to transition a WordPress site to use Less, and how we can remove the need to manually compile styles with the use of a Grunt plugin.

Chapter 10, Using Bootstrap with Less, continues our journey through frameworks with a look at the popular Bootstrap system and how it uses Less to create its styles. We'll take a look at its file structure and some of the mixins it uses before configuring it for use on a demo web page as a part of developing a workflow for using Bootstrap with Less.

Chapter 11, Abstracting CSS Frameworks with Less, illustrates one of the pitfalls of using frameworks, where the supplied code can be nonsemantic and inefficient. In this chapter, we'll learn why frameworks aren't always the answer to everything and that they can make it hard to transition to a different solution if we want to change. We'll take a look at how we can use Less to help simplify complex styles, keep our HTML clean, and ultimately make frameworks work for us, and not the other way around.

Chapter 12, Color Processing with Less, covers one of the most important aspects of any website — colors! CSS styling can make maintaining colors difficult. In this chapter, we'll take a look at how we can bring the power of image processing to our CSS development with the use of Less. We'll also learn how, with a little care, we can begin to reduce our reliance on graphic packages such as Photoshop as part of our development workflow.

Chapter 13, Animation with Less, takes us on a journey to show how Less can be used to help simplify the pain experienced when animating elements and objects on a web page. In this chapter, we'll see how animations work, briefly cover the different types of animations available, and see how Less can simplify the markup, before taking a look at using our skills to produce a simple animated menu that could be used on any site.

Chapter 14, *Extending and Contributing to Less*, is the concluding chapter in our journey through the world of Less with a look at how we can give back to the project and help develop the library further. We'll see how to report bugs, where to find the documentation for the library, and contribute any code fixes or improvements to the library.

Appendix, *Color Functions in Less*, lists details of each function, within four groups of defining color formats, channeling colors, performing color operations, and blending colors.

What you need for this book

All you need to work through most of the examples in this book is a simple text or code editor, a copy of the Less library, and a browser. I recommend that you install Sublime Text—either Versions 2 or 3—as we will go through how to configure it for use with Less, both for syntax and compilation purposes.

Some of the examples make use of additional software, such as WordPress or Crunch!—the details are included within the appropriate chapter along with links to download the application from the source.

Who this book is for

The book is for frontend developers who need to quickly learn how to use Less in order to write CSS styles more efficiently with less code. To get the most out of this book, you should have a good working knowledge of HTML, CSS, and JavaScript, and ideally be comfortable with using jQuery.

Conventions

In this book, you will find a number of styles of text that distinguish between different kinds of information. Here are some examples of these styles, and an explanation of their meaning.

Code words in text, database table names, folder names, filenames, file extensions, pathnames, dummy URLs, user input, and Twitter handles are shown as follows: "In our example, we've added a reference to the Less object and then used the `modifyVars` method to change the color of the `@button-color` variable, which we've specified in `object.less`, to `#61783F`."

A block of code is set as follows:

```
header {
  margin-bottom: 25px;
  nav {
    height: 25px;
    a { color: white }
  }
}
```

When we wish to draw your attention to a particular part of a code block, the relevant lines or items are set in bold:

```
.shape1 {
  color: #5cb100;
  border: 1px solid #5cb100;
}

.shape2 {
  background: #fff;
  color: #5cb100;
}

.shape3 {
  border: 1px solid #5cb100;
}
```

Any command-line input or output is written as follows:

```
npm install -g grunt-cli
```

New terms and important words are shown in bold. Words that you see on the screen, in menus or dialog boxes for example, appear in the text like this: "Click on **Continue** to begin the installation."

 Warnings or important notes appear in a box like this.

 Tips and tricks appear like this.

Reader feedback

Feedback from our readers is always welcome. Let us know what you think about this book – what you liked or may have disliked. Reader feedback is important for us to develop titles that you really get the most out of.

To send us general feedback, simply send an e-mail to feedback@packtpub.com, and mention the book title via the subject of your message.

If there is a topic that you have expertise in and you are interested in either writing or contributing to a book, see our author guide on www.packtpub.com/authors.

Customer Support

Now that you are the proud owner of a Packt book, we have a number of things to help you get the most from your purchase.

Downloading the example code

You can download the example code files for all Packt books you have purchased from your account at http://www.packtpub.com. If you purchased this book elsewhere, you can visit http://www.packtpub.com/support and register to have the files e-mailed directly to you.

Errata

Although we have taken every care to ensure the accuracy of our content, mistakes do happen. If you find a mistake in one of our books – maybe a mistake in the text or the code – we would be grateful if you would report this to us. By doing so, you can save other readers from frustration and help us to improve subsequent versions of this book.

If you find any errata, please report them by visiting http://www.packtpub.com/support, selecting your book, clicking on the **errata submission form** link, and entering the details of your errata. Once your errata are verified, your submission will be accepted and the errata will be uploaded on our website, or added to any list of existing errata, under the Errata section of that title. Any existing errata can be viewed by selecting your title from http://www.packtpub.com/support.

Piracy

Piracy of copyright material on the Internet is an ongoing problem across all media. At Packt, we take the protection of our copyright and licenses very seriously. If you come across any illegal copies of our works, in any form, on the Internet, please provide us with the location address or website name immediately so that we can pursue a remedy.

Please contact us at copyright@packtpub.com with a link to the suspected pirated material.

We appreciate your help in protecting our authors, and our ability to bring you valuable content.

Questions

You can contact us at questions@packtpub.com if you are having a problem with any aspect of the book, and we will do our best to address it.

1
Introducing Less

Are you tired of writing the same old CSS styles for client websites only to find out that you're repeating yourself? Wish you could cut down on what you write and still produce the same results…?

Well, you can. Welcome to the world of CSS preprocessors, and in particular, Less! CSS preprocessors such as Less are designed to help you reorganize your styles to smaller, more manageable chunks of reusable code that you can store and reference as and when your projects demand.

Less, designed as a superset or extension of CSS, is very much about making your development work easier — it incorporates variables and functions that are more likely to be seen in scripting languages such as JavaScript while still compiling in valid CSS. While the initial thought of working with code might scare you, you'll see that Less is really just CSS, but with some additions to help make development easier. Less will help you cut down the development time, as you can reuse code from one project in another — how much is all up to you!

In this chapter, we will cover the following topics:

- The roles of HTML and CSS, and the limitations of using CSS
- Why CSS preprocessors are needed
- Why you should use Less
- The advent of CSS4, and what this means for Less

The role of HTML and CSS

If you spend time developing websites for clients, it is likely that you will have used both HTML and CSS to create your masterpiece.

HTML, created in 1990, has been the *de facto* standard for placing content on a web page. Over the years, it has evolved into what we now know as HTML5, which we can use to produce some very detailed websites or online applications. To use a cooking analogy, HTML is effectively the creation of the cake base; it is content that makes sense to any Internet browser. HTML forms the base of any website available on the Internet—it won't look very exciting, but it will have all the elements you need, such as headings, paragraphs, and images, to produce well-formed pages. Well-formed pages are made up of two elements: **accessibility** and **validation**.

Accessibility is the equivalent of building a new house, where we can add ramps or make doorways wider than normal to make it accessible for everyone. Basic accessibility isn't difficult or complex, but it must become a part of the development process; when left to its own devices, it will make it harder to move around the house, for those who need extra help to do so! In tandem with accessibility comes validation, which is very much like the Physics of cooking; if we work within the rules of validation, we can produce a masterpiece, while working outside of best practices is likely to lead to disaster.

It would be hard to produce a website without some form of decoration though; using HTML alone won't produce a very exciting effect! It's for this reason that we employ CSS to add final touches to our website, where we can tweak the positioning, add animation, or alter the colors of the elements on the page. Just as you can't build a house without cement, you can't produce a website without using CSS at some point in its creation.

Using CSS does not come without its limitations though—as it has evolved over the years, the support for its functionality has changed. One can argue that it has come a long way since its incarnation back in 1996, but at its very heart, it will always suffer from some core deficiencies. Let's take a look at these in more detail.

The limitations of using CSS

If you've spent time working with CSS, you will know the pain and heartache suffered when working with CSS—and all in the pursuit of creating that perfect site! Those who are still somewhat new to working with CSS will, at some point, fall foul of some of the limitations of CSS, which include:

- CSS is heavily dependent on browser capability—it is impossible to display the same content in every browser in the same way. We can get around this, but not without the expense of having to add vendor-prefixed statements. This can lead to pages with a lot of repeated code, making them slow and difficult to maintain, where even the smallest change requires a lot of effort.

- Not every browser supports every feature within CSS—this is particularly true of CSS3. This means we need to implement some form of graceful fallback for the affected browsers if we are to maintain some form of visitor experience.

- The advent of CSS made a functionality such as columns on a magazine website much easier, although it is still not perfect. To achieve perfect columns, we will require JavaScript or jQuery to tweak the code, which makes the page less accessible (for example, making it harder for those using screen readers). It also has an effect on the use of progressive enhancement, where content should be enhanced using a functionality, such as CSS3 or jQuery, and not reliant on it.

- It is impossible to target specific ranges of content, without altering the markup to include placeholders; should these placeholders change, then the associated CSS must also change.

- We can't include a rule from one CSS style in another, nor can we name a rule—the latter of which could be used by client-side scripts, even if the selector that is being referenced changes.

By now, you're probably thinking that it is all doom and gloom when using CSS; fear not, we can fix this with the help of CSS preprocessors to help make our development more effective.

The benefits of using CSS preprocessors

If you've spent time working with CSS, one of the first questions you may ask yourself is "Why do I need to use a preprocessor?" It's a valid question and you certainly won't have been the first person to ask this either! Let me explain this in more detail.

CSS is known as a declarative language—this means that the rules we use to declare what happens to an element will be the rules that the browser uses to paint the results on the screen. If, for example, we want a block of text, such as a printed comment, to be in italics, then we will use something akin to the following code:

```
.comment {
  font-style: italic;
  font-size: 12px;
}
```

The browser will then render this on the screen in 12 px italicized text.

This example is very straightforward—it could be used anywhere. The trouble is, we may need to specify the same styling attributes elsewhere. We could use the .comment class, but what happens if we want to change the size? Or, perhaps render the text in bold instead?

Changing the style rules to suit one element could break them for the original element, which is not ideal. Instead, we will need to create multiple style rules that apply to specific elements, but which duplicate this code—this could make for very verbose CSS! Just imagine that we end up having to create a selector such as the following:

```
.article #comments ul > li > a.button {
...some style rules...
}
```

This isn't an easy selector to understand, let alone apply styling to, right? We can eliminate this issue of duplication using Less—it is possible to set one style block at the start of our Less style sheet and then reuse this style at every instance in our code, in the same way as you might use the autotext function to add predefined text to a document in Word, based on a key phrase. If we make a change, we only need to do it once—Less will automatically update our code, avoiding the need to do it manually. Imagine doing this for the dozens of buttons you might have on an e-commerce site and the benefits will soon be apparent!

This might come across as an alien concept in CSS — after all, I am sure we are used to writing code manually and spending many hours perfecting it. You might well have some misgivings about using a CSS preprocessor to take out some of the grunt work, particularly as it is satisfying when you manage to achieve that stunning piece of CSS artwork for a client. It's perfectly natural — let's take a moment to consider some of the common misgivings about using CSS preprocessors.

Why not just write normal CSS?

Many people will often ask, "If we're producing CSS, why aren't we just writing it instead?" It's a common reaction; after all, we use CSS every day to solve any layout problem thrown at us while building beautiful responsive sites that work in any browser. The last thing we want is to not look like we know what we're doing, right?

Let me be clear from the outset: the purpose of using Less is not to write better CSS. If you don't understand how to use CSS now, then Less won't help you fill that gap. What it will do is help you write CSS faster and more easily, while making your style sheets more manageable at the same time. Let's explore some of the reasons why we should switch to using a CSS preprocessor, such as Less, in more detail:

- CSS preprocessors, such as Less, don't break browser compatibility — each CSS preprocessor produces valid CSS

- CSS preprocessors help to make our CSS **DRY (Don't Repeat Yourself)** — we can create variables from reusable CSS properties, which helps us to make our code more scalable and manageable, as we can break it down into smaller files that automatically compile into one larger style sheet

- CSS preprocessors, as we'll see throughout the book, contain some useful features that help remove some of the tedium that frequently appears when writing CSS styles, by automating some of the low-value tasks that have to be performed

- We can take advantage of the nesting capabilities of CSS preprocessors, which leads to a more natural style of writing, where we can use a form of shorthand to produce the desired effect

Now that we've explored some of the advantages of using a CSS preprocessor, let's delve in and get acquainted with Less for the first time. We'll go on a whistle-stop tour in order to give you a flavor of what to expect in Less. Don't worry if you don't understand it just yet; we will cover everything in more detail throughout the book.

Introducing Less as a solution

First created in 2009 by Alexis Sellier, Less is a dynamic style sheet language originally written to use Ruby; this was soon deprecated in favor of the significant increase in speed gained by rebasing the library in JavaScript. It is designed to be used by both the client and the server — the latter with help from Node.js, which we will cover in *Chapter 3, Getting Started with Less.*

Less was built as a superset of CSS, which means that it contains more advanced tools than traditional CSS. This allows us to write less code while still compiling it to valid CSS. The key to this lies in how we can use Less to produce better organized, more readable code. To see this in practice, let's take a look at a quick example of what we mean.

Imagine that you've written the following sample of CSS code — it's a perfectly valid CSS, even though it won't actually produce any useable results:

```
header {
   margin-bottom: 25px;
}

header nav {
   height: 25px;
}

header nav a {
   color: #151b54;
}
```

You might have noticed though that we've had to repeat ourselves a little, which is not ideal, but a necessary evil when writing such styles. The code is readable in our example, but if we had developed this to any degree, the repetitive nature of the selectors (such as `header nav div.first div.thumb .img-wrapper img`) could make it harder to follow the code.

One of the core concepts of Less is to use the DRY principle when writing code — we can take advantage of its **nested metalanguage** syntax to reduce the code by nesting our statements. If we take the previous block of code and reform it using Less, it will look as follows:

```
header {
   margin-bottom: 25px;
   nav {
     height: 25px;
     a { color: #151b54; }
   }
}
```

Here we compile to the CSS we've just seen.

Notice how we managed to reduce the amount of code we had to write while making the code easier to read, by grouping styles and adopting a more natural flow. Nested metalanguages are hierarchy based, where we can group related declarations together and reorder them in some form of hierarchy that abstracts each level while including the higher level. Less will naturally group these related declarations together, which is a great benefit if a CSS style sheet is edited by multiple individuals.

 If you would like to learn more about nested metalanguages, you may want to browse to `http://en.wikipedia.org/wiki/Metalanguage#Nested_metalanguage`. Note that it's a somewhat dry reference (pun intended!).

To prove that this does indeed compile to valid CSS, you can see the results of compiling the previous Less code in Crunch!. Crunch! is a CSS editor and compiler for Less, which we will cover in more detail in *Chapter 2, Building a Less Development Toolkit*. You can code in Crunch! as shown in the following screenshot:

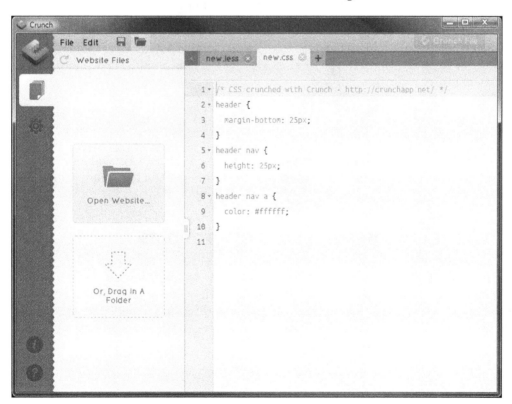

Don't worry if nesting code doesn't mean a great now — we will cover nesting in more detail in *Chapter 4, Working with Variables, Mixins, and Functions*. This is just one of the many functions in Less that will help revolutionize your CSS development. Let's take this a step further by delving into some of the reasons why you should use Less, in more detail.

Why you should use Less

We've already seen that Less is designed to help make CSS easier to manage and maintain. Let's explore some of the key features in more detail, which will give you a taste of what to expect with Less and demonstrate how Less can make writing CSS easier.

Reducing redundancy with variables

How many times have you worked on a website where you needed to declare the value of a color in CSS, such as #ececec? 10 times? 20 times? It's rare that you will get the color in the first time; it is more likely that you will need to revise it, which can create a real burden when working in CSS. No matter how many times it ends up being, one thing is true: it is not easy to remember the hex value for each color.

Less can help by allowing us to define colors as variables, with more memorable names. A variable is merely a mechanism for referencing a value; take a look at the following three examples:

```
@red: #de1446;
@blue: #4a14de;
@green: #32de14;
```

The beauty of Less is that once we've defined these variables, Less will automatically update any instance where they are used if we decide to change the hex values at a later date.

Understanding the syntax of variables

In Less, the @ sign indicates that we are defining a variable; following this (@) symbol, we normally have the name of the variable (with no spaces), and the colon indicates the end of the variable name. This is followed by the value, with a semicolon used to close the statement. In this case, the @red variable refers to the red color we want as a hex value. Once we've defined these variables, we can use them anywhere in our Less style sheet shown as follows:

```
.red-box {
  color: @red;
}
```

When we compile it, the following valid CSS is produced:

```
.red-box {
  color: #de1446
}
```

 In Less, compile just means to go from Less to CSS. We will use this term frequently throughout the book.

Writing and remembering variable names is far easier than remembering unnatural hex values, right? Moreover, when these values need to change, we only need to update them in one location and Less takes care of updating everything else. No more need to perform a "find and replace" when changing colors—this can be a huge timesaver!

Creating reusable blocks of code

So we've created some variables…but reusable blocks of code?

One of the benefits of using Less is that we can group together multiple lines of code and turn them into a reusable block that we can drop in our code. Let's take a look at an example:

```
.serif() {
  font-family: Georgia, 'Times New Roman', serif;
}
```

This is a very simple example of a reusable block of code, or mixin. If you've spent any time developing JavaScript or jQuery, then you may recognize a similar behavior in the form of classes; mixins work in pretty much the same way.

Mixins, by themselves, won't do anything and to make them useful, we need to call them from our code using a placeholder, as highlighted in the following code:

```
p {
  font-size: 10px;
  line-height: 1.25em;
  .serif;
}
```

This compiles to valid CSS:

```
p {
  font-size: 10px;
  line-height: 1.25em;
  font-family: Georgia, 'Times New Roman', serif;
}
```

See how, with just one short keyword, we've asked Less to drop in something more involved? One small point to note is the use of () against the mixin name—Less will compile the reusable code (or mixin) to valid CSS, but it will not render the compiled mixin on the screen. The great thing though is that we can simply call .serif; wherever we need to render text using the defined font-family attribute.

Generating values automatically

In more recent browsers, you are likely to find websites using RGBA (Red Green Blue Alpha) and HSLA (Hue Saturation Lightness Alpha) colors, rather than the typical hex values that we saw in the previous section.

Not every browser supports these color formats—to get around this, we can declare a hex value first, followed by its RGBA or HSL equivalents. As an example, we might write something similar to the following code in order to turn the text set with the h1 attribute to dark brown:

```
h1 {
  color: #963529;
  color: rgba(150, 53, 41, 0.5);
}
```

If we're choosing colors in a graphics package such as Photoshop or GIMP, we might occasionally struggle to get both the values and might need to resort to alternative means. Thankfully, this is not an issue with Less as it allows us to use functions to create new values automatically.

Why will we do this? The answer is simple: all we need to do is provide a color value using one format, such as RGBA. We can then use Less' functions to convert it to a different format—we can then avoid any confusion about ensuring we've provided the right values, as these will be worked out automatically by Less.

Let's take a look at a quick example of how this will work:

```
.brown-color {
  @rgbaColor: rgba(150, 53, 41, 0.5);

  color: fade(@rgbaColor, 100%);
  color: @rgbaColor;
}
```

Here, we've used a simple variable to define the base color before using the `rgba` color function to convert it to its RGBA equivalent value, with the alpha value set to `0.5`. If we compile the Less code, it produces the following CSS:

```
.brown-color {
  color: #963529;
  color: rgba(150, 53, 41, 0.5);
}
```

The alpha channel in our example is set at 50 percent. This means that we can see 50 percent of whatever is behind the color in the browsers that understand RGBA. The use of functions will really come into their own when creating themes for sites — we could potentially create a whole host of colors from just two to three base colors!

We will explore more about the color functions later in this book, in *Chapter 12, Color Processing with Less*.

Forgetting about vendor prefixes

The beauty about using CSS3 is that there's no need to always use images, when we can often achieve the same result using pure styling alone. Trouble is, catering to all these new features, such as background gradients, animations, box shadows, and the like, means that we often have to use vendor prefixes or different syntaxes to ensure that the site can be viewed by the widest possible audience.

This can be a real pain but not so much with preprocessors. As you will see later in *Chapter 4, Working with Variables, Mixins, and Functions*, we can create a mixin or a small block of predefined code that can literally be mixed in our Less style sheet and can be used to create valid CSS. Take, for example, the following block of code, which is used to produce rounded corners:

```
.roundcorners {
  -webkit-border-radius: 4px;
  -moz-border-radius: 4px;
  -ms-border-radius: 4px;
  -o-border-radius: 4px;
  border-radius: 4px;
}
```

With Less, there are hundreds of mixins that are available online (more of which we will cover later in the book), which we can use in our code. Instead of having to remember what each style needs in terms of prefixes and syntax, we can just use the following code:

```
.roundedcorners {
  .border-radius;
}
```

The preceding code produces exactly the same CSS that was once compiled; Less automatically adds all the vendor prefixes, which is a great time saver.

Creating media queries and animation the simple way

The advent of mobile devices has created a need for responsive websites, which will display content only if the rules meet a specific environmental condition or breakpoint. A good example is determining the size of the screen in use when browsing a responsive website.

This normally means having to write a number of queries for each breakpoint in a design. As an example, we could write the following (simplified) CSS to change the typography for a particular device:

```
@media only screen and (max-width: 529px) {
  h1 {
    font-size: 0.7em;
  }
}
```

```
@media only screen and (max-width: 949px) {
  h1 {
    font-size: 0.9em;
  }
}

@media only screen and (max-width: 1128px) {
  h1 {
    font-size: 1.1em;
  }
}
```

Even though this is only setting the size for the h1 attribute, it seems like a lot to remember. We can simplify the code using the power of Less:

```
@smallwidth: ~"only screen and (max-width: 529px)";
@mediumwidth: ~"only screen and (max-width: 949px)";
@largewidth: ~"only screen and (max-width: 1128px)";

h1 {
    @media @smallwidth { font-size: 0.7em; }
    @media @mediumwidth { font-size: 0.9em; }
    @media @largewidth { font-size: 1.1em; }
}
```

We start by declaring three variables, each containing the media query statements. These are static values and will only change if we decide to add or modify any of the supported breakpoints. It isn't essential to use them in this instance, but it will help make the nesting solution easier to read!

We then call each media query using @media, followed by the variable that contains the breakpoint we wish to test against. The key point here is that while it might look like @media is repeated, we can't base our nesting style on @media as the code will fail to compile. Instead, we need to base it on the h1 selector for the code to compile correctly.

Reusing code across multiple projects

One of the limitations of CSS is that we often find ourselves applying the same values across multiple elements, throughout each site that we build. On a small site, this is less of an inconvenience, but for larger sites, there is a greater risk that we may miss updating a value, which could produce unexpected results. We've seen how you can reduce (or even eliminate, with good planning), the risk using variables — what if we could *reuse* our code in future projects?

This is not as crazy as it might seem—we may develop a specific drop-shadow style for buttons that we like and want to reuse. The conventional way is to store this in a text file, database, or the likes, and then dig it out each time we need to reuse it. It's a cumbersome way to do it, even if it does work—the need to do this is eliminated if we use a preprocessor.

We can simply store the code in a file, in the form of **mixins** or reusable blocks of code. If we need to reuse any of them, we simply add the file to our project and use the following command to import the contents:

```
@import "mixinfile.less";
```

The beauty of using Less though means that it will only import those mixins that are needed for our project in the main CSS file.

Compressing CSS automatically for faster websites

So far, we've talked about some of the compelling features of Less—a fraction of what it offers—there is a lot more that we will cover throughout the book as well as taking a look at some of the more practical uses of Less.

There is one key thing to writing CSS that we've not mentioned: the ability to compress your style sheets as part of releasing your site into production. Compressing our style sheets removes white space and allows us to concatenate multiple files in one master CSS file.

Why should you do this? The answer is easy: it will make style sheets a fraction of the size of the original, which saves on bandwidth. While this is probably less of an issue for normal Internet connections, it is critical for those using mobile devices with limited bandwidth.

How will you compress your CSS? Sure, we could compress it using an online tool, but this means using an extra tool, which adds to your already busy development. There is no need to do this when using Less—if you compile your code using one of the GUI tools, such as WinLess, or even the command line, you can set it to compress the code at the same time.

This is just a taste of what Less can offer. Before getting up and running the development tools we will need for using Less, let's take a brief look at what CSS4 will offer and how this might affect preprocessor tools such as Less.

Supporting CSS4 standards within Less

With the advent of CSS2 and CSS3, it is natural to assume that CSS4 will arrive at some point in the future. You are probably wondering how it might affect CSS preprocessors — let's take a look at what CSS4 is likely to mean for Less.

Officially, there is no such thing as CSS4. Strange as it might seem, we won't see the appearance of a new global standard; CSS4 instead will be grouped under smaller headings, of which each will have its own level. There is still a long way to go, but one of the groupings that is closest to being finalized is CSS4 Selectors.

> You can see more details about the proposed changes for CSS Selectors in the W3C's draft proposal at http://dev.w3.org/csswg/selectors4/. There is an interesting discussion on the possibilities of using Selectors at http://vandelaydesign.com/blog/design/some-interesting-possibilities-with-css4/.

Although these have been around since the beginning of CSS, CSS4 brings a number of new logical operators, such as :not and :matches, as well as some new local pseudo classes in the form of :any-link or :local-link. The latter, in particular, brings some useful features to styling links, as shown in the following code example:

```
nav:local-link(0){
    color: red;
}

nav:local-link(1){
    color: green;
}

nav:local-link(2){
    color: blue;
}

nav:local-link(3){
    color: yellow;
}

nav:local-link(4){
    color: gray;
}
```

We can rewrite this using the following code in Less:

```
nav {
  &:local-link(0) { color: red; }
  &:local-link(1) { color: green; }
  &:local-link(2) { color: blue; }
  &:local-link(3) { color: yellow; }
  &:local-link(4) { color: gray; }
}
```

If we compile this code, we can see the results within a page that has a breadcrumb trail—take, for example, the URL as `http://internetlink.com/2014/08/21/some-title/`, and this in the form of a breadcrumb trail as follows:

- Home (`http://internetlink.com/`)

- 2014 (`http://internetlink.com/2014/`)

- August 2014 (`http://internetlink.com/2014/08/`)

- 21 August 2014 (`http://internetlink.com/2014/08/21/`)

- Article (`http://internetlink.com/2014/08/21/some-title/`)

The first link will be red, the second will be green, the third blue, then yellow, and finally gray.

Supporting future CSS standards within Less

Support for future CSS standards (or CSS4, as it is frequently termed) is still very much in its early stages within Less. Some progress has been made to allow the use of selectors in Less, which can be used with the ampersand symbol, as we saw earlier in the *Supporting CSS4 standards within Less* section in this chapter.

At the time of writing this book, the developers have refrained from adding too many new features for CSS4, as most of the current proposed changes are still in the draft state and are subject to change. The main feature added so far is that of support for attributes, which appeared in Version 1.4 of Less—others will appear once the specification has been finalized and support has appeared in more than one browser. The key thing to note though is that any CSS4 standard with CSS3 syntax is automatically supported in Less.

There will still be a need for Less once CSS4 standards become mainstream; Less will evolve to include the new standards while still allowing us to be more efficient when writing CSS.

> **How much support does my browser offer for CSS4?**
>
> As an aside, you may like to test your browser of choice to see how much support it offers for CSS4; browse to `http://css4-selectors.com/browser-selector-test/` and then click on **Start test!** to see the results.

Summary

In this chapter, we started with a brief look at the role of HTML and CSS in designing websites, and covered a few of the limitations that CSS has when styling elements on web pages.

We then talked about how CSS preprocessors can help solve some of these issues; we covered the critical question that people will often ask, which is, why we should need to use them when we are perfectly *au fait* with writing valid CSS. We then introduced Less as one of the preprocessors available and as a possible solution to some of the issues we face with CSS.

We then rounded up the chapter with a look at some of the reasons why Less should become part of your development toolkit, as well as some of the features available for helping you to manage your CSS development. In the next chapter, we'll start to take a more in-depth look at the syntax of Less and how we can compile it to create valid CSS.

2
Building a Less Development Toolkit

We've covered the principles behind Less, and saw how it can help reduce the effort required to manage style sheets with the use of variables, functions, and mixins. We're almost ready to start coding, but before we can do so, there's one small thing missing—we need some tools!

You might wonder whether there is a need for more tools, given that CSS is just plain text and that we don't need anything to edit plain text files, right? Well, plain text editors will work, but as we'll see in this chapter, there are tools available that include support for Less in order to help make editing files easier.

Throughout this chapter, we will look at a selection of tools that you may find useful for working with Less; we will install a selection that will be used for the purposes of the exercises throughout this book, although you can always pick and choose the packages you prefer to use.

In this chapter, we will cover the following topics:

- Choosing and installing an editor to work with Less files
- Watching out for changes to Less files
- Debugging in browsers
- Tools for compiling the Less code
- Automating the development using tools such as Node and Grunt

 The software that we install in this chapter will be for Windows, as this is the author's preferred development platform; comments will be added to indicate whether alternatives for Apple Mac or Linux are available.

Choosing an IDE or editor

We need to start somewhere, and what better place than an editor. After all, we can't produce anything if we don't have something that we can use to write it! Editing Less files is very easy—they are plain text files, which can be edited in almost any editor.

The downside is that there are dozens of editors available, either free or at a cost. However, there are some editors that have support for Less either included by default or available as an add-on package, which includes the following:

- **Sublime Text**: This is a shareware application for Windows, Mac, or Linux and is available at `http://www.sublimetext.com`; a license costs USD 70 at the time of writing this

- **Notepad++**: This is an open source editor for PC and is available at `http://www.notepad-plus-plus.org`

- **Coda**: This is available at `http://www.panic.com/coda` (Mac only); the license cost is USD 99 at the time of writing this

- **Codekit**: This is a shareware application that is available at `http://www.incident57.com/codekit`; license costs vary

There are more editors available; you can see a complete list of editors available at `http://lesscss.org/usage/#editors-and-plugins`.

 You might have noticed that I have not mentioned IDEs such as Dreamweaver. While these will work perfectly well with Less files, their method of working can affect the experience of learning how to write Less code effectively.

In the meantime, let's take a look at installing my personal favorite, which is Sublime Text 2.

Installing Sublime Text 2

Sublime Text is a shareware cross-platform text editor, which is available at `http://www.sublimetext.com`. Its popularity stems from an uncluttered interface that allows for easy editing, yet is equally powerful. Sublime Text comes with a Python-based API, for which you can write plugins.

To install Sublime Text, we can download it from `http://www.sublimetext.com/2`. Different versions are available for Apple Mac, Linux, and Windows; please download and install the version that is appropriate to your platform, accepting all defaults.

 The next version of Sublime Text, Version 3, is available at the time of writing this at `http://www.sublimetext.com/3`; it is in beta at present but is reasonably stable for use if you don't mind working with beta software!

Adding Less syntax support

Next, we need to add syntax support for Less, which requires several steps — the first of which is to install Package Control Manager, which is required in order to install plugins for Sublime Text. Let's begin by browsing to the installation page of the Package Control website at `https://sublime.wbond.net/installation#st2`.

We need to copy the code shown in the Sublime Text 2 tab, and then open Sublime Text 2. Once it is open, click on **View** and **Show Console** before pasting the code into the console. Press *Enter* to run the installation. Once you see the following appear in the Console window, restart Sublime Text:

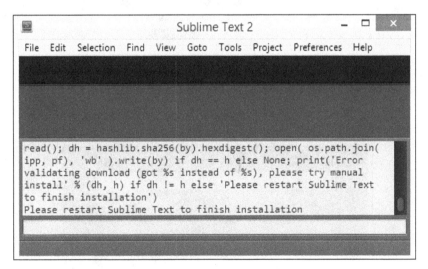

We now need to install syntax support for Less. For this, you will need an Internet connection, so you might not find it possible to do this while commuting, for example!

Assuming you have access to the Internet, go ahead and press *Ctrl + Shift + P* to bring up Package Manager, then type in **Package Control: Install Package**, and press *Enter*, as shown in the following screenshot:

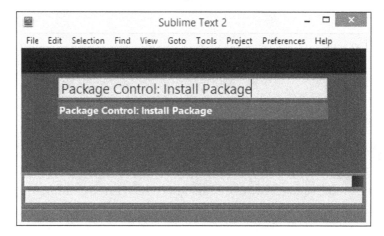

There will be a short delay while Package Manager retrieves the latest list of packages that are available; you can monitor their progress in the status bar.

Once this is retrieved, the package list will be presented; in the package name box, enter LESS, as shown in the following screenshot, and press *Enter*:

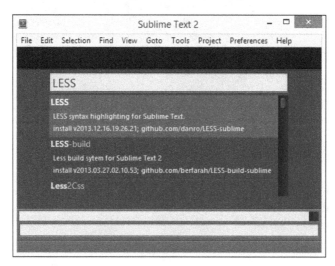

Sublime Text will now install the package. There will be a delay while it is installed; we can monitor its progress in the status bar at the bottom of the window. Once this is completed, you will see **Line 1, Column 1; Package LESS successfully installed** appear in the status bar. Syntax support is now installed—if we open up a test Less file in Sublime Text (such as `buttons.less`, from *Chapter 4, Working with Variables, Mixins, and Functions,* in the accompanying code download for this book), we can see that the code is now in color and not in black and white as before:

At this point, we're ready to start editing Less files—we still have some more tools we need to look at, though, before we have a complete toolkit! Once we've produced a Less file, we need to compile it into a valid CSS, so let's take a look at some of the tools that are available for this purpose.

Compiling Less files with a standalone compiler

Once we've produced a valid Less file, we need to compile it into its CSS equivalent. For this, we have two options: the first is to compile from the command line; we will examine this in more detail later in this chapter, in the *Compiling from the command line* section. The second is using a standalone compiler, for which we can use one of the following compilers available for this purpose:

- WinLess (http://winless.org/)
- SimpLESS (http://www.wearekiss.com/simpless/)

- Koala (http://koala-app.com/)
- Crunch! (http://www.crunchapp.net/)

Each of these compilers performs the same basic function of compiling Less files, but in different ways. I would suggest that you try each one out and stick with the one that you find preferable.

We must start somewhere, so first, let's take a look at WinLess.

WinLess

WinLess is a Windows-based open source GUI frontend for less.js, which can be downloaded from http://winless.org/downloads/WinLess-1.8.2.msi. This includes an option to automatically monitor changes to any files stored within specific folders; as soon as they are changed, the corresponding CSS files are updated.

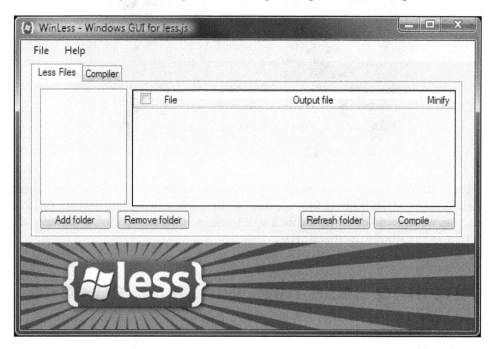

SimpLESS

If something that is a little simpler is sufficient for your needs, then you can always try SimpLESS, which is a cut-down version available for Windows, Apple Mac, or Linux platforms.

You can download this from `http://www.wearekiss.com/simpless`; it is designed to sit and work from the system tray, silently updating any changed Less files.

Koala

Koala is a relative newcomer to the Less preprocessor scene. It is a cross-platform GUI application that compiles most CSS preprocessors available, including Less. It was built using Node-Webkit, so versions are available for Mac OS, Linux, and Windows and can be downloaded from `http://www.koala-app.com/`.

You can find details of other compilers available for use with Less by browsing to `http://lesscss.org/usage/#guis-for-less`. In the meantime, we're going to move on and install Crunch!, as an example of one of the compilers available for Less.

Installing Crunch!

Crunch! is a cross-platform compiler for Less, which works using Adobe AIR. This compiler is different from the others, as it allows us to edit files within the compiler directly.

Installing Crunch! is a two-part process; we begin with installing Adobe AIR:

1. Download the installer from `http://get.adobe.com/air/`, making sure that you select the right version for your platform. Double-click on the AIR installer and accept all defaults.

2. Next, go ahead and download Crunch! from `http://www.crunchapp.net`. Double-click on the **Crunch.1.6.4.air** package, and then click on the **Install** button at this prompt.

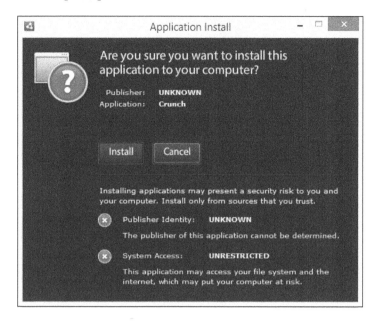

3. Click on **Continue** to begin the installation; we can leave the default settings untouched, as they will suffice for our needs:

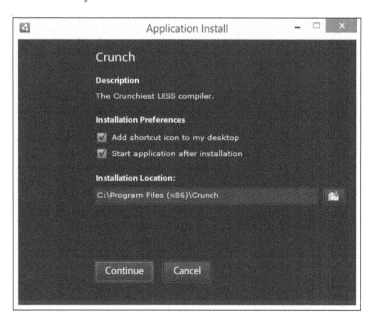

4. After a few minutes, Crunch!'s GUI will appear, ready for use, as shown in this screenshot:

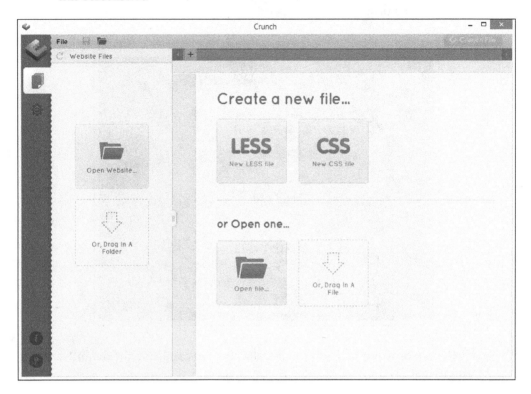

Compiling from the command line

Some of you might prefer not to have to use a standalone application to compile Less code task; after all, who needs to learn yet another application in order to perform a task that can easily be automated and run in the background, right?

Absolutely; instead of using a standalone compiler, we can use the command line to perform the same operation using the JavaScript-based platform, which is Node.js, available at http://www.nodejs.org. Versions of this application are available for the Windows, Linux, Mac, and even SunOS platforms. Otherwise, you can always try compiling from the source if you are feeling adventurous! Let's take a look at how we can use this in more detail.

To download and install Node.js, perform the following steps:

1. Browse `http://www.nodejs.org`, and click on **Download** from the main page; this should automatically determine the right version for your platform. At the time of writing this, the latest version for Windows is `node-v0.10.24-x86.msi`.

2. Double-click on the installer to begin the process; you will see the following welcome screen. Click on **Next**.

3. On the next screen, select the **I accept the terms in the License Agreement** checkbox, and then click on **Next**.

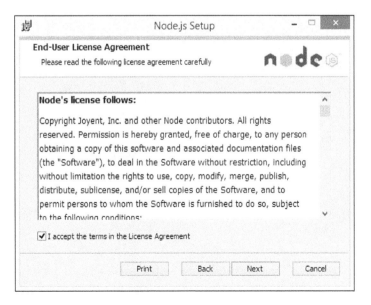

4. At this point, we need to choose the location for where we will install Node. For the purposes of this book, we will assume that it will be installed in the default location of c:\wamp, so go ahead and click on **Next**.

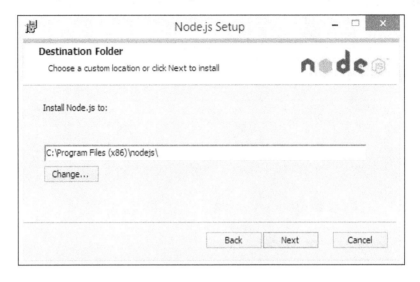

5. On the next screen, you can select from a number of options in order to configure Node. This isn't necessary for the purposes of running the exercises in this book, so we will simply click on **Next**.

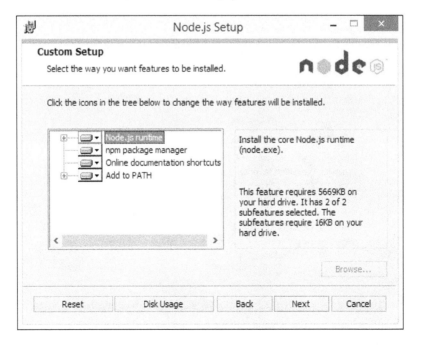

We're now ready to complete the installation, so click on **Install**, and wait for it to complete. Once this is completed, Node is installed and is ready for us to use. We are now ready to install Less for the command line, which we will cover in the next chapter, which is *Chapter 3, Getting Started with Less*.

> If you are interested in learning more about Node.js, then you might like to peruse the book *Mastering Node.js, Sandro Pasquali*, published by *Packt Publishing*.

Watching for changes to Less files

As we will see in the next chapter, it is a simple process to compile Less from the command line; we can open a command prompt, type in a simple command, and then press *Enter* to let it run.

The trouble is that we have to do this every time. After a while, this will get tedious, to say the least! It's something we can easily fix—we first need to install Grunt's command-line interface before taking it a step further by setting Grunt to automatically watch out for, and recompile, any changes to our Less source files.

> There is an alternative watch mode available in Less, called **Watch**. This still requires manual work to configure it; we will take a look at it in more detail in *Chapter 3, Getting Started with Less*.

In the following example, we'll add support for Less by installing a package called `grunt-contrib-less`. Let's start by creating a folder for our project at the root of the C: drive, called `lessjs`. Within this folder, create a new file called `package.json`, and add the following code:

```
{
    "name": "my_grunt_project",
    "version": "0.0.1",
    "devDependencies": {

    }
}
```

Next, fire up a command prompt and enter the following command:

```
npm install -g grunt --save-dev
```

This will download and install a number of additional packages; the `--save-dev` parameter will add any dependencies to the `package.json` file automatically.

If we take a look at the `lessjs` folder, we will see our `package.json` file; if we open it in a text editor, it will look something like this code:

```
{
  "name": "my-project-name",
  "version": "0.1.0",
  "devDependencies": {
    "grunt": "~0.4.2",
    "grunt-contrib-less": "~0.8.3",
    "grunt-contrib-watch": "~0.5.3"
  }
}
```

If the download is complete with no errors recorded, then run this command:

```
npm install -g grunt-cli
```

Add the following code to a new file, and save it in the project folder as `gruntfile.js`. We will go through the file in sections in order to understand what each part does:

```
module.exports = function(grunt) {
  grunt.initConfig({
    less: {
      src: {
        expand: true,
        src:      "*.less",
        ext:      ".css"
      }
    }
  },
```

We start the file with a standard Grunt `exports` statement; here, we initialize Grunt by setting `src` to look for Less files and compile them into CSS files. We've set Grunt to not compress the CSS files when compiled using the `expand` attribute, which is set to `true`. This makes them easy to read while we are still developing, although in reality, we will look to compress the files in a production environment in order to save on bandwidth:

```
watch: {
  styles: {
    options: { spawn: false },
    files: [ "*.css", "*.less"],
```

```
            tasks: [ "less" ]
        }
    }
});
```

As we are defining more than one task, we would ordinarily have to enter the tasks at the command prompt individually. Instead, we can combine all of the subtasks that we define. We can then run them as default when entering the command grunt at the command line, which help saves time:

```
    grunt.loadNpmTasks('grunt-contrib-less');
    grunt.loadNpmTasks('grunt-contrib-watch');

    // the default task can be run just
    // by typing "grunt" on the command line
    grunt.registerTask('default', ['watch']);
};
```

Start a command prompt, switch to the project folder, and enter npm install at the command prompt. This will download and install a number of additional packages. When this is complete, enter grunt at the command prompt. Grunt will begin watching for any changes, as shown in this example:

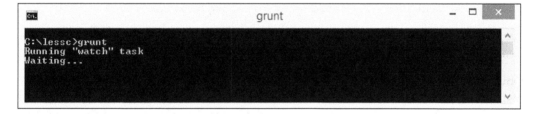

Any changes made will force an automatic recompilation of the Less file.

 If you would like to dig into the source code for these packages, then you will find many of them on GitHub at https://github.com/gruntjs.

As time moves on, and you become more accustomed to developing with Less, you might like to try some of the other watcher packages that are available from the Node Package Manager website at `https://npmjs.org`, such as the following examples:

- less watch (available at `https://npmjs.org/package/less-watch`)
- less monitor (available at `https://npmjs.org/package/less-monitor`)
- less watcher (available at `https://npmjs.org/package/lesswatcher`)

Now that we have Less installed and compiled automatically using Grunt, we can skip to the next chapter in order to create some files in our normal text editor, and then compile them manually. This will work perfectly well, but we can automate the compilation process even further. Let's see how we can do this by adding support to a text editor such as Notepad++ so that we can compile the files directly from within the editor.

Compiling Less files directly from text editors

There are hundreds of text editors available for use; some are free or open source, while others will be available at a cost. A good example of a free editor is Notepad++; the current version is 6.5.3 at the time of writing this and can be downloaded from `http://notepad-plus-plus.org/download/v6.5.3.html`.

For now, we'll get it set up and ready for use. You will see it in action in *Chapter 3, Getting Started with Less*, when we use it to compile code from the editor.

Download the installer for Notepad++, and then double-click on it to launch the installation process. Click on **Next** to accept each default setting, which will suffice for our needs. When the installation is complete, start Notepad++, and then click on **Run** from the **Run** menu in order to launch the **Run** dialog, and add the following line (including the quotes):

```
"C:\Program Files (x86)\nodejs\node_modules\.bin\lessc.cmd" -x
"$(FULL_CURRENT_PATH)" > "$(CURRENT_DIRECTORY)\$(NAME_PART).css"
```

Click on **Save** to add the run command to the list of existing preset commands; in the **Shortcut** dialog, choose the **CTRL + L** shortcut and add `Compile LESS files` for the command, and then click on **OK**.

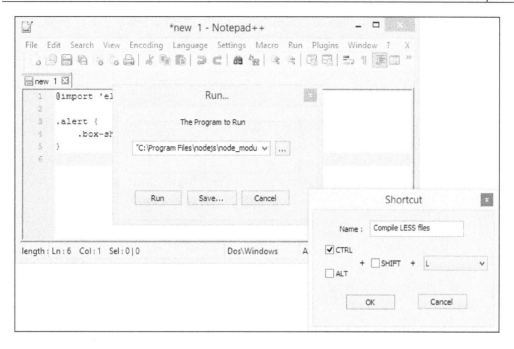

When the **Shortcut** window is closed, click on **Save** to save the changes. For now, click on **Cancel** to close the window. We're not ready to run our shortcut yet—this will happen in the next chapter. Notepad++ is now set up so that we are ready to compile any changes to Less files from within the application.

Installing the compilation support via a package

So far, we've seen how you can set up an editor such as Notepad++, but we're not limited to having to wire up every editor using this technique. For some editors, an extension or package has already been created for this purpose, so the installation will be simplified. One such example is Sublime Text—there is a package that exists, which we can install in order to provide support for Less.

Start by firing up Sublime Text, and then press *Shift + Ctrl + P* to bring up Package Manager, which we installed earlier in this chapter, and then enter Package Control: Install Package and press *Enter*.

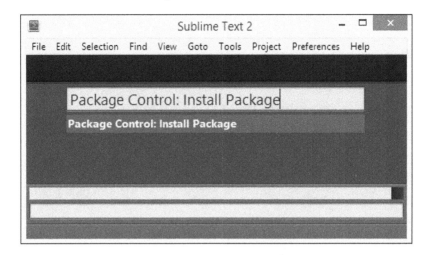

Next, enter lesscss—we need to install the Less2CSS package, so when this appears in the autocomplete, click on it and press *Enter*:

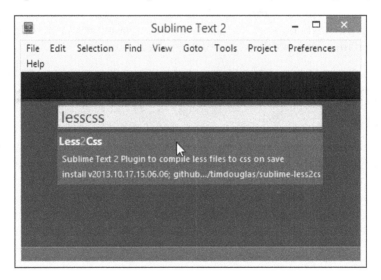

At this point, Sublime Text will install the package, which will take a few moments—the confirmation will appear in the status bar when it is successfully installed. We're now ready to compile Less files directly from within Sublime Text—we'll be using this feature in the next chapter.

Debugging Less in browsers

A key part of developing code of any description is the fixing of any errors or bugs; working with Less code is no exception. We can, of course, do this manually or use a linting tool such as CSS Lint (`http://www.csslint.net`), but either is likely to require working directly with the compiled CSS code, which will make it harder to trace a fault back to your existing Less code.

Fortunately, we have a couple of options that will help in this respect—we can either debug directly in Firefox using the FireLESS plugin, or we can set up a source map that will translate a compiled style back to the line number in the original Less file. Let's take a look at installing FireLESS first and get ready for when we start developing code in the next chapter.

Debugging the Less code using Firefox

To enable support for debugging Less in Firefox, we first need to ensure that Firebug is installed; for this, you can download it from `https://addons.mozilla.org/en-US/firefox/addon/firebug` using the normal installation process for Firefox add-ins.

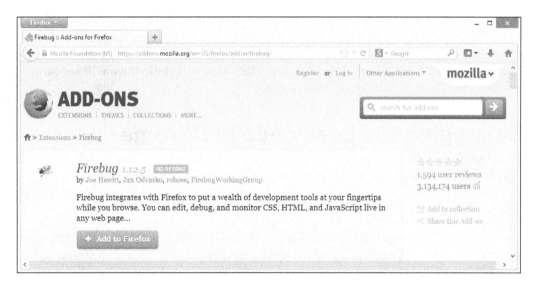

At the time of writing this, the latest version of Firebug is 1.12.5, which will work for Firefox Versions 23 to 26. The installation process is painless and does not require a restart of your browser.

Next, we need to install FireLESS. First, browse to `https://addons.mozilla.org/en-us/firefox/addon/fireless/`, and then click on **Add to Firefox** to initiate the installation. You might get a prompt to allow Firefox to install Firebug—click on **Allow**. After Firefox has downloaded the plugin, click on **Install Now** (shown in the following screenshot) to begin the installation:

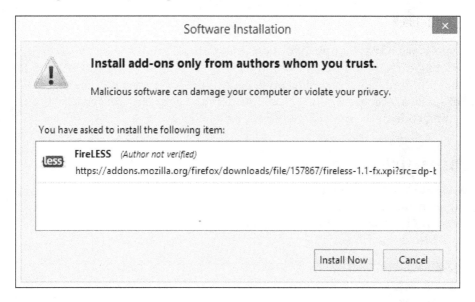

Click on **Restart Now** when prompted. FireLESS is now installed; we will see how to use it in *Chapter 3, Getting Started with Less*.

Debugging the Less code in Chrome

We're not limited to just using Firefox to debug our source code. We can also use Chrome; for this, we need to install the support for source maps in Less.

Source maps are a relatively new feature, which can work with JavaScript- or CSS-based files; the concept is based around providing a mechanism to map back the compiled JavaScript- or CSS-based code to the original source files. This becomes particularly effective when the content has been minimized—without a source map, it would be difficult to work out which piece of code was at fault!

This example relies on the use of a web server to work correctly. We will go ahead and install WampServer for this purpose, so let's do this now.

Installing WampServer

WampServer can be downloaded from `http://www.wampserver.com`—the various versions for Windows are available from within the **Download** tab; make sure that you select an appropriate one for your platform. If you work on an Apple Mac, then you can try installing MAMP, which you can download from `http://www.mamp.info`. Linux users should have a suitable option available as part of their distro.

Start by opening the installer file you downloaded earlier. In the welcome prompt, click on **Next**. Select **I accept the agreement**, and then click on **Next**, as shown in the following screenshot:

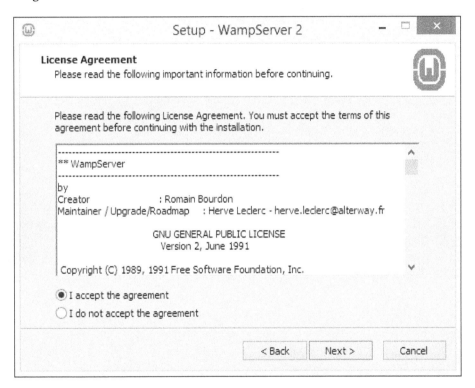

We need to assign a location somewhere to install the application files (and later, host our test pages). By default, WampServer will get installed into `c:\wamp`—this is ideal, as it avoids the use of spaces, which will otherwise translate into `%20` in our URLs.

For the purposes of this book, I will assume that you've used the default; if you've used something different, then you will need to remember the new location for later when we host our example files.

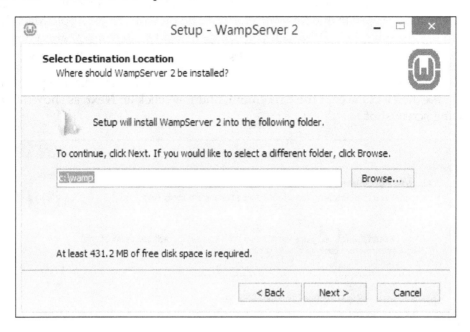

The setup will then prompt you whether you want to create quick launch or desktop icons—at this point, you can choose whichever you prefer to use. Clicking on **Next** will show you a **Ready to Install** screen, which gives you a summary of our install actions. If all is well, click on **Install** to complete the process.

We will then see the **Preparing to Install** window, before **Setup** then runs through the installation. Just before the completion, you will see this message, where we should click on **No**:

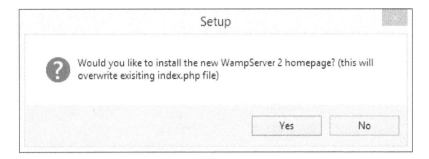

In addition, we also need to install Grunt and Node, as outlined earlier in the *Watching for changes to Less files* section of this chapter.

Now that WampServer is installed, open a command prompt and change the location to your project folder — for this example, I will use a folder called `lessc`, which will be stored at `c:\wamp\www\lessc`.

> In this example, we've used a demo folder — this will need to be your folder from which the content is served when working in production.

In the prompt, enter the following command:

```
lessc namespaces.less > namespaces.css –source-map=namespaces.css.map
```

Here, `namespaces.less` and `namespaces.css` are the names of your Less and CSS files, respectively. When compiled, `lessc` produces a `.map` file, which the browser will use to find the various definitions in Less files that equate to a specific CSS style rule in your code.

Copy the `namespaces.less`, `namespaces.css`, `main.html`, and `namespaces.css.map` files to your web server's `www` folder — in this instance, this will most likely be `c:\wamp`.

Open Google Chrome, and then browse to `http://localhost/lessc/main.html`. If all is well, you will see something like the following screenshot, assuming that you have pressed *F12* to display the developer toolbar:

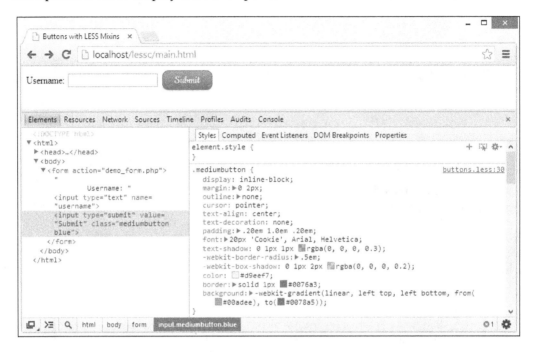

Here, you can see the various CSS styles that make up the `.mediumbutton` class; Chrome shows you the compiled output styles, but in place of indicating where each rule appears in the CSS, we can see where the original rule is shown within the Less file.

We will be able to achieve the same results using Opera (as recent versions are now WebKit-based). Safari has introduced support for source maps, but only from Version 7 onwards. **Internet Explorer** (**IE**) is the only major browser that is yet to include any support for source maps.

For now, don't worry about how source maps work, as we will revisit this in more detail later in the book.

Other useful tools

We've almost come to the end of this chapter, but before we move onto starting to develop the Less code, we should take a look at a few tools that you might find useful once you've spent some time developing CSS with Less:

- **Adobe Kuler**: You can find this tool at `https://kuler.adobe.com/`. Although this is not immediately associated with Less, you might find this useful when choosing a color scheme for your site. Kuler has some useful tools that help you choose a suitable color palette from which we can take and use the color values within our Less styles.

- **Live.js**: If you spend any amount of time editing styles, you will have to manually refresh the pages after each change; this can get tedious if you are making lots of changes! Fortunately, we can get around this with the use of the Live.js script. This tool is developed by Martin Kool and is available at `http://www.livejs.com`. It automatically forces a refresh to the page being worked on so that we can see changes as soon as they are applied.

- **CSS3 Please**: You can find this tool at `http://css3please.com/`. This is a nifty site that allows you to edit any listed CSS3 rule with your own values; it automatically applies the same rule changes to each of the vendor prefixes for that rule so that you have an updated rule that will work in each of the major browsers. This is particularly helpful when you start creating your own mixins, as we will see in the next chapter.

- **SpritePad**: You can find this tool at `http://wearekiss.com/spritepad`. Billed as the "easiest way to create your sprites", SpritePad is an excellent tool for creating image sprites online, which automatically generates the appropriate CSS for each image. We can then use this to create mixins – this is particularly useful if we're creating a site with a lot of small images that feature regularly throughout the site.

- **Prefixr**: You can find this tool at `http://www.prefixr.com/`. Although this site is not designed for use with Less, it is useful nonetheless. We can develop a site for a particular browser (such as Firefox), and then use Prefixr to add other vendor prefix equivalents for any CSS3 rule that still requires them.

- **WinLess Online**: You can find this tool at `http://winless.org/online-less-compiler`. Earlier in this chapter, we touched on using WinLess as a Less compiler; this also has an online version for those who do not use Windows as their platform. Although some of the configuration options are not present (such as minifying the compiled code), it is a useful tool nonetheless.

- **Less2CSS**: You can find this tool at `http://www.less2css.org`. This site performs the same function as WinLess Online but has a few more options, such as adding the media queries required for working with source maps. This developer also recommends that you use this site to verify your code in the event that you come across any issue where you need assistance.

This is a selection of the tools I've used for developing with Less; there are likely to be others that will be as useful as the ones listed here. Please feel free to use these. If you have suggestions for others in a future edition of this book, then they are welcome!

Summary

Working with Less can be very rewarding when you have the right tools installed and available for use in your workflow. We started with a look at some of the editors that are available; these include support for Less, such as Sublime Text or Notepad++. We then moved on to installing Sublime Text 2 and added support for Less.

Next up came a discussion on the options available for compiling Less code – the first option covered how you can use a standalone compiler such as WinLess to produce the final CSS code; we took a look at each of the main compilers available, and followed it by installing Crunch!.

We then moved on to examining how you can use the command line to compile the code – we looked at how using a standalone compiler meant adding another layer into your development workflow, which isn't ideal. We ran through a basic installation of Node.js, which we then first configured to compile Less files before adding an automatic watch facility and finishing with a look at how you can link this to editors such as Notepad++.

We then rounded off the chapter with a look at the options available for debugging code in browsers. We examined how FireLESS and Firebug make this a cinch when using Firefox, while it requires a little more work to configure Chrome (and Opera) in order to use source maps to achieve the same effect. We also covered some of the other tools you might find useful for developing with Less, such as LESS2CSS or Adobe Kuler.

In the next chapter, we're going to really get stuck in and start to produce valid Less code. We'll take a look at downloading and adding Less and start to examine its syntax before writing some styles and seeing the results from compiling using the command line or through a standalone compiler.

3
Getting Started with Less

In the first two chapters of this book, *Chapter 1*, *Introducing Less*, and *Chapter 2*, *Building a Less Development Toolkit*, we learned what Less is, some of its benefits, and the reasons why you should get to grips with a preprocessor that is rapidly gaining serious traction in the development world.

In this chapter, we're going to start by downloading and installing Less and then setting up our base project that we can reuse throughout this book, which is already set to our preferences. While it might seem a little mundane, it is nevertheless an essential part of working with Less! Once we have our base project ready, we will then delve into a whistle-stop tour of some of the main code features of Less, before looking at how you can compile your Less code into valid CSS and seeing the effects of any changes made to the Less code.

In this chapter, we will delve a little deeper into Less by covering the following topics:

- Incorporating Less into your website
- The dangers of using Less on the client side
- Exploring the syntax used by Less
- Creating some basic styles
- Compiling the code and viewing the results
- Altering the Less code and viewing the effects of changes

Ready? As they say in temporal mechanics, there's no time like the present to get started...!

Creating the foundation page

Now that we have downloaded the library, the next stage is to set up our base project that we can reuse throughout this book. This is going to be a simple HTML5 document, which will contain the basic skeleton we will need for our projects.

For my code editor, I will be using Sublime Text 2, for which we set up support for Less back in *Chapter 2, Building a Less Development Toolkit*. This is available for download from Sublime Text's website at `http://www.sublimetext.com/2`, although you can use whichever editor you are most comfortable with.

Let's start by creating our base project file. In a new folder called `lessjs`, create a new file and add the following code:

```html
<!DOCType html>
<head>
  <meta charset="utf-8">
  <title>Untitled</title>
  <link rel="stylesheet/less" href="css/project.less">
</head>
<body>
</body>
</html>
```

> **Downloading the example code**
>
> You can download the example code files for all Packt books you have purchased from your account at `http://www.packtpub.com`. If you purchased this book elsewhere, you can visit `http://www.packtpub.com/support` and register to have the files e-mailed directly to you.

Save this as `project.html`. We'll make reference to this throughout the book and it will be the basis for each of our projects when using Less.

Downloading and installing Less

Now that we have a test page created, it's time to download the Less library. The latest version of the library is 1.7.3, which we will reference throughout this book.

To obtain a copy of the library, there are two main options available: downloading the latest release as a standalone library or compiling code using Node. We'll start with downloading the standalone library.

Installing Less on the client side

To use Less in our code, we can download it from the Less site by browsing to `http://lesscss.org/#download-options-browser-downloads` and then clicking on the **Download Less.js v.1.7.3** button.

Save the contents of the file, displayed in the browser window as `less.min.js`, in a subfolder called `js`, under the main `lessjs` project folder; you will end up with something like this screenshot (this shows the files you will create later in this chapter):

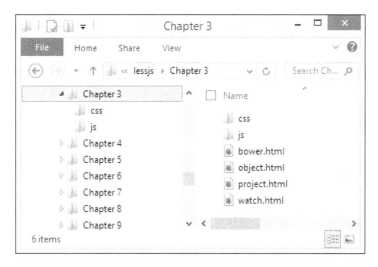

In a copy of the `project.html` file we created at the start of this chapter, add the code as highlighted:

```html
<!DOCType html>
<head>
  <meta charset="utf-8">
  <title>Untitled</title>
  <link rel="stylesheet/less" type="text/css" href="css/project.less">
  <script src="js/less.min.js"></script>
</head>
<body>
```

That's it—once this has been added, Less will compile the styles into valid CSS dynamically and render the results in the browser. The key point to note is that for Less to compile the styles correctly, the reference to the Less style sheet file must be included in your code first, before the reference to the Less library.

Can I get the source code for Less?

If you want to delve into the Less library and examine the code in more detail, then you might like to download a copy of the uncompressed version of the library, which is available at `https://github.com/less/less.js/archive/master.zip`.

Using a CDN

Although we could download a copy of the library, we don't need to when hosting it in a production environment. Less is available on a content delivery network hosted by CDNJS. You can instead link to this version in your code.

If you host an international site with a lot of network traffic, using a **Content Delivery Network (CDN)** hosted file will help ensure that the library is downloaded to a visitor's computer from a server that is geographically close to them. This helps in making the response quicker, as the browser will use a cached version on subsequent visits to the page, which saves on bandwidth. This is *not* recommended for development however!

If you want to use a CDN link, then it can be found at `http://cdnjs.cloudflare.com/ajax/libs/less.js/1.7.3/less.min.js`.

Installing Less on the server side

As an alternative to compiling code on the fly, we can always use the command line to perform the same function—Less comes with a built-in command-line compiler that requires the JavaScript-based Node platform to operate.

Installing Less using Node

We took a look at how you can install Node in *Chapter 2, Building a Less Development Toolkit*; I will assume that you have installed it using the defaults, as outlined in that chapter. At this point, we now need to install the Less compiler, so bring up a command prompt, change to the location of the project folder we created earlier, and enter the following command:

```
npm install -g less
```

You will see it run through a download and install of Less at the command prompt:

```
npm http GET https://registry.npmjs.org/delayed-stream/0.0.5
npm http 200 https://registry.npmjs.org/delayed-stream/0.0.5
npm http GET https://registry.npmjs.org/delayed-stream/-/delayed-stream-0.0.5.tg
z
npm http 200 https://registry.npmjs.org/delayed-stream/-/delayed-stream-0.0.5.tg
z
C:\Users\Alex\AppData\Roaming\npm\lessc -> C:\Users\Alex\AppData\Roaming\npm\nod
e_modules\less\bin\lessc
less@1.5.1 C:\Users\Alex\AppData\Roaming\npm\node_modules\less
├── mime@1.2.11
├── mkdirp@0.3.5
├── clean-css@2.0.4 (commander@2.0.0)
├── source-map@0.1.31 (amdefine@0.1.0)
└── request@2.30.0 (aws-sign2@0.5.0, json-stringify-safe@5.0.0, oauth-sign@0.3.0
, tunnel-agent@0.3.0, forever-agent@0.5.0, qs@0.6.6, node-uuid@1.4.1, tough-cook
ie@0.9.15, hawk@1.0.0, http-signature@0.10.0, form-data@0.1.2)

C:\Users\Alex>_
```

Once the installation is complete, we can enter the following command to compile a Less file, which uses this syntax:

```
lessc srcfile [dstfile]
```

Less will compile the output to stdout; if we want to use a different one, then we can redirect the output:

```
lessc srcfile > dstfile
```

We're now ready to compile Less files at the command prompt—we will see this in action, later in this chapter.

Installing Less using Bower

Using Node with the command line is not the only option we have—we can also install Less using the cross-platform Bower package manager system, available at http://www.bower.io.

Based on Node, Bower is designed to help with the installation of packages for the web, such as jQuery, AngularJS, the Font Awesome icon library, and of course, Less. Let's take a look at how to install it for Windows, as this has an added dependency of Git for Windows, which must also be installed if we are to use this platform.

To get the full benefit from this demonstration, you will find it better to use a local web server, such as WAMP. For the purposes of this book, I will assume this has been installed with the default settings.

Start by visiting `http://msysgit.github.io` and downloading the latest installer, which is `Git-1.8.5.2-preview20131230.exe` at the time of writing. Double-click on the installer and click on **Next** to accept all defaults, until you get to this screen:

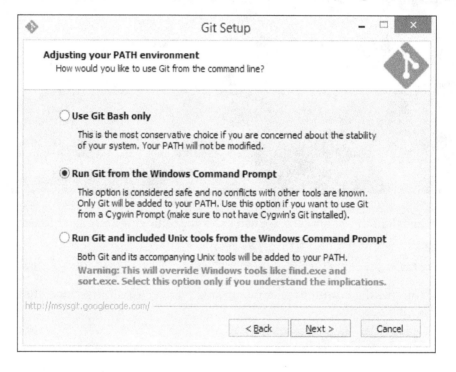

Change the selected option to **Run Git from the Windows Command Prompt**, then continue by clicking on **Next** to accept the defaults for the remaining settings. The Git installer will install and configure the client, and once completed, it will display the installation notes for reading if desired.

In a command prompt, enter the following command:

```
npm install -g bower
```

This will download and install the various packages that make up Bower — it will display a confirmation if the installation has been successful:

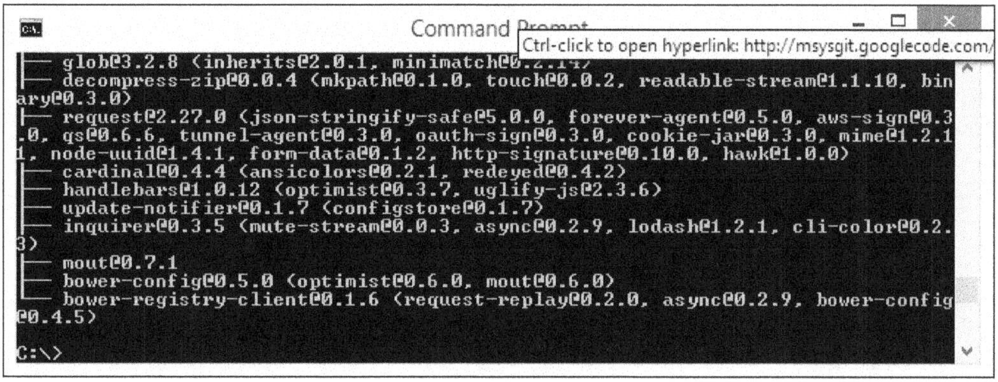

Once the Bower installation has been completed, change to the www folder within your web space and enter the following command to install the Less package for Bower:

```
bower install less
```

This will perform a similar process to download and install the Less package for Bower, as shown in the following screenshot:

At this point, Bower is now installed and available for use.

Using the Bower package

Now that Bower is installed, we can use it in our code—the major difference though is that it doesn't contain a version of `lessc`, so we are limited to only using it to compile dynamically in our code, and that developing code, which relies on using Node, is not supported.

With this in mind, we can still use it in a development capacity, to at least prove that our code works—for this, we only need to make one change to our code. If we open a copy of `project.html`, we can change the highlighted line to use the Bower version of Less, instead of the original version:

```
<link rel="stylesheet/less" href="include.less">
<script src="http://localhost/chapter3/bower_components/less/dist/
less-1.7.3.js"></script>
  <script type="text/javascript">
  </script>
```

We can, of course, take this much further—Bower operates very much in the same manner as Node, allowing us to produce `.json` packages, just as we did for Node in the previous chapter.

 If you want to learn more about producing packages for Bower, then Bob Yexley has a useful article at `http://bob.yexley.net/ creating-and-maintaining-your-own-bower-package/`.

Let's now turn our attention to getting accustomed to the Less syntax. Before we do so, there is one important point we need to be aware of that concerns the dangers of using Less on the client side.

The dangers of using Less on the client side

So far, we've worked through how you can install Less in your code and use it to compile code into valid CSS, as each page is displayed.

Surely we should be good to start using Less, right? After all, we have the library in place, we know how to add it in, and know something of what to expect when styles have been compiled...or perhaps not. There is one critical point we've missed; let me explain.

When Less first came out, it was originally written using Ruby; this meant code had to be compiled first, before including the results in website pages, as valid CSS. Although this was a perfectly valid procedure, it made development slower, as extra steps were required in order to compile the Less code and include it in web pages.

The rebasing of the library in JavaScript led to a 30 to 40 percent increase in speed — this led to the temptation to include the library directly in code, along with the raw Less code. This worked well enough, while removing the need to compile the code separately.

This, however, is no longer deemed good practice, at least for production sites, for a number of reasons:

- JavaScript can be turned off — a reliance on JavaScript to control the styling for a site means that it will break, resulting in a messy site!

- A reliance on a JavaScript-based library means that another HTTP request has to be made to the server, which can result in increased loading times, particularly for script-heavy sites.

- On a content-heavy site, with a lot of styles, this can lead to a noticeable increase in rendering times, as the styles have to be compiled dynamically before content is rendered on.

- Most mobile platforms cannot handle the compilation of Less (nor the associated JavaScript file) dynamically and will just abort the execution, which will result in a mess.

This doesn't mean compiling on client side is a complete no-no, it should just be limited to working in development environments, or in instances where it is beneficial to store the library locally, such as within an HTML5 application.

You will note that many of the examples throughout this book will use Less client-side. This is to ensure that you, as the reader, are exposed to the whole experience; as we are working in a development/demonstration capacity, this is not an issue. When working on production sites, the Less code should always be precompiled first, before adding it to the site.

Exploring the syntax used by Less

Enough theory about installing! Let's move on and take a look at the syntax that makes up Less. Over the next few chapters, we will explore each part of the library in depth; before doing so, we will start with a whistle-stop tour through some of the more important parts of the library, beginning with variables.

Working with variables

If we need to write CSS styles, it's likely that we will include one or more styles that appear in multiple places. A great example is a number of shapes, where we might need to use the same value for borders or foreground colors:

```
.shape1 {
  color: #5cb100;
  border: 1px solid #5cb100;
}

.shape2 {
  background: #fff;
  color: #5cb100;
}
.shape3 {
  border: 1px solid #5cb100;
}
```

We could, as web designers, simply use the same color values throughout our code, and where appropriate, this is a perfectly valid option. However, what happens if we've set up a specific set of colors, only to find they all need to be changed?

Each style can be changed individually, although this assumes we manage to change every instance — on a style-heavy site, and with the best will in the world, there will always be one that we miss!

We can solve this easily by using variables to store a constant value for each color, and use it throughout the style sheet:

```
@my-color: #5cb100;

.shape1 { color: @my-color; border: 1px solid @my-color; }
.shape2 { background: #fff; color: @my-color; }
.shape3 { border: 1px solid @my-color; }
```

This means that if we choose to change the original color for something else, then all we need to do is change the color value assigned to the relevant variable, and Less will automatically update each instance of the variable throughout the rest of the code.

In our example, we set up a variable to store the color value of #5cb100 — if we wanted to change this, then we will only need to change the assigned variable at the start. Less will then handle the updating of every instance where the variable has been used, so we can be confident that the change has taken effect throughout our code.

We will explore more of variables in *Chapter 4*, *Working with Variables, Mixins, and Functions*.

Changing variables programmatically

Although we can set variables as static values, we might come across instances where it will be beneficial to programmatically change a value assigned to a Less variable, from within our code.

Hopefully, this is not something you will have to do too often, but it is useful to at least know how it works. Let's take a quick look at how this works, using an example form that has a couple of input fields and a simple **Submit** button.

In a new file, open a copy of the `project.html` file we created earlier, then alter the code as shown:

```
<link rel="stylesheet/less" href="css/object.less">
<script src="js/less.min.js"></script>
<script type="text/javascript">
  less.modifyVars({
    '@ button-color': '#61783F'
  });
</script>
```

Next, add the following code in between the `<body>` tags:

```
<form action="demo_form.aspx">
  First name: <input type="text" name="fname"><br>
  Last name: <input type="text" name="lname"><br>
  <input type="submit" value="Submit" id="submitbtn">
</form>
```

Finally, add the following Less styles to a new file, saving it as `object.less`:

```less
@button-color: #4D926F;

input { margin-top: 10px; }

#submitbtn {
  background-color: @button-color;
  margin-top: 10px;
  padding: 3px;
  color: #fff;
}
```

In our example, we've added a reference to the Less object, then used the `modifyVars` method to change the color of the `@button-color` variable, which we specified in `object.less`, to `#61783F`. We will cover variables in more detail in *Chapter 4, Working with Variables, Mixins, and Functions.*

Creating mixins

The next key element of Less is the creation of mixins, or predefined blocks of Less code that we can reuse from one ruleset, as part of another ruleset. So, we take the following block of CSS as an example:

```css
.green-gradient {
  background: #5cb100;
  background: linear-gradient(to top, #5cb100, #305d00);
  background: -o-linear-gradient(top, #5cb100, #305d00);
  background: -webkit-linear-gradient(top, #5cb100, #305d00);
}
```

Here, we've added a gradient color of dark green to a preset style rule called `.green-gradient`. So far so good; this will produce a perfectly usable gradient that fades from green to very dark green.

We could repeat this block of code for each instance where an object needs a similar style, but that would quickly lead to a lot of unnecessary code bloat. Instead, we can include the block of code as a mixin, within another style:

```less
.shape1 {
  .green-gradient;
  border: 1px solid #ccc;
  border-radius: 5px;
}
```

This produces the following valid CSS — the mixin code is highlighted:

```
.shape1 {
  background: #5cb100;
  background: linear-gradient(to top, #5cb100, #305d00);
  background: -o-linear-gradient(top, #5cb100, #305d00);
  background: -webkit-linear-gradient(top, #5cb100, #305d00);
  border: 1px solid #ccc;
  border-radius: 5px;
}
```

Using this method means that we can cut down on the code we need to write and still produce the same results. As you will see in *Chapter 4, Working with Variables, Mixins, and Functions*, we will take this a step further — with some careful planning, we can begin to build up a library of mixins that we can reuse in future projects. The key to this is creating mixins that are sufficiently generic, which can then be reused as needed. Others have already created such libraries and made them available online — we will use some of the more well-known ones, such as **3L, More or Less** and **LESSHat**, in our code examples.

The great thing about Less is that when we include these mixin libraries, Less will only include those mixins from the libraries where they are being referenced in our code. While it might initially seem like we're including a lot of extra code, the reality is that only a fraction of the code is used — it all comes down to careful planning as to how much we need to use!

Nesting styles in Less

Moving on, let's turn our focus to another key part of the Less library: the ability to nest styles. No, I'm not talking about bird habits (if you excuse the pun!), but a way to reduce repetition when creating your styles. Let me explain more.

Imagine you have a block of code similar to the following code, where a number of CSS styles have been created for child elements against their parent element:

```
#header { color: black; }
#header .navigation { font-size: 12px; }
#header .logo { width: 300px; }
```

On the face of it, this would appear normal code, right? Absolutely, there's nothing wrong with it. However, we can do better than this — as part of defining the class styles for each child element, there is a necessary degree of repetition in each style rule.

Using Less, we can embed or nest our styles more effectively. Our code will appear as this:

```
#header {
  color: black;
  .navigation {
    font-size: 12px;
  }
  .logo { width: 300px; }
}
```

Granted that it might not always reduce the number of lines required when writing code in your editor. However, this is not necessarily the aim of the exercise—the key here is to make the code more readable, as styles that relate to a specific element are grouped together, so it is clearer what role they play. You will find, particularly on larger sites, that this can sometimes mean a reduction in the number of lines we need to write—it all comes down to careful planning! We will cover nesting in more detail in *Chapter 5, Inheritance, Overriding, and Nesting in Less.*

Calculating values using operations

So far, our whistle-stop preview has taken us through creating variables, basic mixins, and reordering our code through the use of nesting. We're now going to step things up a little and have a look at the use of operators in our code.

Operators? Suprised? I am sure you are. Let's see what happens when we use them in our code. Imagine we have a number of shapes on screen, which are perfectly sized and positioned. We could use individual style rules for each element, but it would require careful calculations to ensure we had everything in the right place, particularly if any element needed repositioning.

Instead, we can use simple maths to work out the size and position of each element automatically, based on one or more given values:

```
@basic-width: 100px;

.shape1 { width: @basic-width; }
.shape2 { width: @basic-width * 2; }
```

It will, of course, require that each calculation be worked out, but once this is done, then all we need to do is change the initial value set, and it will automatically update every other value.

It's worth noting that a strict math option is available in Less, which only calculates math that is encapsulated in parentheses, such as this code:

```
.class {
  height: calc(100% - 10px);
}
```

You can read more about this option at http://lesscss.org/usage/#command-line-usage-strict-math.

In our example, we've set an initial variable, @basic-width, of 100 px, then used it to double the width of shape2. Once the code is compiled, it will produce the following CSS:

```
.shape1 { width: 100px; }
.shape2 { width: 200px; }
```

If we were to change the value for .shape1 to 75px for example, then the width of .shape2 will be recalculated as 2 x 75px, or 150px. We'll be exploring more on the use of operators later in this book.

Extending existing styles in Less

This is a relatively new feature in Less and works almost as a direct opposite to a normal mixin. It takes a little time to get used to it, so let's examine a simple example – imagine you have a div tag that uses the following style rule:

```
div { background-color: #e0e0e0; }
```

The div tag produces a very light gray color as its background color. We can use this to extend another element:

```
p:extend(div) { color: #101010; }
```

This compiles to the following code:

```
div, p { background-color: #e0e0e0; }
p { color: #101010; }
```

Instead of adding a whole bunch of properties of a mixin class to an existing class, it adds the extending selector to the existing selector so that the output of the extended class includes both sets of styles.

The beauty of this is that it results in a similar effect to using mixins, but without the associated bloat that you sometimes get when using mixins. It works by taking the contents of the existing selector, in this instance `background-color: #e0e0e0`, and assigning it to the new selector, `p`. This way, we can be more selective about reusing styles from existing elements, without the need to introduce new mixins.

 Note that extend will not check for duplicates. If you extend the same selector twice, it will add the selector twice. For more details, see `http://lesscss.org/features/#extend-feature-duplication-detection`.

Compiling the code and viewing results

Now that we've seen something of the syntax of Less, let's change tack and focus on how to compile our Less styles to produce valid CSS. There are several ways to achieve this, of which we touched on some back in *Chapter 2, Building a Less Development Toolkit*. For the moment, we're going to concentrate on using Crunch! to compile our code; we will switch to using the command line later in this section.

Using a standalone compiler

We will start with the variable example shown earlier in this chapter. Let's begin by starting up Crunch! and then clicking on the **New LESS file** button in the main code window. By default, it will create a new placeholder file called `new.less`; paste in the code from our example.

Press *Ctrl + S* to save the file, then save it in the `lessjs` project folder we created earlier, as `variables.less`:

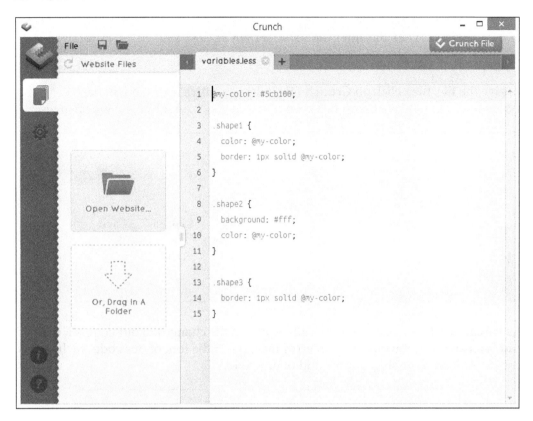

Click on **Crunch File** to view the results of the compiled code—it will prompt you to assign a filename, so give it the default, which is the same name of the Less file, or in this instance, `variables.css`:

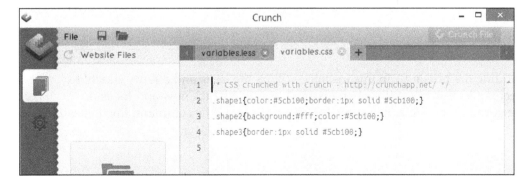

That was easy, huh? Any time we make a change to our Less file, all we need to do is save it, then click on **Crunch File** and the file is automatically updated. Let's test this by changing the color value assigned to the @my-color variable.

In the variable.less file, alter the value shown against @my-color as follows:

```
@my-color: #3f004b;
```

Resave the file, then click on **Crunch File** — the variable.css tab will flash momentarily to indicate that it has been updated. Click on it to view the changes:

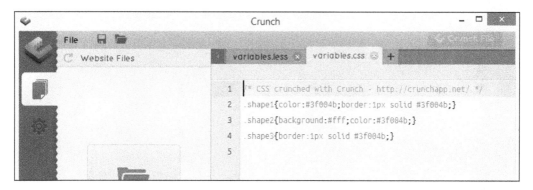

As we can see, Crunch! has successfully updated the changes to our code — if there had been an error, it would flag an error message at the foot of our code, such as this one, to indicate a missing } at the end of our code:

Adding the missing } in this instance will fix the issue and allow Crunch! to recompile our code without any issue. Let's switch tack now and focus on performing the same operation, but this time using the command line instead.

Using the command-line compiler

So far, we've used a standalone editor to compile (or Crunch!—pun intended!) our code. It has successfully produced some valid CSS for us, which can be used in a normal HTML page if desired. This works well, but might not be the preferred choice for everyone!

Instead of having to use a standalone compiler, we can achieve the same result by using the command line instead. Granted that this is a little bit more of a manual process, but it does give us the opportunity to hook in the compilation process as a command that we can run directly from most text editors.

Compiling Less files using the command line

The process to compile Less files via the command line is very easy. Start by bringing up a command prompt and changing the location to your project folder, which is the `lessjs` folder we created earlier. At the command prompt, type in the following command and then press *Enter*:

```
lessc variables.less variables.css
```

That's all that is required for a basic compilation. Less will now compile the `variables.less` file and save the results as `variables.css` in the same folder. It means that you can leave this session open in the background and rerun the command each time you want to make a change to the code.

 Less has a number of other options available when using `lessc` via the command line. To view them, type in `lessc` at a command prompt to display the full list.

Watching for changes in Watch mode

In this exercise, we're going to take a look at a simple, but useful feature called the Watch mode. This allows us to make changes to any Less file while still in development, and for us to reload the page without having to force a complete reload of the page from the server. It is worth noting that the Watch mode can be used with the local filesystem, or with a web server—both will produce the same effect. For the purposes of the book, we will assume the use of the latter; in this case, we will use WampServer, which we covered back in *Chapter 2, Building a Less Development Toolkit*. If you are a Mac user, then you can use something such as MAMP; Linux users will have a selection of local web servers available within their distro.

We're going to test it by creating a simple form with the username and password fields.

Assuming that we have installed WAMP, or have web space available, start by opening up your text editor, then add the following code:

```
<!DOCType html>
<html>
  <head>
    <meta charset="UTF-8">
    <title>Adding watch support</title>
    <link rel="stylesheet/less" href="include.less">
    <script src="less.min.js"></script>
    <script type="text/javascript">
      less.env = "development";
      less.watch();
    </script>
  </head>
<body>
  <form action="demo_form.aspx">
    Name: <input type="text" class="input" />
    Password: <input type="password" class="input" />
    <input type="submit" id="submitfrm" value="This is a button"
      />
  </form>
</body>
</html>
```

 Notice how `less.env = "development"` has been added. This sets Less to work in the development mode – this is one of several options we can set in this mode. For more details, it is worth reading the documentation on Less' site at `http://lesscss.org/usage/#using-less-in-the-browser`.

Save it as `watchr.html` in the www folder, which should be `c:\wamp\www` by default. Next, in a separate file, add the following and save it as `include.less`:

```
@color-button: #556644;
#submitfrm {
    color: #fff;
    background: @color-button;
    border: 1px solid @color-button - #222;
    padding: 5px 12px;
}
```

Fire up your browser, then navigate to it by entering the appropriate URL into your browser; if all is well, you will see something like this:

Keep your browser window open. Now, let's make a change to our Less code; in the Less file, change the `@color-button` value to `#334466`:

```
@color-button: #334466;
#submitfrm {
    color: #fff;
    background: @color-button;
    border: 1px solid @color-button - #222;
    padding: 5px 12px;
}
```

Save the change to the Less file. Within a few moments, we will see the color of our button change from dark green to dark blue, as shown in the following screenshot:

When working with Less, compiled styles are stored in the **localStorage** area of the browser, and they remain there until the **localStorage** area is cleared. We can see this by pressing *F12*, then clicking on **DOM**, and scrolling down to the **localStorage** entry — assuming Firebug is installed:

```
window
    length                                          0
  localStorage                                     2 items in Storage http://localhost/chapter3
                                                   /include.less="#submitfrm {\n  color: #...
                                                   padding: 5px 12px;\n}\n", http://localhost/chapter3
                                                   /include.less:timestamp="Sat, 18 Jan 2014 10:51:07 GMT"

      http://localhost/chapter3/include.less       "#submitfrm {
                                                       color: #fff;
                                                       background: #ff0000;
                                                       border: 1px solid #dd0000;
                                                       padding: 5px 12px;
                                                   }
                                                   "
      http://localhost/chapter3/include.less:timestamp "Sat, 18 Jan 2014 10:51:07 GMT"
```

To view any changes, we have to force a refresh from the server — using the watch facility forces the browser into the development mode, which prevents the browser from caching the generated CSS files.

It is worth noting that there are other methods you can use to watch for changes, such as using Grunt or Gulp. Two great examples include observr, which is available at `https://github.com/kevinburke/observr`, or lessc-bash, downloadable from `https://github.com/pixelass/lessc-bash`. We covered using Grunt to watch for changes in *Chapter 2*, *Building a Less Development Toolkit*.

Summary

We're now ready to start exploring the Less syntax in more detail. Before we do so, let's recap what we learned throughout this chapter.

We began with how you can download and install Less; we first covered how you can download this as a standalone library, before incorporating it into our pages. We also took a brief look at how you can use a CDN link instead of downloading the code; while this isn't recommended for development purposes, it nevertheless is worthwhile for production sites, where the browser can cache the library if a visitor has already accessed the library on a previous site.

Moving on, we then took a look at how you install Less server-side, using the Node platform. We saw how easy it is to compile Less files, using a single command, and that we can perform this as many times as we like, by rerunning the command when needed. We discussed how to install Less by taking a look at the dangers of using it client side and how this should really be limited to use in a development environment only, due to the extra demands placed on the hosting server.

We then changed focus and took a whistle-stop tour on some of the key parts of the Less syntax, as a precursor to exploring it in more detail in later chapters. We covered the use of variables, mixins, nesting, operations, and extending in Less before switching to compiling some basic code to see how the compilation process works. We examined how you can use either a standalone compiler or the command line to perform the same operation. We finished the chapter with a look at how to use the watch() function within Less—this can be set to watch for any changes in the Less file and force the browser to automatically refresh the page, without the need for manual intervention.

We've now covered the basics of how to install Less and get it up and running in our code. Let's move on and begin our journey through the functionality of Less, starting with a look at mixins, functions, and variables.

4
Working with Variables, Mixins, and Functions

So far in this book, we've built up the basics of what will become our development toolkit for working with Less and taken a whistle-stop tour through some of the syntax and concepts that are associated with Less as a CSS preprocessor. I am sure some well-known actor once said in a film somewhere, "It's time...."

Yes, it's time to get stuck with using Less! However, hold on; this chapter says it's about working with variables, functions, and the like; surely, this means we're developing in programming code, right?

Wrong. Don't worry, my friends; granted, we will look at functions, but they are nothing like the functions you might see when developing using languages such as C# or Visual Basic. Indeed, the only similarity is the name—as we will see, functions within the world of Less are more akin to using a scientific calculator than complicated code.

This is just a small part of what we will cover. Throughout this chapter, we will look at some of the building blocks of Less, including:

- Creating and scoping variables
- Developing simple and parametric mixins
- Using Less functions
- Using prebuilt libraries

Intrigued? Let's get started...

Discovering variables in Less

As with all good things, we must start somewhere—it seems like an opportune moment to ask ourselves a question: for those of you who are already familiar with the basics of programming, when is a variable not a variable? It's a constant—but hold on, this section is about variables, right...? If this seemed like double Dutch to you, then don't worry, let me explain.

Variables in Less are very much like the variables in most programming or scripting languages—they act as a placeholder for a value. Consider the following code:

```
#somediv { width: 200px; height: 200px; }
```

Instead of the previous code we could write this:

```
@width: 200px;
@height: 200px;

#somediv { width: @width; height: @height; }
```

This code will produce the same result.

You might ask yourself though, "Why write double the code for the same result?" Surely, we can simply use the first method, right?

Yes and no—on its own, this example isn't actually that effective. However—and this is where the big difference lies when using Less—it comes into its own when you are using the same rule to style multiple items of the same type, with the same effect.

If we had the need to style a number of buttons throughout a site, for example, then we would normally set the style either inline or using classes. This is likely to require updating of styles at several different places in our style sheet, if we need to make a change; this is time-consuming and prone to errors!

Instead, we set up variables at the start of our Less styling, which are used throughout our code. This means that with a single stroke, we can automatically update all the instances of a particular value; this can be a real timesaver, particularly if a client is unsure what they want to see!

The key to setting up variables is planning; with a little care and forethought, we can set up our variables at the head of the style sheet and then use them as appropriate throughout our Less code. To see what I mean, let's put this into practice with a simple example.

Creating Polaroid images

In the first example of this chapter, we're going to use Less to create the tried-and-trusted **Polaroid effect**, as developed by the Canadian developer Nick La (http://www.webdesignerwall.com), and apply it to a number of images, as shown in the following screenshot:

The beauty of this is that there is no need for any JavaScript or jQuery in our code; it will use pure Less, which we will compile into valid CSS.

For the purpose of this book, it is assumed that we will be using Sublime Text that has been configured to automatically compile Less files to valid CSS, as we saw in *Chapter 2, Building a Less Development Toolkit*.

 If you are using a different means to compile the Less code, then you will need to adjust the steps accordingly.

In a copy of the code download that accompanies this book, extract a copy of variables.html—we will use this as the basis for our Polaroid image effect.

With our framework in place, let's add some styling. In a separate file, let's start adding in the Less styles, beginning with the variables that will define our colors:

```
@dark-brown: #cac09f;
@light-grayish-yellow: #fdf8e4;
@dark-grayish-yellow: #787568;
@image-width: 194px;

@caption-text: ' ';
```

Now that we have created our variables, it's time to use them; let's begin by styling each list item, to turn them into the container for each image:

```
li { width: @image-width; padding: 5px; margin: 15px 10px; border:
1px solid @dark-brown; background: @light-grayish-yellow; text-
align: center; float: left; list-style: none outside none; border-
radius: 4px; box-shadow: inset 0 1px rgba(255,255,255,.8), 0 1px 2px
rgba(0,0,0,.2); }
```

We can now turn our attention to styling the contents of each Polaroid; let's begin by setting the main images to appear within each container, and not displaced to right:

```
figure { position: relative; margin: 0; }
```

Next comes the addition of each flower image, along with its overlay effect:

```
figure:before { position: absolute; content: @caption-text; top: 0;
left: 0; width: 100%; height: 100%; background: url(../img/overlay.
png) no-repeat; border: none; }
```

Finally, let's add the styling for each image caption:

```
figcaption { font: 100%/120% Handlee, Arial, Helvetica, sans-serif;
color: @dark-grayish-yellow; width: @image-width; }
```

Save the file as `variables.less`. Sublime Text will automatically compile this into a valid CSS file, although for the purpose of this demo, we will compile the Less code dynamically as it is not very complex.

The keen-eyed among you will notice that we are using a nonstandard font for the caption—this is the Handlee font, available from Google Fonts. To ensure that this works as expected, add this line immediately after the `<title>` tag in `variables.html`:

```
<link href='http://fonts.googleapis.com/css?family=Handlee'
   rel='stylesheet' type='text/css'>
```

If you preview the results in a browser, you will see something similar to this:

In our example, we've created a number of variables to handle the colors being used; instead of displaying hex codes throughout our code, which aren't easy to understand, we can use names, such as @dark-brown, which are easier to understand:

```
@dark-brown: #cac09f;
@light-grayish-yellow: #fdf8e4;
@dark-grayish-yellow: #787568;
@image-width: 194px;
```

We can also use variables to define text, such as:

```
@caption-text: ' ';
```

It is important to note that while using variables to define colors is the most common, it is by no means the only use for variables. We can also use variables to define strings, as we have done here, or even include them in URLs:

```
// Variables
@images: "../img";

// Usage
body { color: #444; background: url("@{images}/white-sand.png");}
```

This will compile to:

```
body { color: #444; background: url("../img/white-sand.png"); }
```

 It is worth reading through the variable examples on the main Less site (http://less.github.io/features/#variables-feature).

In our example, we compiled our styles dynamically; so, Less will automatically substitute every instance of each variable name for the appropriate value throughout our code. At this point, we could easily substitute the Less file for the compiled CSS file — it will produce the same effect. This is something we should do for a production environment; we should also go one step further and minimize the code to ensure that bandwidth usage is kept to a minimum.

Loading variables and setting the scope

When setting and using variables, there is one key element that we need to be aware of: setting variable scope when loading variables in Less.

Variables in Less are **lazy-loaded**, which means they don't have to be declared before being used. If we have declared an instance of a variable, then redeclare it with a new value. Less will always use the last definition of the variable, searching upwards from the point where it is called. Consider this:

```
@var: 0;
.style1 {
  @var: 1;
  .style {
    @var: 2;
    three: @var;
    @var: 3;
  }
  one: @var;
}
```

In this instance, you might expect to see `.style1` contain a rule of `one: 3`. Instead, it will compile to `one: 1`, as the `@var: 3` is contained in the `.class1` class rule, which is not within the same scope. It becomes even more important that variables are correctly assigned at the right point in our Less code, as we don't have to declare them upfront before using them. As an example, consider the following two methods of writing the same code, both of which will compile to equally valid CSS. Consider the first method:

```
lazy-eval { width: @var; }

@var: @a;
@a: 9%;
```

The other method of writing the code is as follows:

```
.lazy-eval-scope { width: @var; @a: 9%; }

@var: @a;
@a: 100%;
```

Both will compile to:

```
.lazy-eval-scope { width: 9%; }
```

See what I mean? The first method is more concise—there is no need to use the second method if it produces the same result! On this note, let's change tack and focus on how we can remove repetition in our Less code by introducing the use of mixins.

Exploring mixins

When writing code, how many times have you written a similar code, but for different projects? Ever wondered if you could, with a little change in the writing style, convert to using prebuilt blocks of CSS that you can drop in a project at a moment's notice?

Sure, you could start to create your own library of code—this would work perfectly well. However, it suffers from at least one potential drawback: you will very likely have to manually modify any stored code to fit the needs of a new project. While this will work, you might find yourself expending more time updating code than if it had been written from scratch!

What if I said you could still maintain a code library, but you don't have to keep modifying each block of library code that you reuse? It is possible—with the use of Less' mixin functionality.

Mixins are blocks of code that do as the name suggests—they can be mixed-in to your project code and called when required. They can even be moved to a library style sheet, which you can include in your projects—the beauty is that while you may have a library style sheet that is huge, only those styles that are actively used in the code are called and compiled in the resulting CSS style sheet.

The uses for mixins are as wide as your imagination—it can be as simple as defining a block of static code to call in your CSS, all the way through to passing specific values as parameters to mixins, otherwise known as parametric mixins. To see how mixins can work, let's begin by creating a simple web form using normal CSS.

Creating a web form

If you've spent any time looking at websites—and in this modern day of technology, it would be difficult not to—then you will have come across, or needed to use, the ubiquitous contact form. They pop up everywhere—you could almost take the cynical view that people use them as a means of avoiding human contact!

Nonetheless, they still serve a valid purpose. Over the next few sections, we're going to develop a simple contact form and enhance it using Less mixins to illustrate how they can be used to reduce the amount of code that we need to write.

 For this example, you will need to avail yourself of a copy of the code download that accompanies this book, as we will be using content from it during the exercise.

Start by opening a copy of `project.html`, which we created earlier, and then updating the `<head>` section, as follows:

```
<head>
  <meta charset="utf-8">
  <title>Demo: Mixins</title>
  <link rel="stylesheet" href="css/buttons.css">
</head>
```

Next, add the following markup in between the `<body>` tags:

```
<body>
  <form id="submitfrm" action="demo_form.asp">
<label for="fname">First name:</label>
<input type="text" name="fname"><br>
<label for="lname">Last name:</label>
<input type="text" name="lname"><br>
<input class="button red" id="submitbtn" type="submit"
  value="Submit">
  </form>
</body>
```

Save this as `mixins.html` — a copy of this file is also available in the code download. From the code download, retrieve a copy of the `buttons.css` file that is in the `css` subfolder, in the code folder for this chapter. Space constraints mean all 59 lines of the file can't be reproduced in full here, but once they are saved in the same folder, we can preview the results:

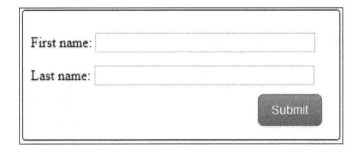

As we can see from the CSS styles, there is definitely a fair amount of repetition — even for an example as simple as ours! Let's change this by introducing mixins in our code.

Adding basic mixins

We can start by adding in two simple mixins to our code—let's begin by editing a copy of `buttons.css` and then adding the following code at the start of the file:

```
.shadow() { box-shadow: 0 1px 2px rgba(0,0,0,.2); text-shadow: 0
  1px 1px rgba(0,0,0,.3); }

.formfont { font-size: 14px; font-family: Arial, Helvetica, sans-
  serif; }
```

Next, we can remove the original code from the `.button` style block, as this is no longer needed—it will be replaced by the names of our three simple mixins:

```
.button {
  .shadow;
  .formfont;
  display: inline-block;
  outline: none;
  cursor: pointer;
  text-align: center;
  text-decoration: none;
  padding: .5em 2em .55em;
  border-radius: .5em;
}
```

Save this as `mixins1.less`; we can then remove the `buttons.css` link that is already in the code. Don't forget to add in a link for our Less file, within `mixins1.html`:

```
<link rel="stylesheet" type="text/less"
  href="css/mixins1.less">
```

Save the HTML file as `mixins1.html`—if we preview the results in a browser, we should not see any difference in the outcome, but we can rest assured with the knowledge that our three styles can be reused at any time in our code.

In our example, we've made a simple change to hive off styles in the blocks that we can reuse—in this instance, our three mixins could be called by any of the buttons used on a site, but they need to be of a similar style to ours. In each mixin, we've grouped together the styles that complement each other, such as `font-family` and `font-size`. There are no hard and fast rules about what should and shouldn't be grouped; it all comes down to what makes sense and helps reduce the amount of code we need to use.

We can further develop mixins by passing in parameters—this makes them more useful, as we can use the same code to produce different results, depending on our needs. However, when working with mixins, there are a couple of *gotchas* that we need to be aware of—the first one is code repetition.

Hiding the original mixin

When working with mixins, Less will compile (and display) both the mixin and the calling code so that we end up with duplicated code in the CSS style sheet. This isn't desirable, as it will make the style sheet larger than it is necessary and harder to debug in the event of any issue.

To get around this, we need to make a small modification to our existing styles—in the `mixin1.less` file, alter both the Less mixins, as follows:

```
.shadow() {
  box-shadow: 0 1px 2px rgba(0,0,0,.2);
  text-shadow: 0 1px 1px rgba(0,0,0,.3);
}

.formfont() {
  font-size: 14px;
  font-family: Arial, Helvetica, sans-serif;
}
```

Save the file as you normally do—Sublime Text will recompile the Less file. We can prove this by examining the code in Firebug—the following screenshot shows the effect of not using `()` in our mixins:

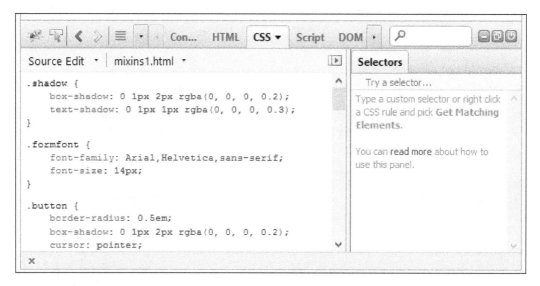

When the code has been compiled, you can clearly see that the styles have been removed—they are still present but are incorporated into the CSS style rules and not as separate mixins:

Using the !important keyword

When working with mixins, we can also specify the !important attribute, in the same way as we might do with normal CSS. All we need to do is to add it immediately after any style that must take precedence over subsequent definitions of the same rule:

```
.mixin (@a: 0) { border: @a; boxer: @a; }
.unimportant { .mixin(1); }
.important { .mixin(2) !important; }
```

This will be compiled by Less as follows:

```
.unimportant { border: 1; boxer: 1; }
.important { border: 2 !important; boxer: 2 !important; }
```

As the second style rule has been assigned the !important attribute, this will take precedence over the first rule. The !important override should be used with care though—it has gained something of a bad reputation since its introduction in CSS1 as it has often been misused. When used with care, it can perform an important function—although some might say that if you need to rely on it, then it is worth checking your CSS to ensure that you can't achieve the same results without it!

For a good explanation of the role of the `!important` tag in CSS as a whole, you might want to refer to Ian Devlin's article on how to best use this attribute, which you can find at `http://www.iandevlin.com/blog/2013/05/css/using-important-in-your-media-queries`.

Let's move on and take a look at how you can make mixins more powerful by passing attributes.

Developing parametric mixins

So far, we have examined how you can use mixins to create blocks of code that can easily be reused throughout your style sheets. On principle, this works great. However, what if you found yourself wanting to reuse the same block of code but couldn't, as the values were different?

Well, this is possible with Less; we've already covered how we can create mixins as reusable blocks of code. Let's take this a step further and introduce the use of parameters—here, we can pass values between the main Less file and individual mixins. When compiled, Less will use the appropriate values that are being passed to produce the desired CSS. Let's see this in action by making some changes to our simple form, which we created earlier in this chapter.

Crack open a new file and add the following mixins:

```
.background (@bkgrd) { background: @bkgrd; }

.border-radius(@radius) {
  -webkit-border-radius: @radius;
    -moz-border-radius: @radius;
        border-radius: @radius;
}

.box-shadow (@x: 0; @y: 0; @blur: 1px; @color: #000) {
  -webkit-box-shadow: @x @y @blur @color;
    -moz-box-shadow: @x @y @blur @color;
        box-shadow: @x @y @blur @color;
}

.formfont() {
  font-size: 14px;
  font-family: Arial, Helvetica, sans-serif;
}
```

Save the file as `mixinlibrary.less`. Next, let's modify a copy of `mixins1.less`, as there are some styles contained in it that are now redundant. In `mixins1.less`, make the following changes to the `.button` mixin, as highlighted:

```
.button {
  .formfont;
  .border-radius(.5em);
  .box-shadow(1px; 2px; rgba(0,0,0,.2));
  display: inline-block;
  outline: none;
  cursor: pointer;
  text-align: center;
  text-decoration: none;
  padding: .5em 2em .55em;
}
```

At the top of `mixins1.less`, we need to link in our `mixinlibrary.less` file; otherwise, the compilation will fail with errors—to fix this, add the following line at the top of `mixins1.less`:

```
@import "mixinlibrary.less";
```

We need to make a few more changes; in `mixins1.less`, we have three style rules for the `.red` class, namely `.red`, `.red:hover`, and `.red:active`. Within each, we need to change the rule for `.background-color` to use the Less mixin we've included in our mixin library. So, let's go ahead and make the following changes, as highlighted:

```
.red {
  .background(#ed1c24);

.red:hover {
  .background(#f14b52);

.red:hover {
  .background(#f14b52);
```

Save the file as `parametric1.less` — don't forget to update `parametric1.html` with a new link for the Less style sheet! If we preview the results in a browser, we can see that there has not been any change to our design (which we would expect):

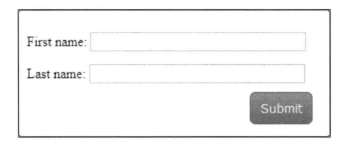

However, on closer inspection using a DOM inspector, such as Firebug (under the **Console** section), we can see that our mixins from `mixinslibrary.less` have been imported successfully:

```
less: XHR: Getting 'file:///F:/Learning%20LESS%20Book/lessjs/Chapter%204/css/parametric.less'          less.min.js (line 13)
less: XHR: Getting 'file:///F:/Learning%20LESS%20Book/lessjs/Chapter%204/css/mixinlibrary.less'         less.min.js (line 13)
less: parsed file:///F:/Learning%20LESS%20Book/lessjs/Chapter%204/css/parametric.less successfully.     less.min.js (line 13)
less: css for file:///F:/Learning%20LESS%20Book/lessjs/Chapter%204/css/parametric.less generated in 181ms   less.min.js (line 13)
less: css generated in 183ms                                                                            less.min.js (line 13)
```

We covered a couple of useful techniques in this exercise — it's worth taking a moment to go through this in some detail.

In previous exercises, we used mixins by defining them as static blocks of code that we can drop in at a moment's notice. This is great, but while the code blocks are static, they are limited to what's contained within each block; we will need to modify them to use different values if required, which makes them less useful.

Instead, we've incorporated parameters, such as this example:

```
.background(#ed1c24);
```

These are passed from the calling statement to the mixin and used to produce different results, depending on the values being passed. When compiled using the mixin in `mixinlibrary.less`, this will produce the following CSS:

```
background: #ed1c24;
```

This makes them infinitely more useful — one mixin can now serve a variety of different uses, depending on which values are passed to it.

Now, did the keen-eyed among you notice that I said we introduced a couple of useful techniques here? Well, the second one is the use of the `@import` statement. It is worth getting to know this keyword well, as it is a key part of Less. It allows you to break down long, complicated Less files into smaller, more manageable ones.

Hold on, I hear you ask: doesn't this mean more CSS files? No, that's the beauty of Less; it doesn't matter how many Less files you create, you will always end up with one compiled CSS file. Ideally, we would limit the number in practice, for practical purposes (7-10 is a good guideline, to allow uses such as WordPress). If you find yourself using more than 10, then I would suggest that you revisit your page design! We will return to importing Less and CSS files later in this chapter, in the *Using external libraries* section and also in *Chapter 5*, *Inheritance, Overriding, and Nesting in Less*.

Let's move on and take this a step further; we introduced the use of multiple parameters with the use of the `.box-shadow` mixin, but it would be worth taking out time to explore these further, as we can make more useful changes to our page's Less design.

Passing multiple parameters

So far, we've seen how you can pass a single parameter to a mixin, such as the radius size when using the border-radius rule. This is a great start, but as always, we can do more—how about passing in *multiple* parameters?

This opens up a world of possibilities, as we can widen the scope of what can be passed to our mixins. For example, if we're creating gradients, then we will have to hardcode color values in our mixins, which doesn't make them very flexible! Instead, if we use parametric mixins, then this allows us to pass colors as parameters to the mixin, thereby making the mixin far more flexible and useful.

Let's take a look at how this works in practice, by updating our existing code for `linear-gradient` (and the associated vendor prefixes), to use a Less mixin.

In a copy of `mixinlibrary.less`, add the following mixin at the end of the file:

```
.button (@color1, @color2, @color3) {
  background: -moz-linear-gradient(top, @color1 0%, @color2 6%, @color3 100%);
  background: -webkit-gradient(linear, left top, left bottom, color-stop(0%, @color1), color-stop(6%, @color2), color-stop(100%, @color3));
  background: -webkit-linear-gradient(top, @color1 0%, @color2 6%, @color3 100%);
```

```
    background: -o-linear-gradient(top, @color1 0%, @color2 6%, @color3
100%);
    background: -ms-linear-gradient(top, @color1 0%, @color2 6%, @color3
100%);
    background: linear-gradient(to bottom, @color1 0%, @color2 6%, @
color3 100%);
    filter: progid:DXImageTransform.Microsoft.gradient(startColorstr='@
middle', endColorstr='@stop', GradientType=0);
    border: 1px solid #980c10;
}
```

We now have redundant code in our Less file; so, in a copy of `parametric1.less`, remove the six background statements in each block, along with the filter and border statements. In their place, add the following, as highlighted:

```
.red {
  .background(#ed1c24);
  .button(#ed1c24, #e93a3f, #aa1317);
}

.red:hover {
  .background(#f14b52);
  .button(#f14b52, #ee686c, #d8181d);
}

.red:active {
  .background(#c61017);
  .button(#c61017, #d8181e, #7c0e11);
}
```

Save the file as `parametric2.less` — don't forget to update the `parametric.html` file with the new name of our Less file.

In this exercise, we continued with the theme of using parametric mixins, but this time, we called the same mixin with different parameters in each instance. In theory, it doesn't matter how many parameters are passed as long as Less can match them with valid inputs in each mixin. However, if you end up with more than 4-5 parameters being passed, then it would be a good point to reassess your mixin and perhaps see if it should be rewritten!

If we preview the results in a browser, we should not expect to see any visible results in our form, but we can see the change from within the HTML tab in Firebug:

```
14
15    .button:active {
16      position: relative;
17      top: 1px;
18   }
19
20    .red {
21      .background(#ed1c24);
22      .button(#ed1c24, #e93a3f, #aa1317);
23   }
24
25    .red:hover {
26      .background(#f14b52);
27      .button(#f14b52, #ee686c, #d8181d);
28   }
```

Applying conditions to mixins

When using static or parametric mixins, there is one thing that we should note—the mixin will be applied, no matter what the circumstances are and provided that any parameters passed to a mixin can be correctly matched and processed.

This isn't always a good thing; fortunately, we can fix this by attaching conditions to mixins so that they only execute if they can fulfill the condition(s) attached. These are known as **guarded mixins**—we will cover these in more detail in *Chapter 8, Media Queries with Less*, where we will see how Less can be put to good use when producing responsive websites.

Using special keywords

If you spend any time working with mixins, then there are two useful variables that you will come across at some point in your Less development. They are `@arguments` and `@rest`. Let's take a look at how they work, in the context of the `.box-shadow` mixin we created in the last exercise.

In the last exercise, we created the `.box-shadow` mixin to handle our `box-shadow` styling:

```
.box-shadow (@x: 0; @y: 0; @blur: 1px; @color: #000) {
  -webkit-box-shadow: @x @y @blur @color;
     -moz-box-shadow: @x @y @blur @color;
          box-shadow: @x @y @blur @color;
}
```

We referenced this mixin using the following command, which works perfectly well:

```
.box-shadow(1px; 2px; rgba(0,0,0,.2));
```

However, if you don't want to deal with all of the individual parameters (and particularly if there are a few involved), then you can replace `@x @y @blur @color;` with the `@arguments` variable:

```
.box-shadow(@x: 0; @y: 0; @blur: 1px; @color: #000) {
  -webkit-box-shadow: @arguments;
     -moz-box-shadow: @arguments;
          box-shadow: @arguments;
}
```

This handles the individual parameters in exactly the same way and produces valid CSS when compiled by Less.

If, however, you want to alter the number of parameters accepted by a mixin, then you can use Less' ability to reference named variables. Less will automatically match them with the variables in the mixin and produce the appropriate result when compiling the code. For example:

```
.mixin(...) {          // matches 0-N arguments
.mixin() {             // matches exactly 0 arguments
.mixin(@x: 1) {        // matches 0-1 arguments
.mixin(@x: 1; ...) {   // matches 0-N arguments
.mixin(@x; ...) {      // matches 1-N arguments
```

You can also use the `@rest` keyword—we first pass different values to any named variable in the parameter list and then use `@rest` to tell Less to work with the remaining variables as they are now:

```
.mixin(@x; @rest...) {
  // @rest is bound to arguments after @x
  // @arguments is bound to all arguments
}
```

These two simple tricks will be of great help when you start working with mixins—there is one trick that we have not covered yet, which is a little more advanced: using mixins as if they were functions. Let's fix this now and see what this means for developing mixins.

Creating mixins as functions

On our journey through creating and developing mixins, we've seen how you can hive off styles into groups and vary the output if needed, if it is set to receive values from the calling statements. We have not covered one area though, which is the use of functions within mixins – let's remedy this and take a brief look at what this means.

Any variable created inside a mixin is visible to the outside world and can be referenced from the calling statement. This means that within a mixin, we can call another mixin and reference any variable from within the second mixin:

```
.mixin() {
  @width:  50%;
  @height: 100px;
}

.caller {
  .mixin();
  width:  @width;
  height: @height;
}
```

The previous code, when compiled, results in:

```
.caller {
  width: 50%;
  height: 100px;
}
```

Taking this further, we can use the variables defined within a mixin, as if it were a return value – this applies to any variable that is being called within the mixin:

```
.average(@a, @b) {
  @average: ((@a + @b) / 2);
}

div {
  .average(6px, 30px); // "call" the mixin
  padding: @average; // use its "return" value
}
```

The preceding code will result in the following:

```
div { padding: 18px; }
```

This is really useful, as it means that we don't have to have a bunch of declarations for variables at the start of our code, but we can convert them into mixins that we can store in a mixin library and reuse in future projects. We will cover this in more detail, as a real-world example, in the *Moving calculations to a mixin* section of this chapter.

Using external libraries

Until now, we've developed a number of mixins and referenced them from either our main Less file or from a library file that we've created to store a number of our mixins. This is all good, but—hold on for a minute—one of Less' core concepts is DRY or Don't Repeat Yourself. While we are creating these mixin library files, we are (in a sense) repeating what other individuals may have already done, by creating—and publishing—their own solution.

With this in mind, it is worth researching online to see if anyone has already made their own mixin library available for use; there are a number of good libraries you can try, which include:

- **LESS Elements**: This is available at `http://www.lesselements.com`
- **LESS Hat 2**: This can be downloaded from `http://www.lesshat.com`
- **3L**: This is hosted on GitHub at `http://mateuszkocz.github.io/3l/`
- **ClearLess**: This is available at `https://github.com/clearleft/clearless`

The Less library available as part of Bootstrap also contains some useful mixins—we will look at this in more detail, in *Chapter 10, Using Bootstrap with Less*.

There are hundreds more available online—it is worth taking the time to look, as a library may exist that fulfills your need.

To incorporate the library, it is as easy as adding this line to the head of your Less file:

```
@import <name of library file>
```

Call the name of the mixin, including any parameters that are needed. We've already used this earlier in this chapter, in the *Developing parametric mixins* section—the principles used there apply here too, whether it be for calling in a prebuilt library made by someone else or one of your own creations.

Enough talk of mixins—let's change the subject and focus on another area of Less, which is the use of functions in our code.

Introducing functions

Another useful feature of Less is its ability to work out values that should be used in CSS, as a result of calculating the answers to functions and not merely using static values.

If you are already familiar with functions in programming, you might think that using functions in Less will involve writing lots of complicated formulae. Before you put your hands up in horror, fear not—it doesn't have to be that complicated! In this section, we're going to take a look at how you can use some simple math functions to automatically calculate values, using operators and the `data-uri` function as the basis for some examples of the many functions available within Less.

 You can see the complete list of functions, on the main website at `http://lesscss.org/functions/`.

Creating column-based layouts

One of the many tasks that a developer has to perform is to build the outline framework for a site—this could be one of the hundreds of designs, but it is likely that it will involve the use of columns in some format.

In some cases, this can be fraught with problems, particularly when dealing with differences between each browser. Thankfully, Less can help here—we can use some of its maths operators to construct a suitable layout with ease. To give you an idea of what can be done, here's a screenshot of the finished article from our next exercise:

Working with Variables, Mixins, and Functions

In a copy of the code download that accompanies this book, extract a copy of functions1.html — we will use this as the basis for styling our simple page layout.

If we preview the results now, the design will look terrible. Let's fix this by adding in the all-important styling rules. In a new file, add the following Less styles:

```
@baseWidth: 800px;
@mainWidth: round(@baseWidth / 1.618);
@sidebarWidth: round(@baseWidth * 0.382);

div { padding: 5px; margin-top: 5px; margin-bottom: 5px; font-family:
'Kite One', sans-serif; }
#container { width: @baseWidth; border: 1px solid black; margin-left:
auto; margin-right: auto; margin-top: 5%; margin-bottom: 5%; border-
radius: 4px; box-shadow: 4px 4px 4px 0px rgba(0, 0, 0, 0.5); }
#title { color: #FFF; font-family: 'Kite One', sans-serif;
font-size: 32px; font-weight: 400; padding-left: 100px; padding-top:
30px; position: absolute; }
#header { height: 150px; font-size: 18px; background-image: url("../
img/leaves.jpg"); }
#leftmargin { width: @sidebarWidth; border-right: 1px solid #ccc;
float: left; box-sizing: border-box; -moz-box-sizing:border-box;
height: 575px; }
#leftmargin li { list-style: none; }
#leftmargin a { text-decoration: none; }
#leftmargin a:hover { text-decoration: underline; }
#content { width: @mainWidth; float: left; box-sizing: -box;
-moz-box-sizing:border-box; height: 575px; padding: 10px; }
#footer { border-top: 1px solid #ccc; clear: both; font-size: 12px; }
```

Save the file as functions.less. Sublime Text will automatically compile this into a valid CSS file as functions.css. If we preview the results, we should see a simple, yet perfectly acceptable page appear:

[98]

In this example, we've used a number of styles to produce a simple two-column web page. The key to this trick lies in the following code:

```
@baseWidth: 800px;
@mainWidth: round(@baseWidth / 1.618);
@sidebarWidth: round(@baseWidth * 0.382);
```

Here, we've set three variables; the first variable, `@basewidth`, sets the overall size of the content container and is crucial for working out the widths that we will use for each column. Next, we've set the `@mainwidth` value, which calculates the value from `@basewidth`, divided by `1.618` (or approximately 61 percent)—this gives a value of `494px`. Lastly, we use the same principle to work out the value for the column—the formula for this becomes `800 x 0.382`, which gives `305.6px` or approximately 39 percent of the total width.

Using this calculation means that we can be sure that the columns will maintain the correct width, irrespective of the size of our container.

Moving calculations to a mixin

In the last example, we used some simple maths to determine the sizes needed to produce a two-column layout; this formed the basis of a simple, but useful page layout that could be used to produce any number of websites with relative ease.

However, there is still a nagging thought that we could do better—what if we could turn our statements into a mixin and use it as if it were a function? Sounds crazy? Well, perhaps not—we covered the basics of how to do this earlier in the chapter, in the *Creating mixins as functions* section. Let's put some of that theory into practice and see it in action.

Start by opening a copy of `functions.less`, which we used to create our Less styling for the page demo earlier. At the top, remove the top three variable statements. Next, add the following mixin immediately below it—this is our replacement for the statements we have just commented out:

```
.divSize (@x) {
  @baseWidth: @x;
  @mainWidth: round(@baseWidth / 1.618);
  @sidebarWidth: round(@baseWidth * 0.382);
}
```

We need to adjust the three `<div>` elements, where we use the variables from within this mixin; so, go ahead and make the following changes, as highlighted:

```
#container {
  .divSize(800px);
  width: @baseWidth;

#leftmargin {
  .divSize(800px);
  width: @sidebarWidth;

#content {
  .divSize(800px);
  width: @mainWidth;
```

Save the changes as `functions.less`. If you preview the results in a browser, you should not see any change to the page visually. However, this gives us the opportunity to hive off the mixin into a mixin library, if we've been creating one—a great example is the `mixinlibrary.less` file, which we put together earlier in the book. Even though this will, by now, contain a number of mixins that we wouldn't need to use here, Less will only ever pull in those mixins that it needs to use if it encounters a direct call for them as part of the compilation process.

Working with the data-uri function

At this point, we're going to completely change tack and look at the other functions available within Less—the use of the `data-uri` option.

`Data-uri` is a function available in Less, which inlines a resource to your style sheet; it avoids the need to link to external files by embedding the content directly in your style sheet. Although it may not help with document sizes, it will help reduce the number of HTTP requests from your server; this is one of the key factors that can affect how fast a page loads on the Internet. We will cover more of some of the pitfalls at the end of this section.

Let's get started with writing some code—there are a few steps involved in this process, so to give you a flavor of what we are going to produce, here's a screenshot of the finished article:

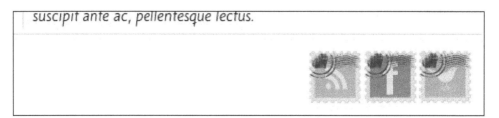

Let's start by opening a copy of `functions1.html` and altering the `<div>` footer, as follows:

```
    </div>
    <div id="footer">
        &copy; samplesite.com 2014
      <div id="social"></div>
    </div>
  </div>
```

Save this as `functions2.html`. We need to add some social media icons at this point—there are thousands available on the Internet; the ones I've used in our example are the icons from *Vintage Social Media Stamps: Icon Pack* by John Negoita, which are available at `http://designinstruct.com/free-resources/icons/vintage-social-media-stamps-icon-pack/`.

If you would like some inspiration, you may want to take a look at the various packs listed at `http://www.hongkiat.com/blog/free-social-media-icon-sets-best-of/`—there are some stunning examples on display!

In this example, we're using three icons: the RSS, Facebook, and Twitter icons, although you may prefer to use different icons from the pack, depending on your needs.

Next, to make positioning of the icons easier, we're going to convert them into an image sprite. For the uninitiated, image sprites are a really useful means of reducing the number of requests for resources from the server. This is particularly useful if you have lots of small images, such as arrows or icons, on your site; once you've downloaded the initial image, it will be cached for further use elsewhere on the site.

 If you would like to learn more about using CSS image sprites, then visit `http://css-tricks.com/css-sprites/`.

There are a number of ways to create image sprites; the easiest way is to use an online service such as the one at `http://spritepad.wearekiss.com/`, which we will use in our example.

Browse to the site and then drag-and-drop each image onto the grid. Position them until you have an even gap around each image—aim to leave 3-5 pixels between each image. When you are happy with the layout, click on **Download** to obtain the converted sprite and associated CSS styles that are produced by the site.

From the compressed archive that we've just downloaded, extract the image to the lessjs project folder; store it within the img subfolder. Switch to a new document in your text editor and then add the following, assuming that you've used the same icons as those outlined earlier:

```
#social {
    background-image: data-uri('../img/sprites.png');
    width: 175px;
    height: 60px;
    float: right;
}
```

Save the file as social.less — don't forget to add a link to social.less in the <head> section of functions2.html:

```
<link rel="stylesheet" href="css/social.less">
```

Sublime Text will have compiled the code into valid CSS — while the benefits of using this method won't be apparent immediately, you will see the effects once you look at the social.css file that is produced (and which is available in the code download for this book). To give you a flavor, this is an extract from our compiled social.css file:

```
#social{background-image:url('data:image/png;base64,iVBORw0KGgoAAAANSU
hEUgAAALgAAA...
```

If you save the files and preview the results in a browser, you will see the icons appear in the footer of your page, similar to this screenshot:

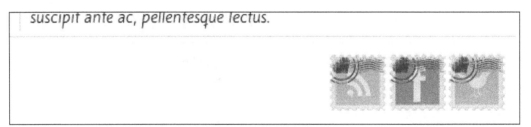

In our example, we've taken three images and converted them into a single image sprite. We've then referenced this from our Less style sheet, using the data-uri function, and positioned this on our page using standard CSS attributes to determine the height and width (necessary for the background-image rule to work correctly).

Using the data-uri function – some words of caution

While it is in a developer's best interests to ensure that his/her page sizes are kept to a minimum, there are some pitfalls that we need to be aware of when using `data-uri`s:

- Updating sites that use `data-uri` to render images throughout can make it harder to maintain—it's better to use `data-uri` where icons or images are frequently repeated.

- It's a good practice to set a long expiry time on the CSS style sheet so that it remains cached as much as possible, particularly for often-repeated images.

- Some browsers will have strict limits on the size of `data-uri` that can be used. For example, IE8 has a maximum of 32KB; this will limit the size of the images that can be used.

- You will find that embedded code means larger file sizes—this isn't necessarily an issue as long as the document is cached; you can help reduce this by using the **gzip** compression if needed.

This shouldn't put you off from using `data-uri`—it just means that you need to be careful about its use in your pages! `Data-uri` is a really useful way of reducing the number of requests to the server, as long as the content to be used is chosen with care. A good example is small credit card images—these are repeated frequently throughout an e-commerce site, so they could easily be used inline within a CSS style sheet.

Summary

Phew! We've covered a lot in this chapter! Let's recap what we learned.

We kicked off with a look at how to create variables in Less, and with care, we used them to good effect in creating our take on the time-honored Polaroid effect on a series of images. We saw how this can be a real timesaver, by reducing the number of alterations required to code, while at the same time, noting that the scope of variables can be varied, and how this can impact our code.

We then moved on to looking at mixins—both the static and parametric varieties. Here, we saw, with a little forethought, that we could create reusable blocks of code that can be dropped in with ease either within our main Less file or a code library file. We used this technique to iteratively alter the code required to build a very simple web form in order to prove that the improvements made will not affect the overall outcome.

Next up, came an introduction to using functions, where we saw that with the use of some simple operators or math functions, we can produce some useful results with little input. We saw how easy it is to create a simple two-column page layout using a small mixin, and that this can be developed further to incorporate more columns, if desired.

Last, but by no means least, we took a look at using another of Less' functions, in the form of the `data-uri` operator. We saw how easy it is to convert the image into something that can be rendered inline in our code, helping to reduce the number of requests to render content from the server and increase the speed of accessing our page.

We're going to move on and change tack to cover another key area of Less in the next chapter, by looking at inheritance, overriding, and nesting within Less.

5
Inheritance, Overriding, and Nesting in Less

So far in our journey with Less, we've seen how you can begin to reduce the code you need to write; it's time to take it up a level and begin to look at some more advanced concepts within Less.

Let me begin by asking you a question: what is the one thing that irritates you about writing styles where the same selector has to be repeated many times, such as when designing a menu system using an unordered list element? Hopefully, the answer is duplicated styles. In this chapter, we will take a look at how you can group styles to avoid the need to duplicate selectors in your code. We will also cover how you can inherit styles that can have a dramatic effect on reducing duplication; I'll also provide some hints and tips on using these techniques and others to help reduce code bloat.

Enough chat, let's take a look at what we will cover throughout this chapter:

- Nesting styles within Less
- Inheriting styles
- Namespacing in Less
- Scope of styles in Less
- Hints and tips on avoiding code bloat
- Importing style sheets into Less

Curious? What are you waiting for? Let's get started...

Nesting styles in Less

If you spend any time writing styles, I am sure you will frequently have written some that are duplicates of existing ones elsewhere in the same style sheet; this is particularly true if you are creating styles for elements of a site, such as a menu system using `<ul>` or `<li>`.

It can add a lot of extra code bloat from duplicated styles. Thankfully, there is a way we can reduce this, by using Less' ability to nest styles. Let's take a look at how this principle works, by creating the online equivalent of a business card.

For this exercise, we will need a few things. As a start, we'll need an image on our card; in this instance, we'll use an avatar, as this business card will be displayed on websites. There are thousands of icons available for this purpose; I will assume you have picked a suitable one and saved it as `avatar.png`. I've used the Office Client Male Light Icon, available at `http://www.iconarchive.com/show/vista-people-icons-by-icons-land/Office-Client-Male-Light-icon.html`.

Next comes the telephone, e-mail, and figurehead icons; these are from the Modern Pictograms font family found at `http://www.fontsquirrel.com/fonts/modern-pictograms`. You will need to convert it into a format that can be embedded into a webpage; this can be done using a free service at `http://www.convertfonts.com`.

Finally, before we can start work on creating our card, we need some social media icons. I've chosen to use the hand-drawn ones by Chris Spooner, which can be downloaded from `http://blog.spoongraphics.co.uk/freebies/hand-drawn-sketchy-icons-of-your-favorite-social-sites`; alter the code accordingly if you decide to use other icons instead.

Creating a business card

Start by opening a copy of `nesting.html` from the code bundle that accompanies this book. This contains the markup we need to create our basic vCard.

Next, we need to add some styling to make it look presentable. There are a few styles involved, so grab a copy of the code download file that accompanies this book and extract a copy of `nesting.less` from within the archive.

Save the file as `nesting.html`. If you preview the results in a browser, you'll see something similar to the following screenshot:

Examining the process in detail

If we take a look through `nesting.less`, you will notice a number of styles using a similar format. These examples are all variations on a theme of nesting, where instead of adding individual child selectors (and thus duplicating code), we can group together similar child selectors and implement one parent selector.

Our first example uses the standard `a` selector, to which we've grouped together the style rules for `:focus`, `:hover`, and `:active`:

```
a {
  &:focus { outline: thin dotted; }
  &:hover { outline: 0 none; }
  &:active { outline: 0 none; }
}
```

This produces the following code when compiled:

```
a:focus { outline: thin dotted; }
a:hover { outline: 0 none; }
a:active { outline: 0 none; }
```

 In this example, we've used `a` only to illustrate how the process works—in reality, this is an example of where you wouldn't gain any benefit from such a short selector name; the benefit is only seen when longer names are used.

Our second example is a little more advanced – here, we've included some standard CSS styles and mixed in style rules for two additional child selectors that go several levels deeper:

```
.social {
  background-color: #e6e6e6; padding: 10px; width: 100%;
  ul { text-align: right; }
  ul li { display: inline-block; height: 48px; width: 48px; }
  ul li a { display: inline-block; height: 100%; overflow: hidden;
text-decoration: none; text-indent: 100%; white-space: nowrap; width:
100%; }
}
```

The key to nesting is careful examination of any classes or selectors, where there is duplication; let's take a look at the CSS styles that will be displayed in a browser, for the .social code block we've just covered:

```
.social { background-color: #e6e6e6; padding: 10px; width: 100%; }
.social ul { text-align: right; }
.social ul li { display: inline-block; height: 48px; width: 48px;
    }
.social ul li a { display: inline-block; height: 100%; overflow:
hidden; text-decoration: none; text-indent: 100%; white-space: nowrap;
width: 100%; }
```

To work out whether a style can be converted to use nesting, we can take a look at similar selectors; nesting will only work where the selectors use common IDs. In this example, .social is the common selector, hence it's used in our Less example.

A key point to note – at first glance, it would appear that .social ul could have been used instead. This would work, but only for two additional child selectors (.social ul li and .social ul li a). The parent .social class cannot be included if we go in at this level, as we can only work top-down and not bottom-up when considering which styles to nest.

 There is a general rule of thumb that the selector or class used as our grouping ID, should not be more than two levels deep; any more is considered bad practice and should really be revisited!

Let's change focus and take a look at another functionality of Less, which is inheriting and overriding styles, using the extend option.

Inheriting and overriding styles with extend

Up until now, we've used mixins to help reduce the need to write extra code, as we can call these blocks of code from our Less statements easily, to produce the desired effect.

Unfortunately this is still not without its own drawback. Let's say we create two rules, that both call the same mixin, and produce identical results (save for the rule name), then Less will interpret these as two separate blocks of code, even though they both perform the same styling on two different objects. What if we could merge these two rules together so that there is only one block of code, but which can be called by either rule?

Well, we can, with the use of the extend function in Less. This is a really powerful function, introduced for this purpose. Let's take a look at the concept to see how it works.

Imagine you have a mixin, such as this simple one:

```
.stuff { color: red; }
.foo { .stuff; }
.bar { .stuff; }
```

If we compile it using something like Crunch!, then it will display this:

```
.stuff { color: red; }
.foo { color: red; }
.bar { color: red; }
```

This works perfectly well, but shows the aforementioned duplicated styles. To remove this duplication, we can use the extend keyword and rework the code as follows:

```
.foo { color: red; }
.bar { &:extend(.foo); }
```

You can immediately see the difference in the output. Instead of splitting each rule onto two lines as it did before, we've been able to merge the rule into one block, but it can be called by either class:

```
.foo, .bar { color: red; }
```

It is worth reading the documentation on the main Less site on the subject of extend—there are some interesting features that you will need to be aware of, when using the function in your code. You can view the documentation at http://lesscss.org/features/#extend-feature.

The rule of thumb for choosing whether to use extend or a mixin is to choose the technique that requires the least final output (or that works best for you).

Using extend to create information alerts

To see how extend works in practice, let's take a look at a little exercise to create some imaginary dialog boxes that contain messages to alert the user about the outcome of an operation.

Before we can get to work on our example, we first need to download some icons that are suitable for use in dialog boxes. I've chosen to use the free icons created by Andy Gongea; it will be assumed that you are using these icons, for the purpose of the exercise. Visit http://www.graphicrating.com/2012/06/14/koloria-free-icons-set/ to download the icons. You will need to extract the info.png, error.png, warning.png, help.png, and valid.png images and drop them into an img folder at the root of your project folder.

Let's start writing the code! Open a copy of project.html, which we created in *Chapter 3, Getting Started with Less*, and then modify the <head> section as shown in the following code:

```
<title>Demo: Extending</title>
<link rel="stylesheet/less" href="css/extend.less">
<script src="js/less.min.js"></script>
```

Next, remove the existing markup in the <body> tag and replace it with this:

```
<div class="info">Info message</div>
<div class="success">Successful operation message</div>
<div class="warning">Warning message</div>
<div class="error">Error message</div>
<div class="validation">
  <li>First name is a required field</li>
  <li>Last name is a required field</li>
  <li>Email address has been typed incorrectly</li>
  <li>Preferred language has not been selected</li>
</div>
```

Save this as `extend.html`. On its own, it won't win any awards for style if we were to preview it now, so let's fix that by adding some! In a new file, add the following styles:

```
body{ font-family: Arial, Helvetica, sans-serif; font-size: 13px; }
.demo { font-style: italic; }

.box { border: 1px solid #000; margin: 10px 0px; padding:15px 10px
15px 50px; background-repeat: no-repeat;
  background-position: 10px center; width: 300px; padding-top: 15px; }

.info:extend(.box) { color: #00529B; background-color: #BDE5F8;
background-image: url('../img/info.png'); }
.success:extend(.box) { color: #4F8A10; background-color: #DFF2BF;
background-image:url('../img/valid.png'); }
.warning:extend(.box) { color: #9F6000; background-color: #FEEFB3;
background-image: url('../img/warning.png'); }
.error:extend(.box) { color: #D8000C; background-color: #FFBABA;
background-image: url('../img/error.png'); }
.validation:extend(.box) { width: 280px; padding-left: 70px; color:
#D63301; background-color: #FFCCBA; background-image: url('../img/
error.png'); }
```

Save the file as `extend.less` in the `css` subfolder; if you have configured Sublime Text to compile Less files on save, then it will also produce the compiled CSS equivalent file. We can use this to compare the results shown in the file, with those displayed in the browser, when using a DOM Inspector such as Firebug. If we preview the file in a browser, we should see something like the following screenshot:

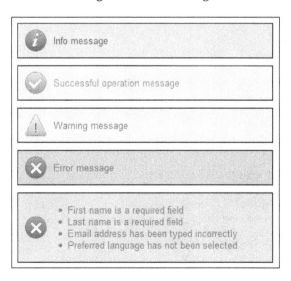

Although this is a relatively simple example, it is worth taking a moment to study the code to see how the `extend` function operates.

If you use a mixin, you often find that you have to include a base class (.stuff in our earlier example) as your mixin, which contains the styles that you need to inherit within your calling classes (in this instance, .foo and .bar).

This will work perfectly well, but will duplicate the code as we have already seen; instead, we used the extend function to apply the existing .box class to each of the classes we used for the dialogs, namely .info, .success, .warning, .error, and .validation.

As extend is a Less pseudo-class, all trace of the extend function will be removed, leaving the resulting compiled styles. The real benefit of using this function can be seen when using Firebug; instead of seeing a lot of duplicated styles, we will see styles neatly merged together where they perform the same function, with the remaining styles left to operate on the remaining elements where appropriate.

Extending using the all keyword

Once you have begun using the extend keyword in your Less code, you might find that you want to extend styles that are nested.

Unfortunately, extend can only match a selector based on what is given in the extend request; it is not always able to match child selectors below a parent, unless a child selector is specified. Let's take a look at an example to see what this means.

Imagine you have this simple bit of nested Less:

```
.module {
  padding: 10px;
  h3 { color: red; }
}
```

Using extend will produce this:

```
.news { &:extend(.module); }
```

The h3 style will not be extended and will instead be compiled as a separate style:

```
.module, .news { padding: }
.module h3 { color: red; }
```

To get around this, we can use the all keyword as shown in the following line of code:

```
.news { &:extend(.module all); }
```

The all keyword will extend everything to produce the desired effect:

```
.module, .news { padding: 10px; }
.module h3, .news h3 { color: red; }
```

The key to it is to think of it as performing a nondestructive search and replace operation on the original selector, to produce a new one. Let's take a look at it in practice, by modifying the previous extend demo to use the all keyword.

Start by opening a copy of extend.html, which we created from the previous exercise, then encompass each of the dialog text messages in the <h3> tags, as highlighted:

```
<div class="info"><h3>Info message</h3></div>
<div class="success"><h3>Successful operation message</h3></div>
<div class="warning"><h3>Warning message</h3></div>
<div class="error"><h3>Error message</h3></div>
<div class="validation">
  <h3>
    <li>First name is a required field</li>
    <li>Last name is a required field</li>
    <li>Email address has been typed incorrectly</li>
    <li>Preferred language has not been selected</li>
  </h3>
An example using <span class="demo">extend:(...all):</span>
<div class="rebase"><h3>Info message</h3></div>
```

Save this as extendall.html. In a copy of extend.less, we need to move the rule for font-size from body to <h3>, so we can then include it as a nested rule later in our code. Amend the style rule for body, and then immediately below this, add a new rule for <h3>, as shown in the following code:

```
body { font-family: Arial, Helvetica, sans-serif; }
h3 { font-size: 12px; }
```

In the validation code block, add the three lines (as highlighted); this will style the <h3> tags we added earlier to our HTML code:

```
.validation:extend(.box) { width: 280px; padding-left: 70px;
  color: #D63301; background-color: #FFCCBA; background-image:
url('../img/error.png');
  h3 { font-size: 14px; }
}
```

We can now take advantage of the all keyword; immediately below the .validation style block, add the following code:

```
.rebase:extend(.validation all) {}
.rebase {
  color: #fff;
  background-color: #9a0074;
  background-image: url('../img/help.png');
}
```

Save the file as extendall.less. If we preview the results in a browser, we will see the added dialog box appear below the last dialog box, as shown in the following screenshot:

Now that we have seen this in action, let's take a moment to examine how it works.

Using the all attribute with extend is very easy, as we have seen, but it does mean that the styles that need to be replicated should be as close to the desired result as possible, to make the use of extend worthwhile.

This doesn't mean to say that you can't add additional, or indeed override, existing styles as we have done here, but we've kept them to a minimum. Here, we've used extend all to replicate the .validation class and rename it as .rebase; this includes the additional styling for the <h3> tag, which would otherwise not have been included if the all tag had not been used. We've then simply overridden three of the styles to change the image used, background-color and text color, to make it a little more unique.

We've only scratched the surface with what you can do using extend—before we change focus and move to looking at namespacing, let's take a moment to look at some of the other highlights of using the extend keyword:

- Extend can be used with pseudo-class selectors such as :hover or :active; multiple extends can be used, along with spaces. However, if only one extend is used, then this must be the last part of the statement.

- You can use &:extend within a ruleset; this is a shortcut to adding extend to every single selector within the ruleset.

- Extend can be used with nested selectors; as long as the calling extend can be matched against a valid Less rule, it will be extended to use the new class or selector ID.

- By default, extend will look for an exact match, for example, *.class and .class, which are equivalent, won't be considered as exact matches by Less, when using extend.

- If you want to match using type identifiers such as [title="identifier"], then it doesn't matter whether quotes are used or not; these are effectively ignored.

The extend keyword is a very useful tool within the Less article, but can cause issues if not used correctly. It is well worth reading the main documentation on the Less site at http://lesscss.org/features/#extend-feature, to get your head around some of the quirks of using the function.

Namespacing in Less

There is one thing I am sure you will find asking yourself as time goes by and your CSS style sheets get larger: *can I group similar styles to make things easier to find?*

Sure, you can always cut and paste similar styles together, but this is a manual process, right? What happens if two weeks down the line, you need to add a new style, which is similar to the one buried 1500-odd lines down? Surely there has to be a better way to do this—there is. Welcome to namespacing in Less!

Namespacing in Less takes your need to group similar styles and flips it on its head; it groups all of the constituent building blocks of your styles together, then allows you to pick and choose which styles to use when adding styling for a new element on your site. We can, of course, create multiple namespaces if we need to—our only real guide for this is that each namespace should contain styles that share common elements; a great example is buttons, as you will see from our upcoming exercise.

Let's begin creating these buttons by opening a copy of project.html and then modifying the <head> tag as shown in the following code:

```
<title>Demo: Namespaces</title>
<link rel="stylesheet/less" href="css/namespace.less">
<script src="js/less.min.js"></script>
```

Next, remove the existing markup in the `<body>` tag and replace it with the following code:

```
<input type="button" name="buy" value="Buy" class="redbutton">
<input type="button" name="clear" value="Pay by PayPal"
  class="purplebutton">
<input type="button" name="checkout" value="Pay by credit card"
  class="bluebutton">
```

Save this as `namespace.html` in the root of our project folder. We need to apply some styling, so go ahead and add the following Less styles to a new file; we'll break it down into sections and go through it bit by bit, as there are a few important concepts to consider:

```
.background (@color1, @color2) {
  background: -webkit-gradient( linear, left top, left bottom, color-
stop(0.05, @color1), color-stop(1, @color2) );
  background: -moz-linear-gradient( center top, @color1 5%, @color2
100% );
  background-color: @color1;
  border: 1px solid @color1;
}
```

We saw examples similar to this back in *Chapter 4, Working with Variables, Mixins, and Functions*; hopefully, you will recognize this as a parametric mixin. In this instance, we're using it to build up a gradient for each of our buttons; we're feeding it two values that represent the colors used in the gradient fading process, as shown in the following code:

```
#button() {
  .base { border-radius: 6px; color: #fff; font-family: Arial;
font-size: 15px; font-weight: bold; font-style: normal;  height: 32px;
text-align: center; text-shadow: 1px 1px 0px #000; margin-left: 5px;
  &:active { position: relative; top: 1px; }
  }
```

 Note that namespaces such as `#button()` used here can be made from classes or selector IDs; for more details on the recognized behavior, see `https://github.com/less/less.js/issues/1205`.

Next comes the most important part of our Less styling: the opening statement for a namespaced style. It shows the name under which we will group our styles. We've used `()`, as we don't want Less to output the mixin as well as the compiled CSS, when compiling our code:

```
.red {
  .background(#cc1c28, #a01620);
  box-shadow: inset 0px 1px 0px 0px #b61924;
  &:hover { .background(#a01620, #cc1c28) }
}

.purple {
  .background(#800080, #9a009a);
  box-shadow: inset 0px 1px 0px 0px #670067;
  &:hover { .background(#9a009a, #800080) }
}

.blue {
  .background(#004771, #00578a);
  box-shadow: inset 0px 1px 0px 0px #0067a4;
  &:hover { .background(#00578a, #004771) }
}
}
```

These three blocks of code will call the `.background(...)` mixin to set the appropriate gradient, depending on which state is currently set for a specific button:

```
.redbutton { #button > .base; #button > .red; }
.purplebutton { #button > .base; #button > .purple; }
.bluebutton { #button > .base; #button > .blue; }
```

This is where the real magic happens. Here, we've set the styles to be used for three buttons, namely red, purple, and blue. Within each button style, we've chosen to call elements from the `#button` namespace; if several similar namespaces had been created, we could easily pick and choose our styles from each, as we are not limited to just using one namespace. The key thing to note is that when calling a namespace style, you must use the format given in our example.

Okay, enough of the theory. If we preview the results in a browser, we should expect to see something akin to this:

A nice, easy example, huh? Hopefully, it will help show you how you can pick and choose your styles from groupings of styles, particularly when a project uses a lot of similar elements and styles that could benefit from being namespaced.

Lazy loading of variables in Less

So far, we've covered a number of techniques to create and control how styles are applied. There is one key theme that runs throughout all of this though and of which you need to be aware: scope.

Yes, there's that ugly word, scope! No matter how much we try to avoid it, we must always allow for it when using Less; if not, it can come back to bite us at the most unexpected moments. Let me explain what I mean: as we will see in the upcoming exercise, we can always reuse our mixins or variables throughout our Less code.

The downside is that Less must have a means of knowing which instance is the most latest; therefore, it always takes the last instance of any variable or mixin that is included in our code. If you're not careful, it can lead to some odd effects. Let's take a look at what this means in practice, with a quick exercise.

Start by opening a copy of `project.html` that we created back in *Chapter 3, Getting Started with Less,* and then, alter the `<head>` tag as shown in the following code:

```
<meta charset="utf-8">
<title>Demo: Scoping</title>
<link
  href='http://fonts.googleapis.com/css?family=Over+the+Rainbow'
    rel='stylesheet' type='text/css'>
<link rel="stylesheet/less" href="css/scope1.less">
```

Next, remove the existing markup and replace it with the following code:

```
<div id ="container">
  <div id="box1">This is box 1</div>
  <div id="box2">This is box 2</div>
  <div id="box3">This is box 3</div>
</div>
```

Save this as `scope.html`. Finally, even though this is only a simple example, we still need to add some styling; go ahead and add the following to a new file, saving it as `scope1.less`:

```
@boxcolor: green;

html { font-family: 'Over the Rainbow', cursive; font-weight: bold;
font-size: 20px; }
```

```
div {  width: 200px; height: 100px; padding: 3px; border-radius: 3px;
float: left; position: absolute; }

#box1 { margin-left: 0; }
#box2 { margin-left: 225px; }
#box3 { margin-left: 450px; }

#container {
  @boxcolor: red;
  #box1 { background-color: @boxcolor; }
  #box2 { background-color: @boxcolor; }

  @boxcolor: orange;
  #box3 { background-color: @boxcolor; }
}
```

Before we preview the results in a browser, ask yourself this one question: what colors would you expect to see in each box?

No, I've not gone insane; stay with me on this one! If you were expecting to see red in boxes **1** and **2** and orange in box **3**, then I'm sorry to disappoint you:

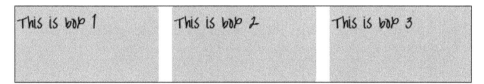

Hold on—all three of them are in orange! This is true; this has to do with the concept of scoping within Less.

If you've spent any time programming, then you will likely be aware of how a variable's value will be used in a statement if it has just been set before the statement. Less uses variables in a similar fashion, but with one important difference: it uses the *last known instance* of that variable assignment, to determine which value to display.

> Variables in Less are merged into code—this is the equivalent of lazy loading, as the last defined instance of a variable is the one that is used, overwriting any previous instance of that variable.

If we look through the code, we can clearly see the last instance of @boxcolor being set a color value, just before box3. As the color set was orange, this is the value that will be used throughout our code. We can clearly see this from a screenshot excerpt of the compiled styles within Crunch!, where #ffa500 is orange:

```
24 ▾ #container #box1 {
25     background-color: #ffa500;
26 }
27 ▾ #container #box2 {
28     background-color: #ffa500;
29 }
30 ▾ #container #box3 {
31     background-color: #ffa500;
32 }
```

It is worth noting the scope that is set when using variables, as we have done here. It is all too easy to be tripped up through the use of an (incorrectly) assigned variable, which produces unexpected results!

The only safe way to ensure that the right values are used is to assign separate variables. We can see the results of this if we modify the Less styles from our previous example:

```less
@boxcolor1: lightgreen;

html { font-family: 'Over the Rainbow', cursive; font-weight: bold;
font-size: 20px; }
div {  width: 200px; height: 100px; padding: 3px; border-radius: 3px;
float: left; position: absolute; }

#box1 { margin-left: 0; }
#box2 { margin-left: 225px; }
#box3 { margin-left: 450px; }

#container {
  @boxcolor2: red;
  #box1 { background-color: @boxcolor1; }
  #box2 { background-color: @boxcolor2; }

  @boxcolor3: orange;
  #box3 { background-color: @boxcolor3; }
}
```

Resave the Less file as `scope2.less`; don't forget to change the markup in `scope.html`! If we preview the results in the browser, we can clearly see the difference it has made, where separate variables have been used:

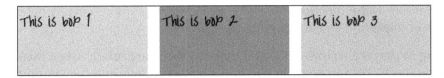

Throughout this demo, we've used `box1`, `box2`, and `box3` as selector IDs — it is worth nothing that these are not semantic names; for this reason, they should not be used in a production environment. As we are working in a demo environment only to illustrate a concept, then use of these names is less of an issue.

Now that we've seen the results of using separate variables, we can also see the difference by looking at the compiled CSS in this screenshot extract from Crunch!:

```
24 ▾  #container #box1 {
25        background-color: #90ee90;
26     }
27 ▾  #container #box2 {
28        background-color: #ff0000;
29     }
30 ▾  #container #box3 {
31        background-color: #ffa500;
32     }
```

Notice the difference? Hopefully, you will see how it is crucial to take care while using variables, as the scope of their use can produce some odd effects if not used carefully! Let's move on, as we need to take a look at some functionality we've already used, but haven't explored in any great depth, namely importing style sheets into Less.

Going overboard with variables

It is all too easy to add lots of variables to cater to values such as colors used in your site. This is not always a sensible thing to do; you should consider setting up a core number of variables, then using functions to work out the values that should be used.

Importing style sheets into Less

Phew! We're almost there. We've certainly covered a lot in this chapter! Before we finish the chapter with some tips on avoiding code bloat, we should take a moment to consider one useful function that we've used, but not explored in any detail—this is the use of importing to manage our Less style sheets.

Importing in Less is a simple but useful trick to learn, particularly when managing large style sheets. We can begin to build up a library of code and then import it straight into any future project.

It makes it much easier to manage smaller files, as we can build a master file that imports each of the subfiles into one master; Less will only compile these styles that are directly referenced from our main code. So for example, if your code library file is more than 2,500 lines long, but a mixin of only 10 lines is all that is used, then Less will only include those 10 lines in the final compiled results.

Using the import option is really easy; all you need to do is add in the following statement somewhere within your Less code:

```
@import (XXXXXXX) "foo.less";
```

Here xxxxxxx is one of any of the following options:

Option:	Allows us to:
reference	This uses a Less file but do not output it, unless referenced from within the code.
inline	This includes the source file in the output but does not process it and is useful if you need to import files that are not Less compatible, but still need to be included in the compiled CSS file.
less	This treats the file as a Less file, no matter what the file extension. This is ideal if you have a need for all Less files to have the .css extension, but where they should be treated as Less files, not plain CSS.
css	This treats the file as a CSS file, no matter what the file extension is.
once	This only includes the file once (this is the default behavior); any subsequent import requests for this file will be ignored.
multiple	This includes the same Less file multiple times. This is the opposite of the default behavior of Less.

You can learn more about the various options from the main Less site, at http://lesscss.org/features/#import-options.

Okay, let's wrap up this chapter by taking a look at some important hints and tips on avoiding code bloat. Some of what you will see comes from the functionality that we've explored throughout this chapter, but it's useful to take a moment to summarize some of the key points we've covered in the book to date.

Avoiding code bloat

When designing websites, one of the key aims that should be dear to every designer is to ensure that they avoid code bloat wherever they can so that their finished article works well and is engaging to their audience.

To help with this, there are a number of tips we can use to help reduce code bloat. We've already used some throughout the book so far, but now seems like an opportune moment to revisit and consolidate them into a useful list you can use for future projects:

- Aim to create a cleaner structure with the use of nesting — this means you can avoid having to reenter duplicate selectors (such as using `<ul>` within a list or menu) and can keep the code organized as related items are grouped together.

- Create variables for faster maintenance — these work very much like variables in other programming languages, such as C#. We can set one instance of a variable at the start, then reference this throughout our code; Less will automatically update each instance for you. Take care how many you create though, as each requires valuable resources; it is better practice to create a core bunch and use operators to dynamically work out new values. This has the benefit of allowing these new values to continue to work, even if original variables are subsequently changed.

- Use mixins to create whole classes that we can reference throughout our code. On larger sites, this can have a dramatic effect in reducing the amount of code that needs to be written. If you are already using mixins, then check through your code to see if they can't be made parametric; this increases their flexibility and will allow you to remove redundant mixins, as they can be served by tweaking other mixins.

- Take an iterative approach to develop your CSS, particularly when using mixins. If you use mixins that are similar to mixins being brought in by external Less libraries, then try to design out the differences, so you can remove your own...

- Use namespaces to pick and choose mixins. This will help you group together common styling rules that apply to similar elements, such as buttons; you can then pick and choose which elements to use. Try to keep the number of selector elements used in each namespace to a minimum too; there is no hard and fast rule, but a good rule of thumb is something like the following code:

```
.redbutton {
  #base > .button
  #base > .redcolor
}
```

If your code uses more than one selector elements in each namespace it is likely that your code isn't as efficient as it should be...!

- If you are using namespacing, then take care of your CSS specificity, otherwise clashing results can be a symptom of nesting too deeply, or overuse of the !important attribute. If you find this happening, then you might need to break your namespacing into smaller groups, which uses fewer levels of nesting.

- Consider using class inheritance instead of selector inheritance. If you are creating a mixin, which you later reference in your selector classes, you might find that you can simply use class inheritance in your HTML instead. So, as an example, instead of using this in your Less file:

```
.gradientBlack { ... }

h3 { .gradientBlack; ... }
.darkBox { .gradientBlack; ... }
td.dark { .gradientBlack; ... }
```

We can eliminate the repeated use of .gradientBlack, by defining it once in our style sheet, then referencing it directly in the code:

```
<h3 class="gradientBlack"></h3>
<div class="darkBox gradientBlack></div>
<td class="dark gradientBlack"></td>
```

- Use extend instead of mixins to reduce code bloat; extend is clever enough to merge together styles that use the same rules, as we saw earlier in the chapter, instead of simply reproducing code blocks for each similar style.

- If you have to stay with using mixins, then use parentheses to hide the mixin code so that only the calling code is compiled and not the additional mixin as well.

- If you have a number of mixins that require vendor prefixing, you can use this mixin to handle them by simply passing the property that needs to be prefixed, along with the appropriate value, as shown in the following code:

```
.vendorize(@property, @value) {
  -webkit-@{property}: @value;
  -moz-@{property}: @value;
  -ms-@{property}: @value;
  -o-@{property}: @value;
  @{property}: @value;
}
```

Note that this isn't necessary for all properties that still require vendor prefixes; if a CSS3 property only needs one or two vendor prefixes, you might find it easier to create a simple mixin to handle this separately.

 It is worth noting that some vendor prefixes use a completely different format to the example we've used—the mixin here won't work for all property values, such as gradients and will therefore need a separate mixin.

Hopefully, there are some useful tips in there that you can use in your projects. The key to all of this is using the right combination of functions, such as extends instead of mixins (or a mix of both), that helps keep your code to a minimum and free of bloat.

Summary

Throughout this chapter, we've covered a few concepts that will help further reduce the amount of code you need to write—let's take a moment to recap, before moving onto some more practical areas of using Less in the next chapter.

We began with a look at how you can group or nest styles within Less; we saw how this can help arrange styles visually, to make it easier to manage, but also remove the need to duplicate styles, when referencing child selectors such as those used in building menu systems.

We then moved on and looked at the extend function to inherit or override existing styles, and covered how it works in a similar fashion to mixins, while at the same time, merging together identical styles, to remove the need to have separate code blocks for identical styles. We also took a look at the use of the `all` keyword to help with inheriting of all of the styles, particularly those otherwise not accessible using extend on its own.

We then covered how you group styles and reference one or more elements using namespacing; this allows us to visually group together common elements, while at the same time, picking and choosing which styles to use. Once chosen, we then saw how Less will compile these into valid CSS.

Last but by no means least, we took a quick look at setting the right scope in Less, to ensure our variables have the right values. We saw from the example how easy it is to get the scope wrong and the importance of using the right scope in our code. We then finished with a look at importing Less files into CSS and some hints and tips on removing code bloat, based on some of the key areas of Less we have seen so far in the book.

In the next chapter, we'll move on from the theory and take a look at some of the practical aspects of moving a CSS-based site over to using Less.

6
Migrating Your Site to Less

So, by now, you've hopefully spent some time using Less and are thinking that this could be really useful for your projects going forward, right?

The trouble is you'll also probably be thinking of existing projects that could easily benefit by using Less, but you're not sure how to go about converting them to use Less. No problem; in this chapter, I will take you through some of the tips and tricks of how to make this transition to use Less, without risking everything.

We'll start by taking a look at the kind of questions we need to ask ourselves and then move on to creating the basic framework that we'll use when beginning the conversion, going through a detailed example of converting a mini website to use Less.

The key to conversion is to remember that Less is, after all, just a superset of CSS—most of the work is about identifying those parts that can be changed easily and those that might require more work. In this chapter, we'll cover the following topics:

- Low-hanging fruit—obvious candidates for Less conversion
- Identifying patterns in your CSS
- Building a library of mixins
- Using prebuilt libraries as part of the conversion process
- Mixing Less with plain CSS
- Working through a practical example

Are you ready to start converting your CSS? Good, let's get started...

Preparing for the initial jump

So, you've read all about using Less and are keen to start using it in some of your older projects. You've started working with it on your newer sites and love how it makes writing CSS so much more manageable...but, you're probably thinking: how can I incorporate it into an older site?

Well, you're in the right place—making the change in older sites doesn't need to be difficult, as long as you keep these tips in mind:

- Make sure you have installed Firebug with Less support, as outlined in *Chapter 2, Building a Less Development Toolkit*. Trust me on this; it will make debugging your efforts so much easier!

- Run your existing CSS through a site, such as W3C CSS Validator (`http://jigsaw.w3.org/css-validator/validator`). If you haven't already done so, this will help spot any errors and ensure that your code validates properly, before beginning to convert it to Less.

- Try to get into the mentality that converting Less should be done in blocks at a time and should be an iterative process—this reduces the risk of missing opportunities or making mistakes in your code; this is particularly important when converting large files, such as a WordPress style sheet!

- Don't forget that Less is a superset of CSS—provided we work through the conversion process in a logical manner. Less will still compile plain CSS code that has yet to be converted to its Less equivalent. This means that we can mix code during the conversion process until all of the styles have been suitably converted.

- Get into the habit of using sites such as `http://less2css.org` or `http://lesstester.com`. These are great for experimenting with the Less code in order to see how it will compile into valid CSS.

Let's put some of these tips into practice and take a look at the initial steps that should form the basis for any initial conversion process.

Creating the initial framework

Once you've made the decision to convert in order to use Less, there are a few steps that we can take, which help with the initial conversion process, before we start writing Less code.

Let's take a look at how we can make this process easier. For the purpose of this example, I'll assume that you have just one style sheet, called `styles.css`, and that you're working in a development environment on a simple HTML-based site in order to get accustomed to the conversion process.

1. Start by renaming the `sitestyles.css` file with a `.less` extension to `sitestyles.less`.

2. In a new file in your text editor, add the following:

   ```
   @import "sitestyles.less";
   ```

3. Save this as `styles.less`. In your HTML code, change the existing link to `sitestyles.css` in order to point to `sitestyles.less`, using the following link:

   ```
   <link rel="stylesheet/less" href="css/styles.less">
   <script src="js/less.min.js"></script>
   ```

Use Crunch! or Sublime Text (depending on what you have set up in *Chapter 3, Getting Started with Less*) to compile the new `styles.less` file in order to confirm whether it is producing a valid `styles.css` file.

 We've referenced the Less file directly in our code — this is for development purposes only and not recommended for production use.

At this point, you might think that having a single statement in the `styles.less` file might sound like an overkill; there is a reason for this: the key to working with Less is to build up the initial framework of the Less file so that we can prove that it compiles to valid CSS first. Once this has been proven, it is simply a matter of adding more `@import` statements for each partial file you want to include. Less will combine all of these into one file when we next recompile `styles.less`, as we will see in the next section.

Mixing Less with plain CSS

If we mix Less with CSS to create a framework for importing individual partials, we will get an additional benefit: we are not obliged to convert all of the Less files in one go! Instead, we can simply break the existing CSS files into smaller **partials** and then import them into the master CSS file (here, `styles.less`) — this makes it easier to manage the conversion process.

Partials are separate files that contain Less code—they are a means to help make managing Less code easier, as multiple files can be imported in one style sheet as part of the compilation process.

We then simply add an `@import` statement for each Less file we need to import, such as the examples shown:

```
@import "sitestyles.less";
@import "fonts.css";
@import "css3.less";
@import "menu.less";
```

Remember that no matter how big the Less file is or how many partials are being imported, Less will only ever import a style in the final compiled CSS file if it is being referenced in the code. While we are still developing the Less file, we can easily compile this dynamically in the browser; once the final version is ready, this can be precompiled, and the resulting CSS file can be imported in our production environment.

Spotting low-hanging fruit

Now that we have our basic framework in place, it's time to go fruit picking—no, I'm not referring to fruit picking in the literal sense, but finding CSS statements that can be easily converted with little effort.

Each project will vary in size and scope, but there will be some easy conversions that we can make, which will apply to any project:

1. An easy change that can be made is to incorporate variables for colors—once converted, we can use operators to calculate new values, such as lightening a specific color by 25 percent. As a start, we can create some variables, such as the following:

```
@color-light-orange: #ffa500;
@color-gray-cyan: #6a7172;
@color-gray-dark: #313131;
@color-grayish-orange: #d7cec3;
```

We can then use variables in our styles, instead of the hex codes; they will appear as follows:

```
body {background: @color-gray-cyan; color: @color-gray-dark; }
a { color: @color-light-orange; }
h1, h2, h3, h4, h5, h6 { color: @color-gray-dark; }
```

Ideally, the names used here should reflect the context that they are used for, such as body-textcolor or heading-textcolor; we've used names here to illustrate how they can replace existing colors, and at least make the color names readable!

2. During the conversion process, you may want to consider moving converted code into a separate Less partial and importing it using the process we covered earlier. Although this will allow you to maintain a distinction between Less and CSS styles, it does mean that we may miss opportunities if the converted Less code is not displayed on the screen while we work on converting the existing CSS styles.

3. If we're using CSS3 styles that contain vendor prefixes, we can convert our code to import mixins from external prebuilt libraries, such as LESS Hat or LESS Elements. This will reduce the code we need to write – after all, why reinvent the wheel if someone has already built a suitable mixin that we can use?

4. A more evolved change that we can make is related to the use of nesting – this will make our code easier to read, as it is clearer how child styles will affect their parent elements. A perfect example of this is a menu system built into the header DIV of a page:

```
header .nav { margin-top: 100px; }
header .nav li { margin-left: 10px; }
header .nav li a { height: 30px; line-height: 10px; }
```

We can then convert it manually or using a site, such as http://css2less.cc; while this site isn't perfect, it will give you a head start in the conversion process:

Online CSS to Less convertors are not perfect—for example, they may struggle to produce good quality code if your CSS file contains a lot of random selectors; Less will also regroup CSS statements during compilation, which may break your code. These sites should be treated as a start point for development; the assumption time is spent in finessing the code manually after the initial conversion.

There will no doubt be other easy changes we can make—it will all depend on the size and scope of the site being converted to use Less. Again, the key point to remember here is that conversion should be an iterative process and that you will do yourself no favors if you try to convert your site in one go!

Let's change our focus slightly and move on to the next stage in the process—once you've dealt with the easy conversions, it's time to ask yourself a series of questions, all of which fall under the banner of identifying patterns in your CSS.

Identifying patterns in your CSS

Identifying patterns in your CSS is all about asking yourself one question: how can I reduce code?

There are a number of ways of doing this; the exact process will depend on the nature of the site being converted. There are some general questions that you can ask yourself though, to help with the conversion process:

- Does your site use any CSS3 styles? If it does, consider using a prebuilt Less library, which we can import in our Less style sheet.

- Does your CSS code contain any statements, such as links to image elements? If it does, you might want to consider using string variables and interpolation to better manage the links, particularly if they need to be updated in the future.

- How many variables does your site use? If any of these variables will be used to define colors, then consider using some of Less' in-built functions or operators to dynamically generate colors, such as making a color lighter by 20 percent or adding a value to an existing color to create a new one.

- How often do you see the same (or very similar) block of code shown throughout your code? With a little care, can it be altered to be the same as others? If so, this would be a prime candidate for conversion into a mixin. The more instances of code we can alter while still maintaining the same effect, the more value we will get from using a mixin.

While there are likely to be more questions that you might ask, since each site is different, not every question will apply. One of the key questions will be related to creating mixins and whether we can separate them in our own library for future use.

Using prebuilt mixin libraries

If we've created a number of mixins, we could turn these into a library. However, this may not always be necessary; instead, we can always look for ways to reuse mixins from libraries that are available for download from the Internet.

Why should we use them? There are two good reasons for doing so:

- We can avoid the need to reinvent the wheel
- We don't need to worry about the support for, or the updating of, the library — this will be handled by the author, frequently with the help of the open source community at large

There are lots of libraries that are available — they can all be imported using the same `@import` statement we've already seen in use. We will cover how to use such a library in more detail in the practical example at the end of the chapter, but in the meantime, here are some examples of libraries that are available for use:

- 3L (`http://mateuszkocz.github.io/3l/`)
- Animate.css (`https://github.com/daneden/animate.cs`)
- ClearLess (`https://github.com/clearleft/clearless`)
- CSS Effects (`http://adodson.com/css-effects/`)
- Cssowl (`http://cssowl.owl-stars.com/`)
- LESS Elements (`http://lesselements.com/`)
- LESS Hat (`http://lesshat.com/`)
- Oban (`http://oban.io/`)
- Preboot (`http://getpreboot.com/`)

There will be plenty more available online; you can search over the Internet to see what is available, as you may find others that are more suited to your needs. We will be using the LESS Hat library in a practical demo later in this chapter.

Building a library of mixins

As part of identifying patterns in our CSS, where we can identify code that can be turned into mixins, we might find that using a prebuilt library, such as LESS Elements or LESS Hat, doesn't always meet our requirements.

This is not necessarily an issue; it may be that the author of the library hasn't created the mixin the way we want it, as he was trying to satisfy another requirement. If existing mixins aren't available, we can always consider creating our own library of mixins as partials that can be included in future projects. We could even consider hosting mixins on GitHub (`http://www.github.com`), as has been done by others:

There are several popular code-sharing platforms available, which you can try—two good examples are Google Code (`https://code.google.com/`) and Bitbucket (`https://bitbucket.org/`).

The trick in creating mixins for libraries here is to stay several steps ahead of yourself and work out how you can convert similar blocks of code so that they can be replaced with one or more mixins.

If you find that the code can be converted into mixins, it is worth giving a thought to how these mixins should be written. A key precept of Less is the DRY principle (Don't Repeat Yourself) — you may find yourself writing a number of mixins that can be reused. The usefulness of these mixins will increase if careful consideration is given to any tweaks that can be made, so that other blocks of CSS code can be replaced by Less calls to the mixins you create.

Once your library has been created, you can host it on GitHub — there are several good reasons for doing so:

- There is a ready-made community at large, who can help with issues or support the library
- It is a good way to say thank you to others, as you may have used their work
- Anyone who uses your mixin library can help suggest improvements to your mixins

Creating your own library and making it available online will give you an enormous sense of satisfaction, from having been able to contribute back to the open source movement — after all, we've only reached where we are today, thanks to the efforts of those who have spent hours creating libraries such as Less!

Now, let's turn our focus to using one of these prebuilt libraries that we've just covered — we're going to take a look at using LESS Hat as part of our practical example.

Working through a practical example

So far, we've looked at a range of tips and tricks that you can use to convert a site in order to use Less — while there are some useful tips, I think you will agree that it is far better to see the conversion process in action! With this in mind, let's take a look at a simple example, in the form of the CSS styling we created in *Chapter 4*, *Working with Variables, Mixins, and Functions*, for the one-page website.

Before we start making changes, let's take a look at the compiled CSS that was created for the page, along with a screenshot of the page:

Introducing the CSS

Now that we've seen a screenshot of the page that we're going to retrofit to use Less, let's take a look at the CSS code we need to convert. The compiled CSS that was generated using Crunch! is as follows—a copy of this is in the code download that accompanies this book, as `conversion.css`. We'll also include a slightly modified version of the styles from `social.css`, within `conversion.css`. This will still produce the same results, but the reason for modifying it here will become apparent in the next section:

```
#social { width: 175px; height: 60px; background-image: url('../img/
sprites.png'); float: right;}
```

At first glance, this should look like an ordinary style sheet, which hopefully uses some fairly common style attributes that could be used in any website project:

```css
1   div { font-family: 'Kite One',sans-serif; margin-bottom: 5px;
2   margin-top: 5px; padding: 5px; }
3
4   #container { border: 1px solid #000000; border-radius: 4px;
5   box-shadow: 4px 4px 4px 0 rgba(0, 0, 0, 0.5); margin: 5% auto;
6   width: 800px; }
7
8   #title { color: #FFFFFF; font-family: 'Kite One',sans-serif;
9   font-size: 32px; font-weight: 400; padding-left: 100px;
10  padding-top: 30px; position: absolute; }
11
12  #header { background-image: url("../img/leaves.jpg"); font-size: 18px; height: 150px; }
13
14  #leftmargin { -moz-box-sizing: border-box; border-right: 1px solid #CCCCCC; float: left;
15      height: 575px; width: 306px; }
16
17  #leftmargin li { list-style: none outside none; }
18
19  #leftmargin a { text-decoration: none; }
20
21  #leftmargin a:hover { text-decoration: underline; }
22
23  #content { -moz-box-sizing: border-box; float: left; height: 575px; padding: 10px;
24      width: 494px; }
25
26  #footer { border-top: 1px solid #CCCCCC; clear: both; font-size: 12px; height: 65px; }
27
28  #social { width: 175px; height: 60px; background-image: url('../img/sprites.png');
29      float: right;}
```

You're probably thinking that with such a simple example, there's little we can do here, right?

Identifying the changes to be made

Wrong! Making the conversion to use Less should not always be about the size of your style sheet but about getting into the mindset that using Less will make it easier to manage your code, no matter what its size. Converting to use Less should be an iterative process that stops only when all of the original CSS has been converted and when Less is being used in your site.

To prove this, let's take a look at the code and highlight some of the areas that can be converted. The style sheet is a simple example, but it is enough to illustrate the processes that you can use to convert a CSS file to its Less equivalent.

- Did you notice the three style rules that use `#leftmargin`? Here is the perfect opportunity to use nesting—we can avoid having to duplicate the rule name, and we can group the styles in a more logical manner.

- We used the box-sizing attribute used for `#content` but didn't include all the vendor prefixes for it. It's a good excuse to look at one of the many mixin libraries available online and see if one of them contains a suitable mixin that we can use. This avoids the need to reinvent the wheel—we can simply link to the mixin and pass values to it, if appropriate. Importing a prebuilt mixin will also handle any vendor prefixes that are required for operation.

- Instead of using hex values for colors, which aren't easy to translate into something meaningful, we can create variables and assign values to them. The names can be set to describe the color value being set. If they need to be updated, then it only requires one update, as Less will handle changing all the other instances automatically.

- In `div` and `#title`, we've included a `font-family` attribute—while this will work perfectly well in normal CSS, we can use the same variable process and create meaningful names for each `font-family` attribute. This makes them much easier to update, should they need to be changed in the future.

- In `#leftmargin` and `#content`, you may or may not have noticed an opportunity here—we're repeating the same code (albeit, with slightly different values) to create our column. Instead, we could use a mixin to control these styles. However, there is a catch: notice that `#content` has additional `padding: 10px` in the style rule? In this instance, it's not an issue—we can add this in `#leftmargin` with no noticeable adverse effect. Remember, it's all about making the initial change and then taking a look to see what we can alter, which will then allow us to add more to the mixin and make it more useful.

- A more advanced change that we can make is to switch to using `data-uri` for importing the social networking image in our CSS in order to save on server requests and bandwidth usage. We used it in the original example in *Chapter 4, Working with Variables, Mixins, and Functions*—it will work perfectly well for small images (such as ours) but is less useful for larger ones, or those that are not reused in the site.

There is no hard and fast rule regarding what can be defined as a "small" image—the image I've used in this example weighs in at 9 KB. This will depend a little on any `data-uri` limit within a browser; for example, IE8 is limited to 32 KB. It is all about choosing carefully—small images such as credit card logos would be perfect, but a large picture clearly isn't!

These are just a few of the concepts that we can use to convert this style sheet to use Less. The key to the conversion process is not about size, but about re-engineering the code to make it easier to maintain and removing duplication if others have already created code that you can import in your own projects. Once you've started converting code, you will see other opportunities for conversion—it is very much a case of practice makes perfect!

Making the changes

Now that we've seen the changes we can make, let's begin to implement some of these changes, beginning with the creation of our Less framework files. Start by renaming the `conversion.css` file to `conversion.less`. Next, add the following line to a new file in your text editor:

```
@import "conversion.less";
```

Save the file as `styles.less`—this sets up our framework, ready for us to convert our code. If you've used Sublime Text or Crunch!, then you will find that a `styles.css` file has been created—this contains a compiled copy of the code from `conversion.less`. Setting up the framework in this manner means that we can add more `@import` statements in the future; the contents of these imported files will automatically be included in the final article, when the `styles.less` file is recompiled.

Using the CSS3 mixins

Next, let's take a look at the CSS3 styles we've used—we can convert to use a prebuilt mixin library. For the purpose of this exercise, we're going to use the LESS Hat library, available at `http://lesshat.madebysource.com/`. Click on the **Download LESS Hat** button—at the time of writing this book, the latest Version is 2.0.15.

We need to extract the `lesshat.less` file, which is in the `build` subfolder—copy this to the `css` subfolder in your project folder. Switch back to the `conversion.less` file in your text editor and then add this line at the start:

```
@import "lesshat.less";
```

This will now import any of the mixins that we need to use from the LESS Hat library.

 We can't include the `@import` statement for LESS Hat in the `styles.less` file—this will cause a compilation error in `conversion.less`, as it can't find the source mixins it needs to use when compiling the code.

Now that we've added the LESS Hat library, we can start adapting our code to use the mixins from this library; there are several places where we alter the code to use mixins, as highlighted:

```
#leftmargin { .box-sizing(padding-box); border-right: 1px solid
#CCCCCC; float: left; height: 575px; width: 306px; }
#content { .box-sizing(padding-box); float: left; height: 575px;
padding: 10px; width: 494px; }
#container { border: 1px solid #000000; .border-radius(4px);
.box-shadow(4px 4px 0 rgba(0, 0, 0, 0.5)); margin: 5% auto; width:
800px; }
```

In this example, there are only three places where we can use LESS Hat. Even though this is only a limited number, we should not forget that it is not so much about the number of instances where we can use external mixin libraries, but more about not reinventing the wheel and that the use of an external library means less work for us to do, provided a suitable library is available for use.

Creating variables for fonts

Let's change our focus and take a look at another concept that we can use when converting to use Less: the use of variables to help maintain values, such as fonts.

In our code, we have a few instances where we're using fonts. These can be a pain to update in normal CSS, so let's create some variables that we can use to automatically update our Less code. Creating variables means that only one value needs to be updated at the start of our code. Less will handle the update of any other instance of these variables automatically.

In a copy of `conversion.less`, add the following line immediately below the `@import` statement:

```
@import "lesshat.less";
@KiteOne: ~"'Kite One', arial, sans-serif";
```

The observant among you will see that we've added a variable—the only difference from the ones we looked at earlier in the book is that this is an encapsulated variable. We're using the tilde symbol to tell Less to reproduce this exactly as shown when compiling our code. This means that instead of using a long sentence, we can now simply use `@KiteOne` as a value:

```
div { font-family: @KiteOne; margin-bottom: 5px; margin-top: 5px;
padding: 5px; }
```

In this instance, we only need to change one rule. In a larger style sheet, the benefits of this will become more apparent, as it removes the need to alter each instance manually when updating styles.

> We will cover more on how to use Less to manipulate fonts in *Chapter 7, Manipulating Fonts with Less.*

Creating variables for colors

We've also used several colors in our code—one should be recognizable as white (`#fff`), but the other is less recognizable as light gray. Let's fix this using the same process to create two new variables for these colors and one variable for black:

```
@KiteOne: "'Kite One', arial, sans-serif";
@lightgray: #ccc;
@white: #fff;
@black: #000;
```

We can now alter our Less code to use these variables, as shown—this will make the code more readable:

```
#container { border: 1px solid @black; .border-radius(4px); }
#title { color: @white; font-family: @KiteOne; font-size: 32px;
font-weight: 400; padding-left: 100px; padding-top: 30px; position:
absolute; }
#leftmargin { .box-sizing(padding-box); border-right: 1px solid
@lightgray; float: left; height: 575px; width: 306px; }
#footer { border-top: 1px solid @lightgray; clear: both; font-size:
12px; height: 65px; }
```

This will make the code easier to read, but it also means that if we ever need to change the values, we only need to do it once at the start—Less will take care of updating all other instances automatically.

Switching to using nesting

Our next change is a little more dramatic; it concerns the four instances of the `#leftmargin` style rules in our code. Instead of having to write each rule manually, we can group them together by using Less' nesting functionality; this makes them easier to read, as they follow a more logical structure.

In a copy of `conversion.less`, remove the four `#leftmargin` lines and replace them with this:

```
#leftmargin {
  .box-sizing(padding-box);
  border-right: 1px solid @lightgray;
  float: left; height: 575px; width: 306px;
  li { list-style: none outside none; }
  a {
    text-decoration: none;
    &:hover { text-decoration: underline; }
  }
}
```

This will make our code easier to read and will avoid the need to have to repeat the element name when writing the rules. Notice also how we've used the ampersand symbol for `:hover`—the ampersand symbol tells Less that `:hover` should be treated as a pseudo selector, which will be compiled as `#leftmargin a:hover` by Less.

> The use of ampersands (as shown in our example) isn't limited to pseudo selectors; it can be used to represent a parent selector or class used in the code—see `http://lesscss.org/features/#parent-selectors-feature` for more details.

Incorporating our own mixins

Our final change is related to column sizes—if you read the code carefully, you will notice that in at least two places, we have almost identical code: `#leftmargin` and `#content`. We can move four style attributes into a separate parametric mixin, as shown—add this immediately below the variables we created earlier in this chapter:

```
.columnsize( @height, @width) { float: left; height: @height;
width: @width; padding: 10px; }
```

Once done, we can alter our style rules accordingly:

```
#leftmargin { .box-sizing(padding-box); border-right: 1px solid @
lightgray; .columnsize(575px, 306px); ...}
```

```
#content { .box-sizing(padding-box); .columnsize(575px, 494px); }
```

It's a simple example of how, with a little care, we can create our own mixin to remove some of the duplication in the code. While it may not reduce the number of lines in our code, it will help make the code more readable and easier to alter if we need to change the values passed through the mixin.

At this point, we've worked through our original code to convert it to use Less. If all is well, we should end up with something that will compile in valid CSS; if you take a look at the code download that accompanies this book, you can see a copy of `conversion.less` and compare it with your own version.

We can test the success of the conversion process by altering a copy of the HTML code we produced in *Chapter 4, Working with Variables, Mixins, and Functions.* Open a copy of `functions2.html` and then look for the lines highlighted below:

```
<title>Demo: Functions</title>
<link href='http://fonts.googleapis.com/css?family=Kite+One'
  rel='stylesheet' type='text/css'>
<link rel="stylesheet/less"  href="css/functions.less">
<link rel="stylesheet" type="text/less" href="css/social.less">
<script src="js/less.min.js"></script>
</head>
```

Change these as shown; then, save the file as `conversion.html`:

```
<link href='http://fonts.googleapis.com/css?family=Kite+One'
  rel='stylesheet' type='text/css'>
<link rel="stylesheet/less" href="css/styles.less">
<script src="js/less.min.js"></script>
```

If you preview the results in a browser, don't expect to see any real changes to the overall page, with the exception of the small amount of extra padding that was added, which has pushed the left-hand navigation down by a small measure. Hopefully, this goes to show that with some care and thought, we can produce the same results while better managing our code!

Importing images into style sheets – a bonus

Before we complete our changes, I thought I would throw in a little bonus; if we look back at the list of changes that we could make, we noted one small change that could be made, which is related to the social media image that is used in the footer of our page.

The CSS for this is controlled by the following line in our Less file:

```
#social { width: 175px; height: 60px; background-image: url('../img/
sprites.png'); float: right; }
```

This will pull in the image as a separate file, which means an additional request to the server. On a small site, this won't be an issue, but on a larger site, this could make the site bandwidth hungry, which will be an issue.

Instead, we can use one of Less' functions, data-uri, which we covered in *Chapter 4, Working with Variables, Mixins, and Functions*, when we created the original version of our page. This is ideal for small images, particularly those that are repeated throughout the site; this will convert them to a base64 statement that can be included in our CSS, thereby removing the need to shell out to the server to request the image.

In conversion.less, look for this line:

```
#social { width: 175px; height: 60px; background-image: url('../img/
sprites.png'); float: right; }
```

If we wanted to use data-uri, we would change the background-image property as shown:

```
#social { width: 175px; height: 60px; background-image: data-uri('../
img/sprites.png'); float: right; }
```

The net effect of this means that while we may have a few hundred lines in our CSS, we've cut down the need to request for the image from the server. This process should be used with care though—it should only be used for small images, which may be repeated throughout the site. It's a useful little trick for saving requests to the server, provided it is used with care!

Viewing the finished article

Now that we've made the changes to our converted CSS file, let's take a look at the end result. To compare, open a copy of `conversion.less` from the code download that accompanies the book and see how you got on with making the changes:

Hopefully, you can see some of the changes we've made — Note that we've not necessarily saved on the number of lines we've written, but we've made it easier to update the code in the future, if changes need to be made. Granted that in a small Less file such as this one, we may not see the full benefits of using Less; in a larger file, the benefits will become apparent when converting from CSS to use Less.

Summary

One of the hardest concepts to understand in Less is how we can convert an existing site to use Less. While there are some easy (or perhaps more complex, depending on your take) questions that we can answer, converting a site can require a certain degree of skill, to ensure that we take full advantage of Less during the conversion process.

Throughout this chapter, we saw some of the questions and tricks that we can use to start the conversion process. We began by taking a look at how to prepare for the initial jump into the conversion process, which was followed by the initial steps anyone should take before considering how to convert their CSS code. We saw how easy it is to split code into separate partials, which can be imported into one master file that Less will compile to valid CSS.

Our initial steps into converting Less code began with a look at spotting the low-hanging fruits, or quick and easy changes that we can make. We saw how, with the use of sites such as `http://css2less.cc`, we can easily start converting code; it was noted that these sites are not perfect but can serve as a good basis for converting code. Next came a look at how to identify patterns in our CSS code—we examined some of the questions that should be asked as part of the process. It was noted that every site will be different; hence, different questions will need to be asked. Nonetheless, there are some basic questions that will apply to any site.

We then saw how to use prebuilt mixin libraries as part of the conversion process and covered some examples that can be used in our projects—this is a good way to incorporate mixins created by others, which will help reduce the effort required for creating our style sheet. We then covered how it might be necessary to create our own mixin library, if an existing one available online does not meets our needs.

We finished the chapter with a detailed look at a practical example of how to convert an existing website to use Less—we used the single web page that was created in *Chapter 4, Working with Variables, Mixins, and Functions*, as a way to prove that it doesn't matter how large the site is, most sites will benefit from the conversion to use Less. We examined how easy it was to apply some simple conversions, using the basic principle of examining the code carefully, in a block at a time, and using the techniques outlined earlier in the chapter. One of the conversions we included was a simple change to the fonts used—we'll explore this further in the next chapter.

7
Manipulating Fonts with Less

We explored how to use the various elements of Less, created a basic page to use Less, and covered how to migrate a site to use Less....so, what's next?

Ah yes, working with text or to be more specific, fonts!

It goes without saying that content is king on any website — part of achieving the right impact is the careful selection of fonts that should be used on your site. We wouldn't use a script-based font if we were designing a news site, as the text should be clean and easy to read. However, a script font would be perfect to represent the flowing lines associated with dresses sold at a dressmaker's outfit.

It's all about selecting the right style; Less is perfect to help us manage the styles, colors, and sizes of any font we decide to use in our pages. Throughout this chapter, you'll see how you can use some simple principles to make managing fonts a cinch with Less. We will cover the following topics:

- Creating font mixins
- Using variables to determine sizes dynamically
- Using prebuilt libraries
- Catering for the `@media` and `@font-face` support in Less

Are you ready to have some fun with fonts? Let's get started!

Creating simple font mixins

The key to working with fonts is to start simple and then build it up—there is no better place to start than to create a simple mixin in order to manage attributes such as font names. Let's create a simple example where we can see this in action; here's what our mixin will produce:

Okay, let's start creating our mixin; we'll begin by preparing the markup for our demo:

1. Open a copy of the `project.html` file we created in *Chapter 3, Getting Started with Less*, and then modify it as shown:

    ```
    <title>Demo: Creating simple font mixins</title>
    <link href='http://fonts.googleapis.com/css?family=Kite+One'
    rel='stylesheet' type='text/css'>
    <link rel="stylesheet/less" href="css/basicfonts.less">
    <script src="js/less.min.js"></script>
    ```

2. Next, add the following markup to the `<body>` section:

    ```
    <h1>H1 - The cat sat on the mat</h1>
    <h2>H2 - The cat sat on the mat</h2>
    <h3>H3 - The cat sat on the mat</h3>
    <h4>H4 - The cat sat on the mat</h4>
    <h5>H5 - The cat sat on the mat</h5>
    <h6>H6 - The cat sat on the mat</h6>
    ```

3. Save the file as `basicfonts.html`. In a separate file, add the following Less styles:

```
.fontfamily() { font-family: 'Kite One', Arial, sans-serif; }
```

```
h1 { .fontfamily; color: #808080; }
h2 { .fontfamily; color: #ff0000; }
h3 { .fontfamily; color: #008000; }
h4 { .fontfamily; color: #ffa500; }
h5 { .fontfamily; color: #800080; }
h6 { .fontfamily; color: #000000; }
```

4. Save this as `basicfonts.less`. If you preview the results in a browser, you will see the six statements appear in decreasing font sizes.

So, let's take a moment to consider what's happened here: we created a simple mixin that replaced `.fontfamily` with `'Kite One', Arial, sans-serif;` as the font family for the statements on the page. Once the Less file has been compiled, each H style will use Kite One as the base font (in various sizes), falling back to use Arial or sans-serif, if Kite One is not available.

Extending the mixin

In the preceding instance, we could stop here—after all, the mixin we've produced works perfectly well. However, it's not the best we can do; if we create similar mixins throughout our code, it will soon become a real handful to ensure that all are updated, should the font names need to change.

Instead, we can make a simple change and use a variable name. To see what this means, open `basicfonts.less` and then add these two lines at the start:

```
@font-family-sans-serif: "Helvetica Neue", Helvetica, Arial, sans-serif;
.fontfamily() { font-family:  @font-family-sans-serif }
h1 { .fontfamily; color: #808080; }
```

You might ask, why make this kind of a change? The answer is easy: this reduces the number of instances where the code has to be updated if a change is made. If you change the fonts being referenced as part of the `@font-family-sans-serif` variable, then Less will automatically take care of updating the code—meaning, one less job to do! Here, we only needed to change one instance; had there been many instances in our code, then Less would have updated them automatically at the point of compiling our code.

Let's move on and turn our attention to changing the size of the fonts that we use—after all, things would be boring if everything was of the same size, right?

Using @font-face with Less

A downside of using fonts in web pages is that they must exist on your end user's PC or laptop. Naturally, with the mix of PC, laptop, and mobile devices now available in the market, it would be almost impossible to guarantee that the font will exist!

I say impossible; there are fonts that we can use on a PC or laptop, such as Arial, Times New Roman, or Verdana; they are not bad fonts, but they are overused and not particularly special. We could, of course, use an external service, such as Google Fonts—as we did in the *Creating simple font mixins* section earlier in this chapter.

However, we can do better than this by using `@font-face` to embed any font in our pages. I say any, but the license for the font must allow embedding in a page. Thankfully, if we use a site such as Font Squirrel (as we will do in the next exercise), we can easily check and eliminate any fonts that fall outside this criteria, when choosing a font.

Enough of the talking; let's turn our attention to using `@font-face` so that we can see how it works. We're going to use it in a very simple demo; while it might not show much, it perfectly illustrates how you can use `@font-face` with Less.

Downloading the font files

Before we get stuck in with writing code, we need to download an appropriate font—after all, using something such as Arial or Times New Roman won't do the demo justice! Perform the following steps:

1. For this demo, we'll use a font from the Font Squirrel site (`http://www.fontsquirrel.com`). Let's start by browsing to the Font Squirrel site and downloading the PT Sans font, which we will use in our demo. We can download it from `http://www.fontsquirrel.com/fonts/PT-Sans`. Here, we can also check the details of the license and see the samples of the font displayed on the screen.

2. Click on the **Webfont Kit** tab and then on the **Download @Font-Face Kit** button to download the font; save the compressed archive in the project folder as `PT-Sans-fontfacekit.zip`.

3. For now, open up the `ptsans_regular_macroman` folder, extract the four Webfont files from within, and place them in a subfolder called `fonts` within our project folder.

We will be revisiting this font in the *Handling different weights* section, later in this chapter.

Embedding the font into our demo

Okay, now that we have the font files in place, let's make a start with the code:

1. Crank up the editor of your choice—I assume that, for the purpose of this exercise, it is Sublime Text.

2. Open up a copy of `projects.html`, which we created at the start of the book, and then modify it as shown:

    ```
    <meta charset="utf-8">
    <title>Demo: Using @font-face</title>
    <link rel="stylesheet/less" href="css/fontface.less">
    <script src="js/less.min.js"></script>
    ```

3. Add the following markup to the `<body>` section:

    ```
    <h1>H1 - The cat sat on the mat</h1>
    <h2>H2 - The cat sat on the mat</h2>
    <h3>H3 - The cat sat on the mat</h3>
    <h4>H4 - The cat sat on the mat</h4>
    <h5>H5 - The cat sat on the mat</h5>
    <h6>H6 - The cat sat on the mat</h6>
    ```

4. Save it as `fontface.html`. As we can clearly see, it's a very simple demo—enough to show off how to use `@font-face`—it was never meant to be complicated! It isn't complete without the all-important styling; so, go ahead and add the following to a new file, saving it as `fontface.less`:

    ```
    .font-face(@family, @filename: @family) {
      font-family: "@{family}";

      @font-face {
        font-family: "@{family}";
        @file: "../fonts/@{filename}";
        src: url("@{file}.eot");
        src: url("@{file}.eot?#iefix") format("eot"),
             url("@{file}.woff") format("woff"),
             url("@{file}.ttf") format("truetype"),
             url("@{file}.svg#webfont") format("svg");
      }
    }

    @name: PTS55F-webfont;
    ```

```
@family: "PT Sans";

h1 {  .font-face(@family, @name);  color: #808080; }
h2 {  .font-face(@family, @name);  color: #ff0000; }
h3 {  .font-face(@family, @name);  color: #008000; }
h4 {  .font-face(@family, @name);  color: #ffa500; }
h5 {  .font-face(@family, @name);  color: #800080; }
h6 {  .font-face(@family, @name);  color: #000000; }
```

5. If you preview the results in a browser, you can expect to see something akin to this screenshot:

This is a simple way to show you how to use @font-face with Less; here, we've displayed a simple sentence using the PT Sans font, styled with different colors for each font size. In each call to the .font-face mixin, we pass the name of the font and the color to be used; the mixin selects the most appropriate format of the font based on the browser being used:

Font format	Browser(s) supporting the format
TTF	This works in most browsers, except IE and iPhone
EOT	This is a proprietary font format for use in IE only—it is currently not a W3C-recommended standard
WOFF	This is a compressed, emerging standard—currently supported by most browsers except Opera Mini
SVG	For use in iPhone/iPad only

If you only have access to one format, then WOFF is the best one to choose; otherwise, try to include fonts in all the four formats where possible.

Using a prebuilt library to handle fonts

In the previous example, we used `@font-face` to embed a custom font into our pages; this removes any constraint on the fonts that we can use, as we can download and use suitably licensed fonts. This is great, but we can do better—one of the precepts of Less is the DRY principle, which we introduced earlier in the book; this is a perfect opportunity to practice what we preach!

Instead of having to create new mixins to handle `@font-face`, we can use a prebuilt library to handle the `@font-face` mixin for us. This means we can remove a good chunk of our code, as we will use the mixin from the prebuilt library—let's take a look at this in action:

1. Open up a copy of `fontface.html` and alter the link to the Less file, as follows:

   ```
   <title>Demo: Using @font-face</title>
   <link rel="stylesheet/less" href="css/fontface-ml.less">
   <script src="js/less.min.js"></script>
   </head>
   ```

2. Save this as `fontface-ml.html`. In a new file, add the following code:

   ```
   @import "lesshat.less";
   @my-font-name: 'pt_sansregular';
   @fontfile: '../fonts/PTS55F-webfont';

   @font-face {
     .font-face(@my-font-name, @fontfile);
   }

   .myfont() {
     font-family: @my-font-name, arial;
   }

   h1 { .myfont; color: #808080; }
   h2 { .myfont; color: #ff0000; }
   h3 { .myfont; color: #008000; }
   h4 { .myfont; color: #ffa500; }
   h5 { .myfont; color: #800080; }
   h6 { .myfont; color: #000000; }
   ```

3. This will be our Less style sheet—go ahead and save it as `fontface-ml.less`.

If you preview the results in a browser, you should see little or no difference in the output, when compared to the results from the previous exercise. So, what's different? I hear you ask: Why use a prebuilt library?

The answer is easy: you're forgetting the one key principle—when using Less, it doesn't matter how big the library is as Less only incorporates those styles that are *directly referenced in the code during compilation*.

If you take a look through the library, you will see the `@font-face` mixin at or around line `1362`:

```
.font-face(@fontname, @fontfile, @fontweight: normal, @fontstyle:
normal) {
  font-family: "@{fontname}";
  src: url("@{fontfile}.eot");
  src: url("@{fontfile}.eot?#iefix") format("embedded-opentype"),
       url("@{fontfile}.woff") format("woff"),
       url("@{fontfile}.ttf") format("truetype"),
       url("@{fontfile}.svg#@{fontname}") format("svg");
  font-weight: @fontweight;
  font-style: @fontstyle;
}
```

In this instance, this is all that is being used—we can prove this using a DOM Inspector, such as Firebug, to view the compiled CSS styles, as shown in this screenshot:

```
 9   h2 {
10     font-family: "PT Sans";
11     src: url("http://127.0.0.1/Chapter%207/fonts/PTS55F-webfont.eot");
12     src: url("http://127.0.0.1/Chapter%207/fonts/PTS55F-webfont.eot?#i
13     font-weight: 800;
14     font-style: normal;
15     color: #ff0000;
16   }
17   h3 {
18     font-family: "PT Sans";
19     src: url("http://127.0.0.1/Chapter%207/fonts/PTS55F-webfont.eot");
20     src: url("http://127.0.0.1/Chapter%207/fonts/PTS55F-webfont.eot?#i
21     font-weight: 800;
22     font-style: normal;
23     color: #008000;
24   }
```

In a small example such as ours, the benefits may not be immediately apparent—once this scales up to a much larger site, this will significantly reduce the amount of code that you have to write. The key to using a prebuilt library in such an instance comes down to choosing the right library—the more we can use from one prebuilt library, the better!

Okay, we now have the right fonts in place; we need to ensure that they can be sized as appropriate on our pages. Thankfully, Less contains some useful functionality that helps make sizing fonts a cinch—let's take a look at how we can use the library to help set font sizes in our pages.

Using variables to calculate sizes

Now that we have chosen the fonts we want to use, we need to ensure that we can set the right size for the occasion; thankfully, Less has a number of techniques that we can use to create our CSS styles.

The simplest technique is to assign a font size to a set variable and then reference this variable throughout your code:

```
@font-size-base: 14px;
```

Once the initial variable is set, we can then create a range of font sizes automatically, by multiplying the base value with a graduated set of numbers:

```
@font-size-large: @font-size-base * 1.25;
@font-size-small: @font-size-base * 0.85;
@font-size-mini: @font-size-base * 0.75;
```

When compiled using a precompiler, Less will convert these into valid CSS font sizes as shown in this screenshot:

This is a very simple way of defining font sizes; if we need to change the font sizes, all we need to do is change the value of `@font-size-base` and Less will take care of updating the others automatically.

Moving with the times

Working with pixels is a consistent, reliable way of defining font sizes — if you specify a value of `14px` for an element, that element will be sized at `14px`. However, for those using IE, sizes do not cascade well when the zoom function is used.

Instead, we can use the `rem` unit — this maintains its value relative to the root (HTML) element, instead of its parent. You might notice that I've skipped over the use of `em` as an option. The `em` value is set relative to the parent, which means elements will not resize well if your visitor decides to use the zooming function in IE!

 For a good discussion on the pros and cons of using `rem`, `em`, and `px` as font size formats, take a look at an article by Jonathan Snook — although it is a few years old, it still contains some useful details — at `http://snook.ca/archives/html_and_css/font-size-with-rem`.

Support for `rem` is good within modern browsers, so we just need to provide fallback support for any version of IE older than Version 8.

With this in mind, we can create a mixin such as the following to handle sizing values using the `rem` values, but with a pixel fallback for those who still need to use IE8 or below:

```less
.font-size(@sizeValue) {
  @remValue: @sizeValue/10;
  @pxValue: @sizeValue;
  font-size: unit(@pxValue,px);
  font-size: unit(@remValue,rem);
}

p { .font-size(13); }
```

When compiled, this produces the following CSS:

```css
html { font-size: 62.5%; }
p { font-size: 13px; font-size: 1.3rem; }
```

Most modern browsers will support the use of the rem element without issues or will fall back to use the pixel equivalent, if appropriate. Perfect! We now have our fonts sized properly; we're good to go, right? Or, are we...?

Handling different weights

Well, perhaps not; what if we're using multiple variations of a particular font? This isn't a problem when using Less—we can reference our font in the normal way and use the Less namespacing facility to pick and choose which font styles to use for each HTML element. Let's take a look at what this means in practice.

Let's start by downloading a copy of the code that accompanies this book; from the code download, extract the weights.html file that contains our basic text and HTML markup. Save a copy of the file within the project folder.

Next, go ahead and add the following to a new document, saving it as weights.less:

```
@Alegreya-Sans: "Alegreya Sans",sans-serif;

#SansFont() {
  &.light { font-family: @Alegreya-Sans; font-weight: 300; }
  &.bold { font-family: @Alegreya-Sans; font-weight: 500; }
  &.extrabold { font-family: @Alegreya-Sans; font-weight: 800; }
}

.para1 { #SansFont > .light; }
.para2 { #SansFont > .bold; }
h1 { #SansFont > .extrabold; }

section {
  background-color: #ffc; border-radius: 5px;padding: 5px;
  border: 1px solid black; width: 400px;
  box-shadow: 3px 3px 5px 0px rgba(50, 50, 50, 0.75);
  h1 { background-color: #c00; margin-top: 0px; color: #fff; border-
top-left-radius: 4px; border-top-right-radius: 4px; padding: 3px; }
}
```

If you preview the results in a browser, you will see something akin to this screenshot:

Media Queries Shortcodes using LESS

Lorem ipsum dolor sit amet, consectetur adipiscing elit. Morbi porttitor pharetra lobortis. Nullam molestie dapibus risus in porta. Duis elementum dapibus metus mattis imperdiet. Ut id imperdiet mauris. Donec nec nibh iaculis, cursus sapien nec, tincidunt urna.

Nunc molestie bibendum sem, vitae imperdiet sem congue in. Etiam non augue non nisi semper volutpat. Nunc volutpat tempus nulla, sit amet imperdiet turpis consequat in. Phasellus erat dolor, condimentum vitae erat porttitor, ornare ullamcorper lacus. Praesent eu elit ut massa ornare eleifend.

Using the Less namespace functionality is a great way to work with fonts. In this example, we've touched again on a technique that we covered in *Chapter 5, Inheritance, Overriding, and Nesting in Less,* where we can pick and choose the styles we want Less to compile into valid CSS.

In this instance, we're pulling in one of Google's Web Fonts to create three styles as a nested block before calling each of them from within `.para1`, `.para2`, and `h1`. It's a great technique to help group common styles together — the real benefit of using it is to help better organize your Less styles; Less will convert the calling styles (that is, `.para1`, `.para2`, and `h1`) into valid CSS.

 Don't forget to include the `()` in your namespace block, to prevent Less from compiling it as a valid CSS block.

Now that we've covered the basics of using Less to help manage our fonts, let's move on and take a look at some more examples of using fonts with Less, beginning with creating the `@media` queries for a responsive design.

Working with @media in Less

In the age of using mobile devices and responsive design, a key element in building sites is to allow their use on mobile devices, such as iPads or smartphones.

The key to responsive design is the `@media` rule—we can use this to define the style at particular breakpoints or sizes of screen estate for different devices. To illustrate how this works when using Less, we'll use a simplified example created by Eric Rasch as a basis for an example web page:

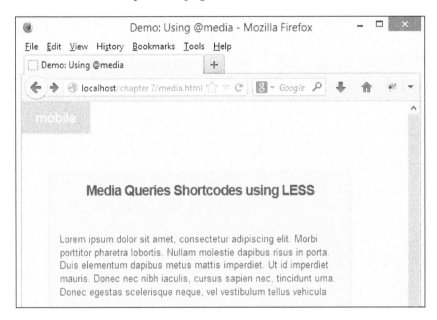

 Eric's original example is available at
`http://codepen.io/ericrasch/HzoEx`.

For this demonstration, we'll break the convention and use the copies of the `media.html` and `media.less` files that are available in the code download that accompanies this book. I recommend that you run the demo in a browser that has a DOM inspector installed, so you can see the different styles in use as we resize the browser.

The `media.html` file contains some simple text generated using the **Lorem Ipsum** generator at `http://www.lipsum.com`; this is to represent a standard web page.

For reasons of space, we'll work through the important elements of the `media.less` file—the rest of the Less markup in this file is purely to make the page look attractive.

Creating a basic media query

Before we take a look at the Less file in detail, let's just remind ourselves of how a basic @media query looks:

```
@media all and (max-width: 699px) and (min-width: 520px) {
  body { background: #ccc; }
}
```

This translates to setting the background color to #ccc (light gray), when the screen size is between 520 px and 699 px.

Examining the Less file

This is a simple enough media query, right? Let's apply this to what we have in our Less file.

In media.less, we can see several sections—the first section declares a number of variables; these include each of the breakpoints we will use, and the font sizes that we will apply to the text in our page:

```
@mobile: ~"only screen and (max-width: 529px)";
@tablet: ~"only screen and (min-width: 530px) and (max-width: 949px)";
@desktop: ~"only screen and (min-width: 950px) and (max-width:
1128px)";
@desktop-xl: ~"only screen and (min-width: 1129px)";

@font-size-base:   14px;
@font-size-large:  @font-size-base * 1.25;
@font-size-small:  @font-size-base * 0.85;
@font-size-mini:   @font-size-base * 0.75;
```

Did you notice the @tablet variable and how similar it is to our example query? Granted, ours will not be for as large a device as this tablet, but the format stays the same, irrespective of the sizes defined.

Next comes the mixin that will apply styles to each @media rule. The body:after statement changes the label at the top-left of our screen to display which breakpoint is being used at a particular screen size. The section rule determines the width and font size to be used for the <section> block:

```
.mediaMixin(@background, @content, @width, @fontsize) {
  body:after { background: @background; content: @content; }
  section { width: @width; font-size: @fontsize;  }
}
```

We finish with the most important part—this ties together all of the mixins and variables we've defined to arrive at the `@media` CSS rules we will have in our compiled style sheet:

```
@media @mobile { .mediaMixin( orange; "mobile"; 85%; @font-size-mini
); }
@media @tablet { .mediaMixin( purple; "tablet"; 37%; @font-size-small
); }
@media @desktop { .mediaMixin( green; "desktop"; 40%; @font-size-base
); }
@media @desktop-xl { .mediaMixin( blue; "desktop xl"; 45%; @font-size-
large );
```

If we run the example from the code download and resize the screen to its maximum (that is, greater than `1129px` for this example), we can see that the breakpoint in use is **desktop xl**:

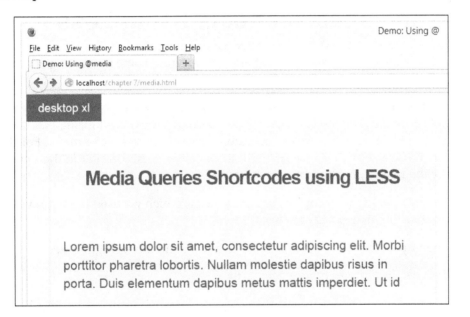

How does our example work? It's easy; we've used a combination of variables and a mixin to reproduce the code required for each `@media` query. Although we can change each breakpoint to match those devices we want to cater for, the ranges used here should cover most devices.

In each statement, we call the `.mediaMixin` mixin and pass to it the desired background, content (to describe which breakpoint we are using), width of the `<section>` containing the content, and font size. Less compiles each instance into a valid CSS rule, which is then interpreted by the browser as appropriate. We will take a more in-depth look at using `@media` in *Chapter 8, Media Queries with Less*.

 If you have Firefox installed, try pressing *Ctrl + Shift + M* to activate the Responsive Design Mode when viewing this demo—it shows off the demo to a great effect!

We've almost come to the end of our journey through using fonts with Less; before we move on, let's take a moment to have a little bit of relief and see some of the effects you can create when using Less.

Creating special effects using Less

The beauty of Less is that if you've created valid Less code, it will compile to valid CSS—this means we can use it to great effect to produce some interesting effects when working with fonts.

If you spend a little time searching on the Internet for CSS3-type effects, you will no doubt come across some good examples—to show you what I mean, let's take a moment to try reworking two effects using Less: letterpress and emboss. For this demo, we'll use a copy of the `weights.html` page we created earlier in this chapter, and alter the title to give it some more emphasis.

Let's start by opening up a copy of `weights.html`, which we used in the previous demo, and saving it again as `sfx.html`.

Next, open up a copy of `weights.less` and add the mixins as highlighted:

```
@Alegreya-Sans: "Alegreya Sans",sans-serif;

.letterpress() { text-shadow: 0px 1px 0px rgba(0, 0, 0, 0.5); }
.emboss() { box-shadow: 0px 1px 3px rgba(0, 0, 0, 0.5); }
```

The mixins won't be used unless we call them from our Less statements; so, go ahead and modify the `h1` block as shown:

```
h1 {
  .emboss;
  .letterpress;
  background-color: #c00;
```

Save the file as `sfx.less`. If you preview the results in a browser, you should see that the title has more emphasis, as shown in this screenshot:

Media Queries Shortcodes using LESS

The great thing about Less is that we can easily apply a similar effect to any text—all it takes is a little care and planning.

In this example, we've used `text-shadow` and `box-shadow`, to which we've passed the right combination of values to produce the letterpress and emboss effects used in the title. It is worth running the demo for this example to see the effect in full color—reproducing it in print doesn't quite do it justice!

It should not be used as an excuse to laden your sites with lots of different text effects—this will more likely put your visitors off. With a little care, text effects such as the two we've used here can add real emphasis to our page, without the use of images.

Taking effects further

Wait—surely, we don't need to do anything more, except plan which effects we're going to use, right? Wrong, here's where the planning comes in: if we're careful about choosing any external mixin libraries we use, we can save ourselves even more work.

For example, we used `text-shadow` here to produce the letterpress example; this is available in at least one external mixin library, namely LESS Elements (which we introduced in *Chapter 6, Migrating Your Site to Less*), and is available at `http://www.lesselements.com`.

Assuming that you are already using LESS Elements in your project, all we need to do is include our calling statement—the mixin will already be part of the LESS Elements library. Yes, while it means that we don't necessarily reduce the overall code in our project, it does mean we have less to write, which must be a good thing!

Summary

Phew, what a tour! We covered a lot of content on using fonts when working with Less; let's take a moment to recap what we have learned in this chapter.

We began our journey by learning how to create a simple mixin that helps with setting the font family and color to use; we then saw how we could extend the mixin to store our font choices as variables. Next, we explored how to use `@font-face` when working with Less, and that this removes any constraint on the fonts we can use within our pages.

We also saw how we can use a prebuilt library in our code, which helps save time on writing mixins, as they can be referenced from libraries such as LESS Hat. We then moved on to take a look at the various means available to manage font sizes, including using `rem` and why using `ems` is not always as good as it might appear.

We then moved on to take a look at using Less to create the `@media` queries as part of responsive design, before rounding up the chapter with a brief look at some of the special effects you can create with fonts when using Less.

In the next chapter, we're going to explore in more detail, a vital technique when building sites for multiple devices—namely, how we can use the `@media` rule when working with Less.

8

Media Queries with Less

Now that we've seen how to use Less to manage the appearance of our content, what about making sure it fits on the page? Ah yes—isn't this where media queries come in to play…?

Before the advent of smartphones, most websites would be built at a fixed width—small enough to fit on laptops or PCs so that most end users would have a consistent experience.

However, now that more and more people are using mobile devices, the need to design content that can be seamlessly viewed on each device has increased. Gone are the days where you had to have the skills of a surgeon to view content, and work a mobile device—people are increasingly more comfortable viewing content on mobile devices.

How do we get around this? Easy—welcome to the world of media queries! An essential component of responsive web design, we can use media queries to build a site that can be seamlessly viewed over multiple platforms.

I guess you're thinking—how can Less help here? No problem. In this chapter, we'll see how Less can make creating media queries a cinch; we will cover the following topics:

- How media queries work
- What's wrong with CSS?
- Setting client criteria
- Building media queries using Less

Ready to have some fun creating media queries? Let's get started!

Introducing media queries

If you've ever spent time creating content for sites, particularly for display on a mobile platform, then you might have come across media queries.

For those of you who are new to the concept, media queries are a means of tailoring the content that is displayed on screen when the viewport is resized to a smaller size. Historically, websites were always built at a static size — with more and more people viewing content on smartphones and tablets, this means viewing them became harder, as scrolling around a page can be a tiresome process!

Thankfully, this became less of an issue with the advent of media queries — they help us with what should or should not be displayed when viewing content on a particular device. Throughout this chapter, we'll take a brief look at what they are, how they work, and focus more on how you can use Less to create them.

Almost all modern browsers offer native support for media queries — the only exception being IE Version 8 or below, where it is not supported natively:

Media queries always begin with `@media` and consist of two parts:

```
30  @media only screen and (min-width: 530px) and (max-width: 949px) {
31    body:after {
32      background: purple;
33      content: "tablet";
34    }
35  }
```

The first part, `only screen`, determines the media type where a rule should apply—in this case, it will only show the rule if we're viewing content on screen; content viewed when printed can easily be different.

The second part, or media feature, `(min-width: 530px) and (max-width: 949px)`, means the rule will only apply between a screen size set at a minimum of `530px` and a maximum of `949px`. This will rule out any smartphones and will apply to larger tablets, laptops, or PCs.

There are literally dozens of combinations of media queries to suit a variety of needs—for some good examples, visit `http://cssmediaqueries.com/overview.html`, where you can see an extensive list, along with an indication of whether it is supported in the browser you normally use.

Media queries are perfect to dynamically adjust your site to work in multiple browsers—indeed, they are an essential part of a responsive web design. While browsers support media queries, there are some limitations we need to consider; let's take a look at these now.

The limitations of CSS

If we spend any time working with media queries, there are some limitations we need to consider; these apply equally if we were writing using Less or plain CSS:

- Not every browser supports media features uniformly; to see the differences, visit `http://cssmediaqueries.com/overview.html` using different browsers.

- Current thinking is that a range of breakpoints has to be provided; this can result in a lot of duplication and a constant battle to keep up with numerous different screen sizes!

- The `@media` keyword is not supported in IE8 or below; you will need to use JavaScript or jQuery to achieve the same result, or a library such as **Modernizr** to provide a graceful fallback option.

- Writing media queries will tie your design to a specific display size; this increases the risk of duplication as you might want the same element to appear in multiple **breakpoints**, but have to write individual rules to cover each breakpoint.

Breakpoints are points where your design will break if it is resized larger or smaller than a particular set of given dimensions.

The traditional thinking is that we have to provide different style rules for different breakpoints within our style sheets. While this is valid, ironically it is something we should not follow! The reason for this is the potential proliferation of breakpoint rules that you might need to add, just to manage a site.

With care and planning and a design-based breakpoints mindset, we can often get away with a fewer number of rules. As you will see in the example towards the end of the chapter, there is only one breakpoint given, but it works in a range of sizes without the need for more breakpoints. The key to the process is to start small, then increase the size of your display. As soon as it breaks your design (this is where your first breakpoint is) add a query to fix it, and then, keep doing it until you get to your maximum size.

Okay, so we've seen what media queries are; let's change tack and look at what you need to consider when working with clients, before getting down to writing the queries in code.

Setting client criteria

The hardest part of working with media queries isn't in the design of the code, but in agreeing with clients as to what devices should be supported!

Some clients might want to have the same experience throughout their site, irrespective of the device or platform being used to view the content. This might have worked when the Internet was still being viewed on normal-sized screens. This is no longer the case; more and more people are viewing content on mobile or other such devices. The use of mobile devices is such that numbers are increasing rapidly, to the extent that they will soon overtake those who still use a desktop PC to view content.

The phrase, "Expectation is the root of all heartache" (from an anonymous source, but often misquoted as being Shakespeare), is particularly apt—it is key in deciding what should and should not be included in each breakpoint; if not, you are more likely to land yourself in trouble with your client!

When creating media queries as part of constructing a client's site, there are some key points to keep in mind, which will form the basis for conversations with your client:

- At the start, make it clear to your client what responsive design is all about—making content fit a particular screen size. Impress on them that it is perfectly acceptable practice for the site not to show all of the content on mobile devices.

- If the desire is to have the same experience on all devices, then this will naturally add a significant amount of code and require extra resources—is it absolutely necessary? It is far better to work with the client to create content that will work on multiple devices from the same site, but not every element will be displayed on each device.

- Be clear with the customer what should and should not be included at each breakpoint—they might want content such as terms and conditions to be displayed, but this might put mobile users off from viewing the site, if they are long.

- If clients have difficulty in grasping the whole concept of responsive design, then get them to look at their site in a mobile device—they should see that it looks poor. Mobile devices work better with content and less so with interaction or searching—media queries can hide these elements on screen.

- A more radical approach will be to limit what can be done on a mobile device—this works perfectly for airline sites, where they might only want customers to book tickets or check their reservations. This requires more work upfront to hide more elements by default, but is worth the effort required to produce a site that is clean, fast, and works well on mobile devices.

- From a technical perspective, it is critical to determine which elements can be scaled, moved, omitted, or even collapsed on screen, at a particular breakpoint. Consideration should also be given to other elements when used in a mobile environment, such as the forms of interaction used, resizing of fonts, and cropping of images.

There is one critical question that needs to be agreed with the client—should the site work for a number of devices, or should it just work when the screen is resized and elements break at certain points? There is an emerging thought that says we can't hope to support every device and that we should just try resizing a screen and then fix any element that breaks at a certain point during the resizing process. We can, of course, use the emulation features available within Chrome or Opera—even after doing this, we still cannot hope to cater for every device!

Okay, let's move on and turn our attention to creating media queries; before we write the code, we will have a quick recap on the options available when creating the queries.

Exploring media queries

When creating media queries, we've seen how they split into two parts—the first part consists of a media type, which defines the environment where the media query should apply (that is, on screen or in print). It should be noted that none of these are specific to Less—they are all valid CSS media types that we can use when creating our media queries using Less.

Defining media types

Although it is likely that we might only need to use print or screen when creating our Less code, there are other options available; here's a full list of elements that might or might not be supported by all browsers:

Feature	Intended for
all	Most devices; this is default, unless otherwise specified
braille	Use in braille tactile devices
embossed	Paged braille printers
handheld	Handheld devices, where screen size is small and bandwidth is limited
print	Producing content that is viewed on screen in the print preview mode
projection	Projected presentations when using devices such as projectors
screen	Color computer screens
speech	Use with speech synthesizers
tty	Media using a fixed-pitch character grid, such as terminals or teletypes
tv	Use with television devices, with low resolution, color, limited scrolling, and sound

Exploring media features

Once the media type has been set, we also need to set the media feature that should be tested; the media query will return true if it can match both the type of device the media is being displayed on and the feature being tested.

Media features are split into three categories—visual and tactile media, bitmap media, and TV. Let's take a look at the full list of options available for visual and tactile media:

Feature	Value	Min/max prefixes	Description
width	Length	Yes	This gives the width of the display area
height	Length	Yes	This gives the height of the display area
device-width	Length	Yes	This gives the width of the device area
device-height	Length	Yes	This gives the height of the device area
color	Integer	Yes	This is the number of bits per color component (if not color, the value is 0)
color-index	Integer	Yes	This is the number of entries in the output device's color lookup table
monochrome	Integer	Yes	This is the number of bits per pixel in the monochrome frame buffer (if not monochrome, the value is 0)
grid	0 or 1	No	If this is set to 1, the device is grid based, such as a teletype terminal or phone display with only one fixed font (all other devices are 0)

The second category is bitmap media types; here's the full list:

Feature	Value	Min/max prefixes	Description
orientation	portrait or landscape	No	This gives the orientation of a device
aspect-ratio	Ratio (w/h)	Yes	This gives the ratio of width to height, expressed as two integers and separated by a slash (for example, 16/9)
device-aspect-ratio	Ratio (w/h)	Yes	This is the ratio of device-width to device-height
resolution	Resolution	Yes	This gives the density of pixels of the output device, expressed as an integer followed by dpi (dots per inch) or dpcm (dots per centimeter)

The third and final category only has one media type—this is `scan`, which is used for TV devices:

Feature	Value	Min/max prefixes	Description
`scan`	`Progressive or interlace`	No	Scanning process used by TV devices

In most cases, it will be sufficient to specify a single media type and feature when creating media queries—there will be instances where we might need to check against multiple features or types in a single query.

Thankfully, Less can easily handle this by using logical operators—let's take a moment to recap the options available when creating media queries.

Using logical operators

As we begin to build more complex queries, there will be instances where we need to perform a check against multiple criteria within a media query. Less can handle this with ease. Before we take a look at putting into practice what we've learned, let's just take a moment to review the operators available:

Operator	Is used to
`and`	Combine multiple media features together, or media features with other media types. For example: `@media tv and (min-width: 700px) and (orientation: landscape) { ... }`
`comma`	Apply a set of styles if any of a comma-delimited list of queries returns true: `@media (min-width: 700px), handheld and (orientation: landscape) { ... }`
`not`	Return `true` if the media query would otherwise return `false`, for example, `@media not all and (monochrome) { ... }` would return `@media not (all and (monochrome)) { ... }`
`only`	Prevent application of styles by browsers that do not support media queries (assuming that fallback support has not been implemented)

Okay, we've covered the theory around media queries; let's turn our attention to building some queries!

Designing media queries

So far, we've seen what media queries are, the options available, and our clients who have helped us to determine what devices we need to support. It's at this stage in the process that we need to determine how we're going to translate these requirements into real code.

To help with this, let's work through a simple example. In this instance, we need to create a simple block of text, with a list of editors shown to the left of the text. Granted, it is somewhat contrived, but it does show perfectly how we can vary the content when displayed on different devices.

Creating a simple example

The best way to see how media queries work is in the form of a simple demo. In this instance, we have a simple set of requirements, in terms of what should be displayed at each size:

- We need to cater for four different sizes of content
- The small version must be shown to the authors as plain text e-mail links, with no decoration
- For medium-sized screens, we will add an icon before the link
- On large screens, we will add an e-mail address after the e-mail links
- On extra-large screens, we will combine the medium and large breakpoints together, so both icons and e-mail addresses are displayed

In all instances, we will have a simple container in which there will be some dummy text and a list of editors. The media queries we create will control the appearance of the editor list, depending on the window size of the browser being used to display the content.

Let's begin by downloading and extracting a copy of `simple.html` from the code download that accompanies the book. This contains the markup that we will use to create our page.

Next, add the following code to a new document. We'll go through it section by section, starting with the variables created for our media queries:

```
@small: ~"(max-width: 699px) and (min-width: 520px)";
@medium: ~"(max-width: 1000px) and (min-width: 700px)";
@large: ~"(min-width: 1001px)";
@xlarge: ~"(min-width: 1151px)";
```

Next comes some basic styles to define margins, font sizes, and styles:

```
* { margin: 0; padding: 0; }
body { font: 14px Georgia, serif; }
h3 { margin: 0 0 8px 0; }
p { margin: 0 25px }
```

We need to set sizes for each area within our demo, so go ahead and add the following styles:

```
#fluid-wrap { width: 70%; margin: 60px auto; padding: 20px;
background: #eee; overflow: hidden; }
#main-content { width: 65%; float: right; }

#sidebar {
   width: 35%; float: left;
   ul { list-style: none; }
   ul li a { color: #900; text-decoration: none; padding: 3px 0;
display: block; }
}
```

Now that the basic styles are set, we can add our media queries—beginning with the query catering for small screens, where we simply display an e-mail logo:

```
@media @small {
   #sidebar ul li a { padding-left: 21px; background: url(../img/email.
png) left center no-repeat; }
}
```

The medium query comes next; here, we add the word Email before the e-mail address instead:

```
@media @medium {
   #sidebar ul li a:before { content: "Email: "; font-style: italic;
color: #666; }
}
```

In the large media query, we switch to showing the name first, followed by the e-mail (the latter extracted from the data-email attribute):

```
@media @large {
   #sidebar ul li a:after { content: " (" attr(data-email) ")"; font-
size: 11px; font-style: italic; color: #666; }
}
```

We finish with the extra-large query, where we use the e-mail address format shown in the large media query, but add an e-mail logo to it:

```
@media @xlarge {
  #sidebar ul li a { padding-left: 21px; background: url(../img/email.
png) left center no-repeat; }
}
```

Save the file as `simple.less`. Now that our files are prepared, let's preview the results in a browser. For this, I recommend that you use **Responsive Design View** within Firefox (activated by pressing *Ctrl + Shift + M*). Once activated, resize the view to 416 x 735; here we can see that only the name is displayed as an e-mail link:

Increasing the size to 544 x 735 adds an e-mail logo, while still keeping the same name/e-mail format as before:

If we increase it further to 716 x 735, the e-mail logo changes to the word **Email**, as seen in the following screenshot:

Authors:

Email: John Smith

Email: Fred Bloggs

Email: Anonymous

Lorem ipsum dolor sit amet, consectetur adipiscing elit. Mauris ullamcorper eleifend leo, non sagittis libero venenatis et. Nullam imperdiet tempus velit vel eleifend. Nulla lobortis hendrerit lobortis. Quisque vitae sollicitudin mauris. Quisque auctor dolor nec neque rhoncus posuere. Suspendisse lacinia ipsum nulla, vestibulum eleifend urna scelerisque ac. Nunc ultricies. lorem at

Let's increase the size even further to 735 x 1029; the format changes again, to a name/e-mail link, followed by an e-mail address in parentheses:

Authors:

John Smith *(john.smith@example.com)*

Fred Bloggs *(fred.bloggs@anywhere.com)*

Anonymous *(example123@test.com)*

Lorem ipsum dolor sit amet, consectetur adipiscing elit. Mauris ullamcorper eleifend leo, non sagittis libero venenatis et. Nullam imperdiet tempus velit vel eleifend. Nulla lobortis hendrerit lobortis. Quisque vitae sollicitudin mauris. Quisque auctor dolor nec neque rhoncus posuere. Suspendisse lacinia ipsum nulla, vestibulum eleifend urna scelerisque ac. Nunc ultricies, lorem at dignissim cursus, odio arcu porttitor neque, a convallis orci nibh vehicula nunc.

In our final change, increase the size to 735 x 1182. Here, we can see the previous style being used, but with the addition of an e-mail logo:

Authors:

John Smith *(john.smith@example.com)*

Fred Bloggs *(fred.bloggs@anywhere.com)*

Anonymous *(example123@test.com)*

Lorem ipsum dolor sit amet, consectetur adipiscing elit. Mauris ullamcorper eleifend leo, non sagittis libero venenatis et. Nullam imperdiet tempus velit vel eleifend. Nulla lobortis hendrerit lobortis. Quisque vitae sollicitudin mauris. Quisque auctor dolor nec neque rhoncus posuere. Suspendisse lacinia ipsum nulla, vestibulum eleifend urna scelerisque ac. Nunc ultricies, lorem at dignissim cursus, odio arcu porttitor neque, a convallis orci nibh vehicula nunc.

These screenshots illustrate perfectly how you can resize your screen and still maintain a suitable layout for each device you decide to support; let's take a moment to consider how the code works.

The normal accepted practice for developers is to work on the basis of "mobile first", or create the smallest view so it is perfect, then increase the size of the screen and adjust the content until the maximum size is reached. This works perfectly well for new sites, but the principle might have to be reversed if a mobile view is being retrofitted to an existing site.

In our instance, we've produced the content for a full-size screen first. From a Less perspective, there is nothing here that isn't new—we've used nesting for the `#sidebar` div, but otherwise the rest of this part of the code is standard CSS.

The magic happens in two parts—immediately at the top of the file, we've set a number of Less variables, which encapsulate the media definition strings we use in the queries. Here, we've created four definitions, ranging from `@small` (for devices between 520px to 699px), right through to `@xlarge` for widths of 1151px or more.

We then take each of the variables and use them within each query as appropriate, for example, the `@small` query is set as shown in the following code:

```
@media @small {
   #sidebar ul li a { padding-left: 21px; background: url(../img/email.
png) left center no-repeat; }
}
```

In the preceding code, we have standard CSS style rules to display an e-mail logo before the name/e-mail link. Each of the other queries follows exactly the same principle; they will each compile as valid CSS rules when running through Less.

Now that we've seen how to construct media queries using Less, it's worth taking a moment to explore how best to view our demos. While it can be argued that simply resizing the browser window might suffice, we can go further and take advantage of a number of tools to help with the process.

Using tools to resize the screen

In the previous section, we took a look at a simple example of creating media queries to show or hide elements when a list of editors is resized. We used Firefox's **Responsive Design View** option to resize the screen for us; this is one option we can use to cleanly resize a screen for mobile viewing; it's a critical tool to work with media queries.

You can use special tools for this purpose, but most modern browsers already have a perfectly adequate tool built in for this purpose. Let's take a look at a few in turn.

For Firefox users, press *Ctrl + Shift + M* to activate **Responsive Design View**, as shown in the following screenshot:

However, if your preference is Google Chrome, then the same functionality is available—it is part of the developer tools set, which can be activated by pressing *Ctrl + Shift + I*:

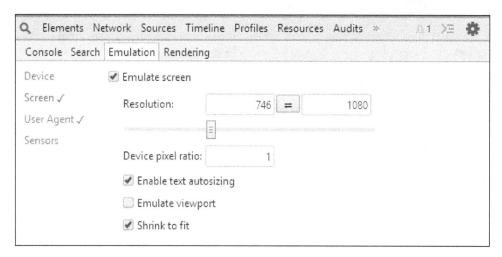

If you are an Opera user, then there is the dedicated Opera Mobile Emulator, which is available at `http://www.opera.com/developer/mobile-emulator`, with versions available for the Windows, Mac, and Linux platforms:

If you need to use IE to display your site in a responsive format, then unfortunately your options are somewhat limited — at least to IE10. IE has a **Resize** option (as shown in the following screenshot), but it resizes the whole window, rather than show a view within a normal-sized window:

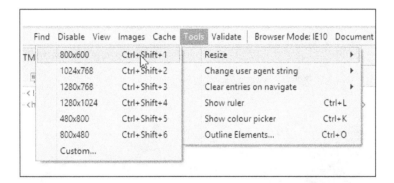

It's not the perfect option, but then the best practice is to develop in browsers that are more standards-compliant (such as Google Chrome or Firefox). We can then effect any tweaks for IE later.

It is worth noting that if IE11 is used, then it can be set to work in a similar way to Google Chrome. We can set the emulation mode to display a small window, within a large/full-size browser window.

If you prefer not to use built-in browser tools, then there are other tools available that can be used instead. Two tools that are of particular note are ish from Brad Frost, available at `http://bradfrostweb.com/demo/ish/`, and ViewPort Resizer by Malte Wassermann, available at `http://lab.maltewassermann.com/viewport-resizer/`.

Let's now change focus and turn our attention to building something more in-depth, where we can use Less in a more real-world example.

Building responsive pages

Adding media queries to any site is possible; the key to it is deciding what breakpoints you want to support and the elements that should be displayed at each breakpoint. This can be as little as just the one breakpoint, or many. It all depends on what happens to the elements when they are resized and whether you need to alter the code to improve their appearance at a particular breakpoint.

Now that we've seen basic media queries in action, we're going to create something more complex, in the form of a basic welcome page that would not be out of place on a portfolio site. We'll start with the basic full-size page, which will look something like this screenshot:

This is a very simple page, created as if it were part of a portfolio site. It's a perfect opportunity to explore how we can use some simple media queries to resize the page for a mobile platform.

Building the basic page

Let's start by extracting a copy of the `responsive.html` file that is in the code download that accompanies this book. This contains a simple demo page, set to appear as if it could form the front page of a portfolio site. Save this file into your project folder.

We also need a copy of the `reset.less` file that is in the same code download; go ahead and extract this to the project folder as well. This provides some basic style resets to mimic what might happen when creating pages for display on your site.

 For the purposes of this demo, I will assume that you are using Sublime Text, which is preconfigured to compile Less files into valid CSS when saving content.

Next, open your text editor of choice and add the following code; we'll go through it in detail, section by section. We start with setting some basic styles, to define each area within the page:

```
#wrapper { width: 96%; max-width: 45rem; margin: auto; padding: 2%; }
#main { width: 60%; margin-right: 5%; float: left; }
aside { width: 35%; float: right; }
a { text-decoration: none; text-transform: uppercase; }
a, img { border: medium none; color: #000000; font-weight: bold;
    outline: medium none;}
```

Next, we need to define some styles for our header. This is one of the elements that will be replaced when we resize the page to a smaller screen:

```
header {
  font-family: 'Droid Sans', sans-serif;
  h1 { height: 70px; float: left; display: block; font-weight: 700;
font-size: 2.0rem;}
  nav {
  float: right; margin-top: 40px; height: 22px; border-radius: 4px;
  li { display: inline; margin-left: 15px; }
  ul { font-weight: 400; font-size: 1.1rem; }
  a {
    padding: 5px 5px 5px 5px;
    &:hover { background-color: #27a7bd; color: #ffffff; border-
radius: 4px; }
  }
  }
}
```

The remaining two basic styles cover the **Skip to Main Content** link that appears when the screen is resized, and the main image on screen respectively:

```
#skipTo {
display: none;
  li { background: #197a8a; }
  a { color: #ffffff; font-size: 0.8rem; }
}

#banner {
  float: left; margin-bottom: 15px; width: 100%;
  img { width: 100%; }
}
```

Save the file as `responsive.less`. If we preview the results in a browser, we will see something akin to the screenshot shown at the beginning of this example.

However, if we resize the browser window using a tool such as Responsive Design View in Firefox, it will begin to break the design—the toolbar loses tabs, the header has a large gap, and the right side of the image has been chopped off, as shown in the following screenshot:

We can fix this by adding in a media query to manage what happens when the screen is resized. Let's take a look at how this works in action.

Adding responsive queries

We've set the basic styles for our portfolio page and can clearly see that elements are beginning to break when the page is resized. Let's fix this by adding in the media query that redefines what happens when the screen is resized.

Start by adding the following at the head of the responsive.less file:

```
@mobile: ~"screen and (max-width: 30rem)";
```

Next, we need to add the replacement styles that will kick in when using a mobile platform. Immediately below the Less styles in responsive.less, go ahead and add the following code, beginning with the styles that control the display of a **Skip to Main Content** button that appears at the top of the page when it has been resized:

```
@media @mobile {
  #skipTo {
  display: block;
  a {
     display: block; padding: 10px; text-align: center; height: 20px;
     &:hover { background-color: #27a7bd; border-radius: 0px; height:
20px; }
     }
  }
```

Next comes the styles required to resize the main content area, side bar, and header:

```
  #main, aside { float: left; clear: left; margin: 0 0 10px; width:
100%; }
  #banner { margin-top: 150px; }
  header h1 { margin-top: 20px; }
```

Finally, we need to alter the styles used to redefine the navigation options that now appear as a stacked list of buttons, when the page is resized:

```
  header nav{
  float: left; clear: left;margin: 0 0 10px; width: 100%;
  li { margin: 0; background: #efefef; display: block; margin-bottom:
3px; height: 40px; }
  a {
     display: block; padding: 10px; text-align: center;
     &:hover { background-color: #27a7bd; border-radius: 0px; padding:
10px; height: 20px; }
     }
  }
}
```

Resave the file as `responsive.less`. If you've used Sublime Text as your editor, it will convert it to a compiled CSS file. Let's now preview the results in a browser:

At full size, there will be no change (which is anticipated), but when the page is resized, we can already see an improvement on the page. The title has been repositioned so there is less of a gap below it, the toolbar has been reset to display as buttons, the image has been resized to better fit on the page, and the content has been repositioned into a vertical format. We can also see the addition of a button to allow us to jump down to the main content on the page.

Excellent, our page now looks and works as we expect in a mobile capacity! If we increase or decrease the size of the browser window, we can see the content reflowing to fit the available space, based on the media query we created in `responsive.less`.

So, what's the magic that's making this work? From the code we've worked with, you might be forgiven if you thought it was all of the code in this section. It's a perfectly valid statement. After all, all of the styles are needed to ensure content is correctly placed when used in a mobile environment.

In reality though, there are only two statements that we've used that are key to the whole process: `@mobile: ~"screen and (max-width: 30rem)";` and `@media @mobile {...}`.

(Okay, I cheated slightly, but only by one character!)

The first statement is a Less variable that we've set as our media type and the feature we will be testing. The second one calls in that variable as the test. Everything in between is standard CSS styling and is being used to rework the layout of the page when used to display content on a mobile device.

In this example, we've used a large image, which has been set with `width: 100%`. While it will resize perfectly when the page size is reduced or increased, it still means that we're potentially loading a large image on a small device—not a good idea! We can improve on this by asking the browser to load different versions of the image, depending on which media query is being applied. Let's take a look and see how Less can help remove some of the burden in managing this process.

Adding responsive images

Hands up if you own a mobile device, such as a tablet or smartphone? If you do, then you will likely have seen how long pages take to load, when they haven't been sized for mobile use.

In the example we've just worked on, we set a 100 percent value for the width of `#banner img`—in most cases this will work perfectly fine; it does mean that we are loading a large photo, which is not ideal on a mobile device! Instead, we can make a simple change to our media rules to load a smaller image when the screen is reduced in size.

For this demo, I've resized a copy of the abstract image to a smaller 461px x 346px version and saved it as `abstract_small.jpg`. This size is small enough to see the change take effect when the screen is suitably resized to smaller dimensions.

Let's start by downloading and extracting copies of `responsive.html` and `responsive.less` from the code download for this book, then saving them as `responsive_img.html` and `responsive_img.less`, respectively.

Open up `responsive_img.html`, then alter the line as shown:

```
<link href="css/reset.less" type="text/less" rel="stylesheet">
<link rel="stylesheet/less" href="css/responsive_img.less">
```

Next, add the highlighted line to the media query, as indicated:

```
#banner {
margin-top: 150px;
img { content:url("../img/abstract_small.jpg"); }
}
```

Save both files. If we then preview the results in a browser, you should not see any visible change (which we would expect). However, we will see a change in the URL for the image if we open up the developer tools within the browser and reduce the size of the screen:

```
@media screen and (max-width: 30rem)
#banner img {
    content: url("http://localhost/Chapter%208/img/abstract_small.jpg");
}
#banner img {
    width: ▶ 100%;
}
```

The beauty of this is that we can save a few kilobytes, which makes it quicker to view the site on mobile devices, as there is less to download into the browser. We can, however, go to the complete extreme by replacing images with high definition resolution versions, but only if the device supports it! Intrigued? Let's take a look at how this works, using the `retina.js` Less mixin, available at `http://imulus.github.io/retinajs/`.

Incorporating retina support for images

In the previous example, we saw how easy it is to adjust our Less code so that a smaller image can be loaded when screen estate has been resized to mimic a mobile device.

However, many of you will own devices (such as iPads or iPhones) that have retina support, or which can support the display of high-resolution images that otherwise would not display very well on regular PCs. We can take advantage of this when working with Less. In fact, a Less mixin has already been created, which we can get from `https://raw.githubusercontent.com/imulus/retinajs/master/src/retina.less`. Save this as `retina.less` within our project folder.

Next, we need to save a copy of the `abstract.jpg` file that we've been using, as `abstract@2x.jpg`—this will become our hi-res version. Take a copy of the original `abstract.jpg` file and compress it using a JPG compressor such as the online service from `http://www.jpeg-optimizer.com`. Save the compressed version as `abstract.jpg`.

Now that our images are prepared, open up `responsive.html` and modify the lines as shown:

```
<link href="css/reset.less" type="text/less" rel="stylesheet">
<link href="css/responsive_hd.less"
  rel="stylesheet/less">
<script src="js/less.min.js"></script>
```

Save this as `responsive_hd.html`. Next, open `responsive.less` and add this line at the head of the file:

```
@import "retina.less";
```

Then, add the following line at the end of the file:

```
#banner img { .at2x('/images/abstract.png', 200px, 100px); }
```

 In a production environment, it is more likely that this would be within a media query—adding it at the end is sufficient to illustrate how it works, for the purposes of this demo.

Save this as `responsive_hd.less`. We can then preview the results in a browser. For best results, I recommend the following:

- Preview the results using a local web server or online webspace—a good local web server to try is WAMP (`http://www.wampserver.de` for Windows) or MAMP (`http://www.mamp.info` for MAC).

- If possible, try to view the results within Google Chrome if you can't view them online via a retina-enabled device. Google Chrome has the ability to emulate different devices; if we enable this feature and set it to show as an iPhone 5, for example:

We can clearly see that the change has been made:

```
Styles | Computed  Event Listeners  DOM Breakpoints  Properties
element.style {                                    + :.
}
@media (-webkit-min-device-pixel-ratio: 1.5), not all,
not all, (min-resolution: 1.5dppx)
#banner img {
    background-image: url("/images/abstract@2x.png");
    background-size: 200px 100px;
}
#banner img {
    background-image: url('/images/abstract.png');
}
#banner img {
    width: ▶ 100%;
}
```

While there should be no material change to the layout of the web page, using this trick means that a higher resolution image can be used when a device supports it, or be replaced with a standard resolution image if the device does not have retina support.

To test whether a device supports the **device-pixel-ratio** test we used here, browse to `http://www.quirksmode.org/css/mediaqueries/devicepixelratio.html`. For example, we can confirm that `webkit-device-pixel-ratio` is supported, when testing with an iPad:

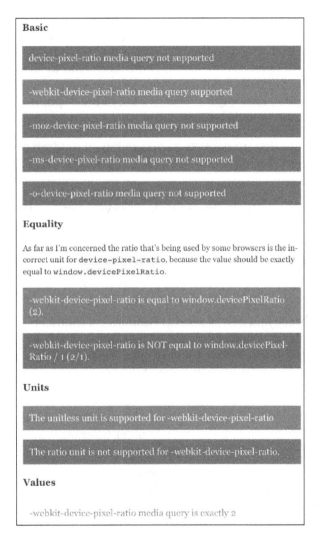

Let's move on and continue with this theme of using external libraries by taking a look at what external libraries are available for use with Less, when working with media queries.

Using prebuilt libraries

So far we've covered the basics of creating media queries using Less—it's at this point that you're probably thinking, "Surely there's a prebuilt library we could use to help us here, right...?"

Well, in this instance, unfortunately there isn't a prebuilt library we can use; it's down to us to build each query manually! This is no bad thing, as media queries can be seen as something of a workaround, which can lead to bloated code if we're not careful. It will be difficult, if not near impossible, to cater for all breakpoints. Each project will require support for a specific set of break points, which will not necessarily be the same for every site.

In addition, media queries are natively supported in all modern browsers; the only exception is IE, where Version 8 or below is not supported. To get around this, there are three options:

- We can use the fallback library media-query-to-type created by Mike Morici, and which we can download from `https://github.com/himedlooff/media-query-to-type`. This converts media queries into media types, which are supported as far back as IE6.

- Alternatively, we can use Modernizr (from `http://www.modernizr.com`) to detect when media queries are used.

- Another library that can be used is Respond.js, created by Scott Jehl and available from `https://github.com/scottjehl/Respond`. This is effectively a drop-in library that can convert most media queries into formats that IE8 or below can understand.

Although this chapter is about using Less to create media queries, it is nevertheless important to consider which browsers should be supported and how far you will be willing to go to get media queries to work in older browsers such as IE6 to 8.

To help maintain clarity, we can use conditional hacks to only load the media-query-to-type or Respond.js libraries when we detect that IE9 or below has been used:

```
#<!--[if lt IE 9]>....<![endif]-->
```

While in some respects we might feel obligated to provide the same environment in all cases (including for old IE), this is not necessarily a worthwhile exercise; supporting a smaller number well is better than average support for a lot of browsers!

Summary

Media queries have rapidly become a de facto part of responsive web design. Throughout this chapter, we saw how to use Less to make the process easier to manage within your code.

We started our journey through media queries with a brief introduction, followed by a review of some of the limitations that we must work around and considerations that need to be considered when working with clients.

Next came a brief exploration of the media types and features that we can use when working with Less; we took a look at the logical operators we can also use to create queries that test for multiple types or features. We then covered how to create a simple media query, with a quick look at how best to show responsive views in browsers, before continuing with a more practical example of a single page from a demo portfolio site. We saw how first we can create our basic page, before adding the requisite code to turn it into a responsive one.

We then moved on to take a brief look at how to improve the image on the page, by first making it more responsive, then switching to displaying high-resolution images when retina support is available and enabled. We then closed out the chapter with a look at what prebuilt libraries are available that can help when working with Less.

In the next chapter, we're going to move onto some more practical uses of Less, with a look at using Less within a CMS, such as WordPress.

Working with Less in a CMS

Working in a CMS…Ah, choices, choices…!

Question: what do the following have in common—Facebook, Beyoncé, Sony, Dallas Mavericks NBA basketball team, and Time?

Worked it out? Well, it's the subject of our next chapter in our journey of learning Less. They all have blogs or sites created using WordPress! Created back in 2003, WordPress has become one of the world's most well-known content management system platforms, used in dozens of scenarios, from simple blogs to full-blown e-commerce systems.

Throughout the next few pages, we're going to learn how to incorporate our favorite CSS preprocessor into WordPress and some of the tricks we can use to help simplify the creation of style sheets. The best bit—most are tricks we've already covered throughout the book so far; we're just going to adapt where we use them.

In this chapter, we will cover the following topics:

- An overview of the WP theme structure
- Incorporating Less into pages
- Some examples of converting code to use Less
- Prebuilt themes for WP, using Less
- Plugins available to use Less with WordPress
- Using Grunt to help Less development in WP

Curious? Let's get started…!

This chapter will assume a certain level of familiarity with the WordPress theme design; if you're new to WordPress, you might like to peruse one of the several books by Packt Publishing on WordPress theme design.

Introducing the WP theme structure

If you've spent any time working with CMS systems, then you will likely have come across the concept of using themes to customize your site and add or remove features as you see fit.

WordPress is no different; it uses a system of themes to customize its appearance; throughout this chapter, we're going to follow this principle and see how we can use Less to help simplify the process. Before we start writing code, it's worth taking a moment to examine the anatomy of a WordPress theme.

First, we need to download the WordPress source files, which are available at `http://wordpress.org/latest.zip`; at the time of writing this, the latest version is 3.9.1. When we open the WordPress archive, navigate to **wp-content** | **themes** | **twentyfourteen**. We'll see something akin to this:

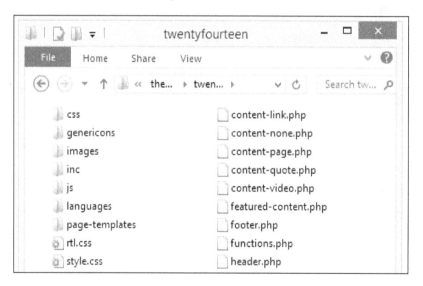

All of these files are required to operate the Twenty Fourteen theme that comes with this version of WordPress; we will be using this theme as a basis for our exercises throughout this chapter.

We are most interested in the `style.css` file—this is the main style sheet for any theme. This file contains the theme information that is displayed within the theme selection area of WordPress, where we can see details such as the name of the theme, author, support URL, and so on. We will also make use of the `functions.php` file to add support for Less, but this will be a one-off process that happens before we really get to work on customizing our theme.

Preparing our environment

Now that we've downloaded WordPress, we need to ensure we have a working environment available in order to work with Less.

Each person's environment might differ, but to get the most benefit out of the exercises that follow, you will need to ensure that you at least have the following:

- A working copy of WordPress that can be customized—ideally, this will be locally hosted using a web server such as WAMP (for Windows, available at `http://www.wampserver.com`), or MAMP (for Mac, available at `http://www.mamp.info`). Alternatively, you might have some online webspace available for use—this will work as well, although you might find the automation exercises at the end of this chapter hard to do.

- For the purposes of the book, I will assume WampServer is installed; change accordingly, if your server is different.

- A copy of Node.js installed along with Grunt; we covered how to install both earlier in *Chapter 2, Building a Less Development Toolkit*.

- A text editor of your choice—there are hundreds available; my personal preference is Sublime Text 2, which I will assume you have installed.

If you do not have WordPress already installed, then you can find full instructions at `http://codex.wordpress.org/Installing_WordPress` on how to install it.

Okay, assuming we have the requisite pieces of software installed, let's move on and take a look at preparing our theme for working with Less.

Creating a basic child theme

Hold on, preparing our theme?

Yes, you read correctly—preparing our theme. While WordPress does come with three themes available for use out of the box, it is not good practice to modify the source files directly.

Modifying the source files means that your theme will break if an update is released for it (and yes, WordPress does release updates to its themes). We can get around this by creating a child theme, which sits in the same theme folder, but is set to inherit the base files of its parent theme.

What this means is that we can retain the original system files for the parent theme, but use new styles created in the child theme to override existing styles. We will make good use of this principle later in this chapter, when we start to write new Less code.

For now, let's quickly run through creating our new child theme:

1.   Navigate to **wp-content | themes**; here, you will see a folder called `twentyfourteen`:

2.   Create a copy of this folder, but rename it `twentyfourteen-child`. It is good practice to append `child` at the end of such a theme, to identify it in the theme folder list.

3.   Within the `twentyfourteen-child` folder, crack open a copy of `style.css`, then remove everything below the closing `*/`, and replace as shown:

```
This theme, like WordPress, is licensed under the GPL.
Use it to make something cool, have fun, and share what you've
learned with others.
*/

@import url("../twentyfourteen/style.css");

/* =Theme customization starts here
-------------------------------------------------------------- */
```

That's all we need to do. If we browse to the **Central Administration** area of our WordPress installation, we will see the child theme present in the **Appearance | Themes** area. All that remains to do is to activate it in the usual manner.

Note that going forward, it is assumed all changes will be made in the child theme, unless directed otherwise.

Adding support for Less in WordPress

With WordPress installed and working, it's time to turn our attention to adding support for Less.

In older versions of WordPress, it was customary to add this directly to the `header.php` file. While it worked fine, it meant we couldn't maintain a clear separation between HTML content and presentational markup. Thankfully, in more recent versions, the WordPress team moved to adding the style sheet by using a function stored in the `functions.php` file. Let's take a look at how to achieve this now:

1. Open a text editor of your choice, then browse to the `twentyfourteen` theme folder, and look for `functions.php`. Add the following code at the bottom of the file:

```
/*
 * Adds support for the Less preprocessor to your theme.
 *
 * @since Twenty Fourteen 1.0
 * @param string $current_user Determines the currently logged in
   user
 */
if ( ! function_exists( 'less_enqueue_scripts' ) ) {
    function less_enqueue_scripts() {

        $current_user = wp_get_current_user();

        if ( $current_user->ID == '1' ) {
          wp_enqueue_script( 'lesscss',
            get_stylesheet_directory_uri() . '/js/less.min.js' );
        }
    }
    add_action( 'wp_enqueue_scripts', 'less_enqueue_scripts' );
}
```

2. Save the changes. If we refresh the screen and then preview the results in a browser, we won't see any visual changes. However, if we preview the compiled source code in a DOM Inspector such as Firebug, we can clearly see the addition of Less:

```
⊞ <script src="http://localhost/wordpress/wp-includes/js/jquery/jquery-
  migrate.min.js?ver=1.2.1" type="text/javascript">
⊟ <script src="http://localhost/wordpress/wp-content/themes/twentyfourteen
  /js/less.min.js?ver=4.0" type="text/javascript">
   1   /*!
   2    * Less - Leaner CSS v1.7.3
   3    * http://lesscss.org
   4    *
   5    * Copyright (c) 2009-2014, Alexis Sellier <self@cloudhead.net>
   6    * Licensed under the Apache v2 License.
   7    *
   8    */
   9
   10  /** * @license Apache v2
   11   */
   12
   13  !function(a,b){function c(b){return a.less[b.split("/")[1]]}function
   14  },unit:function(a,b){if(!(a instanceof d.Dimension))throw{type:"Argu
   15  },eval:function(b){var c,d,e,f,g,h,i,j,k,l,m,n,o,p=[],q=!1,r=[],s=[],
   16  return j<c.length&&k>0&&(l[l.length-1].elements=l[l.length-1].element
  </script>
```

At this point, we have a version of WordPress working perfectly well with Less support—we can go ahead and create a Less file, called `style.less`, and drop this in as a replacement for `style.css`, right...?

Showing Less style sheets to specific users

Not so fast. We told WordPress how to call in Less, but not how to retrieve the right set of Less styles yet! To do this, we need to add another function into the `functions.php` file; this one will not only incorporate a replacement Less-based style sheet, but also show it only to the administrator and display a compiled version for normal use. Bear with me on this; all will become clear shortly:

1. Open a copy of the `functions.php` file that we worked on in the previous exercise. This time, add the following at the bottom of the file:

```
if ( ! function_exists( 'less_filter_stylesheet_uri' ) ) {
  function less_filter_stylesheet_uri( $stylesheet_uri,
$stylesheet_dir_uri ) {
    $current_user = wp_get_current_user();
```

```
    if ( $current_user->ID == '1' ) {
      $style_src = $stylesheet_dir_uri . '/style.less';
    } else {
      $style_src = $stylesheet_dir_uri . '/style.min.css';
      return $style_src;
    }
    add_filter( 'stylesheet_uri', 'less_filter_stylesheet_uri',
10, 2 );
}
```

2. Save a copy of the file, then refresh the browser window that currently displays WordPress. If we open up our DOM Inspector as we did before, we can now see the replacement style sheet in use:

```
⊟ <link id="twentyfourteen-style-css" media="all" type="text/css" href="http://localhost/wordpress
  /wp-content/themes/twentyfourteen-child/style.less?ver=3.9.1" rel="stylesheet">
    1  /*
    2  Theme Name: Twenty Fourteen - Child Theme
    3  Theme URI: http://wordpress.org/themes/twentyfourteen
    4  Author: the WordPress team
    5  Author URI: http://wordpress.org/
    6  Description: In 2014, our default theme lets you create a responsive magazine website wi
    7  Version: 1.1
    8  License: GNU General Public License v2 or later
    9  License URI: http://www.gnu.org/licenses/gpl-2.0.html
```

If we log out of WordPress and log in as another user, the compiled CSS version of the style sheet will be displayed instead.

Adding Less support using a plugin

Adding in code manually works perfectly well, but after a while it gets tedious. Surely we can make things easier using a plugin, right?

Absolutely, we can add support for Less using a plugin; there are several ways to achieve this, but my favorite has to be the plugin created by Justin Kopepasah and available for download from WordPress Plugin Directory at `https://wordpress.org/plugins/less-theme-support/`. Let's take a peek at how to use it; it's really easy to install:

1. Start by navigating to `https://wordpress.org/plugins/less-theme-support/` and then clicking on **Download Version 1.0.2**. When prompted to do so, save it into the `plugins` folder within our installation of WordPress.

2. Browse to the **Plugins** area in WordPress' admin, then click on **Upload** and select **less-theme-support.1.0.2.zip**.

3. Click on **Install Now**, then when prompted, click on **Activate Plugin**.

At this point, the plugin is now active and we need to tell our WordPress theme how to use it:

1. If you have not already done so from a previous exercise, rename the `style.css` file at the root of our theme to `style.less`.

2. Fire up your favorite text editor and open a copy of the `functions.php` file that is located at the root of our `theme` folder.

3. Look for the `twentyfourteen_setup()` function (on or around line 58) and add the following at the end of the function, as shown:

```
    add_filter( 'use_default_gallery_style', '__return_false' );

    // Add support for Less preprocessor
    add_theme_support( 'less', array('enable' => true ) );
}
endif; // twentyfourteen_setup
```

Save the file. If we revert to our WordPress site and refresh the screen, we should see no visual change. The real change will show if we look at the code within DOM Inspector:

```
⊞ <script src="http://localhost/wordpress/wp-includes/js/jquery/jquery-
   migrate.min.js?ver=1.2.1" type="text/javascript">
⊟ <script src="http://localhost/wordpress/wp-content/plugins/less-theme-support-master
   /js/less.min.js?ver=1.7.0" type="text/javascript">
   1   /*!
   2    * LESS - Leaner CSS v1.7.0
   3    * http://lesscss.org
   4    *
   5    * Copyright (c) 2009-2014, Alexis Sellier <self@cloudhead.net>
   6    * Licensed under the Apache v2 License.
   7    *
   8    */
   9
  10   /** * @license Apache v2
  11    */
```

It is worth noting that Less Theme Support comes with a number of configuration options, which we can use to change how it works. This is perfect if we're switching from using it in a development site, to a production one. The values that can be set are Boolean and the default is false:

- `Enable`: This enables Less and enqueues `less.min.js` on the frontend
- `Develop`: This enables a development environment for Less and enqueues `less-develop.js`

- `Watch`: This enables the watch mode for Less and enqueues `less-watch.js`
- `Minify`: This enables usage of a minified style sheet (`style.min.css`) on the frontend for all other visitors (best generated using `lessc -x style.less > style.min.css`)

If used with care, they can be very flexible; for instance, you might want to configure your theme to use Less dynamically when working in development, but not in production:

```
add_theme_support('less', array(
  'enable'  => true,
  'develop' => true,
  'watch'   => true
));
```

If we switch to production use, then we are likely to use the `minify` option instead:

```
add_theme_support( 'less', array(
  'minify' => true
));
```

As we've seen, it's an easy plugin to configure. If you're working with Less on a number of sites, it's often better to use a plugin to install Less so that we don't have to delve into source files and edit them. The key part of this exercise is the use of the `add_theme_support` keyword for WordPress, which allows a theme or plugin to register support for a certain feature within our theme.

> If you are interested in learning more about `add_theme_support`, it is worth browsing the WordPress Codex page at `http://codex.wordpress.org/Function_Reference/add_theme_support`.

This allows us to tell the theme to use Less. We can always do this manually (as we have seen), but it is preferable where possible to use plugins, unless circumstances dictate an alternative method is needed.

Working with Less themes in WordPress

Now that we have support for Less in place, let's move on and take a look at the options available to use Less styles in our themes, either within our own creations, or as part of prebuilt themes available for sale or download via the Internet.

Converting themes to use Less

We now have the basis for a Less style sheet, to which we can start to add our converted styles. Hold on, I hear you ask, "If we're converting a theme such as TwentyFourteen, where on earth do we start?"

It's a very good question. Within excess of 4200 lines in the current style sheet for this theme, it's easy to feel bewildered! However, all will begin to come clear if we follow two simple principles:

- Less allows us to break down our style sheet into multiple files, which are compiled into one by Less. Make use of this; it will be a big help, as smaller files make for easier conversion!

- Don't try to convert all of it in one go; do it bit by bit. Less is a superset of CSS, which means that it is effectively all CSS; Less will happily compile unchanged CSS styles, even in a .less file.

With these principles in mind, let's make a start on converting our theme:

1. Start by opening a copy of the `style.css` file from the `TwentyFourteen` parent theme and look for section 4, which starts on or around line 831 to 926.

2. Copy this section to the `style.less` file in our child theme; paste it in below this line:

   ```
   /* =Theme customization starts here
   -------------------------------------------------------------- */
   ```

3. We'll start by converting the normal green color for the search box to use a variable, then use it to work out the light green color used when hovering over it. Add the following immediately below the `@import` statement in `style.less`, as shown:

   ```
   @import url("../twentyfourteen/style.css");

   /* Define colors */
   @search-box-color: #24890d;
   @search-box-hover-color: @search-box-color + #333;
   ```

4. The next change we'll make will be to the `.site-title` style. We'll convert it to Less' nesting format, so remove these two styles:

   ```
   .site-title { float: left; font-size: 18px; font-weight: 700;
     line-height: 48px; margin: 0; }

   .site-title a, .site-title a:hover { color: #fff; }
   ```

Replace the previous two styles with the following:

```
.site-title {
  float: left;
  font-size: 18px;
  font-weight: 700;
  line-height: 48px;
  margin: 0;
  a {
    color: #fff;
    &:hover { color: #fff; }
  }
}
```

5. We also have an opportunity to incorporate a mixin. This time, it will be in the form of a replacement for the box-sizing style used in the .search-box-wrapper class. Look for this class in the style.less file and modify as shown:

```
.search-box-wrapper {
  .box-sizing(border-box);
  position: absolute;
  top: 48px;
  right: 0;
  width: 100%;
  z-index: 2;
}
```

6. In a separate file, add the following code and save it as mixins.less in the less folder:

```
.box-sizing(@sizing: border-box) {
  -ms-box-sizing: @sizing;
  -moz-box-sizing: @sizing;
  -webkit-box-sizing: @sizing;
  box-sizing: @sizing;
}
```

7. We need to import this into our Less file, so go ahead and add the following line, as indicated:

```
@import url("../twentyfourteen/style.css");
@import "less/mixins.less";
```

8. The final step is to rename the style.css file in our child theme to style.less; although this is not yet fully converted, Less will still compile this as valid CSS.

At this point, we can now save our work, then refresh the browser window, which displays our WordPress site. If all is well, you will not see any visual difference. The only difference you will see is when looking at the compiled code through a DOM Inspector, such as Firebug:

The keen-eyed among you might have spotted something – why are we duplicating code, I hear you ask? There's a good reason for duplicating the code, at least temporarily – while this is something we wouldn't normally want do to do, the irony here is that we can use the unintended duplication to good effect, to help confirm if our new styles are correct.

We took a copy of `section 4` from the original parent theme's CSS file and copied it into our child theme. By default, styles in a child theme are appended to the parent's style sheet. In this instance, our theme has appended the duplicated style, as we would expect. Here comes the rub: we need to then rework the duplicated style to its Less equivalent (as was done here). We can then check against the original theme, indicated by the `style.css` at line 917, to see if our Less version is correct.

If it is correct, we can then either remove it from the original theme, or we can remove the `@import` statement; this breaks the dependency on the parent theme and turns the child theme into a theme in its own right.

Now that we've covered the basics of converting a theme, let's take a moment to consider some useful tips that will help us with creating your own theme.

Creating our own theme

So far, we've spent time converting existing CSS styles in our WordPress theme to use Less. While this works well, it will take time to complete, as WordPress core themes, such as TwentyTwelve or TwentyFourteen, run into several thousand lines!

A more sensible route is to create your own theme. Rather than writing one from scratch, it is preferable to create it as a child theme, so it overrides existing styles within the parent theme.

 Although, we've used an example here, the principles detailed can be used in any instance where you need to create a new theme.

"Why use a child theme", I hear you ask? There are several good reasons to do so:

- Any changes you make to a parent theme will likely break if the WordPress team issues an update.
- It saves you having to redefine a whole bunch of styles; you can concentrate instead on making the critical changes. When ready, you can incorporate the parent theme's styles into your own and convert your child theme into one that can be used in its own right.

Let's now take a look at creating a theme using Less. To get the full benefit from this exercise, we'll need to ensure that a few things are in place:

- Your WordPress installation has a copy of TwentyTwelve installed and activated. TwentyTwelve has a simpler CSS style sheet than the current TwentyFourteen incarnation; it will make the process easier to grasp and hopefully encourage you to move onto working with the newer theme!
- A copy of the TwentyTwelve theme has been saved and reconfigured as a child theme; if you're unsure on how, then refer to the *Creating a basic child theme* section of this chapter.
- A copy of Crunch! has been installed and configured for use on your system.
- A copy of Firefox is installed. This theme was developed using Firefox to keep things simple for the purposes of this exercise.

We'll begin with creating the basic style sheet that is key to the whole compilation process:

1. Start by renaming the existing style.css file within your child theme folder. We'll replace it with a compiled version at the end of the exercise.
2. From the accompanying download, extract and save a copy of the **less** folder within the learningless folder, to the root of your child theme folder.

3. Open your text editor and then add the following to it, saving it as `style.less` in the root of your child theme folder:

```
/*
Theme Name:      Learning Less
Description:     Child theme for the Twenty Twelve theme
Author:          Alex Libby
Author URI:      http://www.not42.net
Template:        twentytwelve
Version:         0.1
*/

// Import parent theme styles
@import url("../../twentytwelve/style.css");
@import "variables.less";
@import "mixins.less";
@import "misc.less";
@import "navigation.less";
@import "header.less";
@import "posts.less";
@import "pages.less";
@import "sidebar.less";
@import "widgets.less";
@import "footer.less";
```

4. Next, we need to compile `style.less` in order to produce our WordPress style sheet. For now, we'll use Crunch! to compile the file, so go ahead and open `style.less` within your installation of Crunch!.

5. Click on **Crunch File**, then when prompted, enter `style.css` as the filename to save the compiled results. It will look similar to the following screenshot:

6. Copy the compiled `style.css` file into the root of your child theme folder.

7. Fire up your copy of Firefox and browse to your WordPress installation. If all is well, you should see something akin to this screenshot:

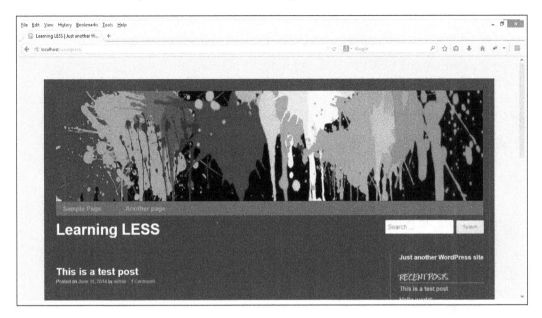

Okay, it won't win any style awards! Nevertheless, it helps to illustrate some key points; let's take a breather and look at these in more detail.

> There are completed version of the `style.less` and `style.css` files within the `learningless` folder; navigate to the less folder, then rename `style-finished.css` to style and copy to the root of your child folder. If you are struggling with the less code, then `style-finished.less` contains a completed copy of the code for this theme.

The crux of this whole process is the `style.less` file. Notice how we created a number of `@import` statements within? This is an essential part of developing themes for WordPress when working with Less; Less allows us to split what could be a lengthy style sheet into smaller, more manageable files.

At this point, you're probably asking, "How do I know how many files to split my code into?" It's a good question and the short answer is: there is no single right answer! Let me explain.

It all depends on how large your style sheet is. A good pointer is to consider what elements you have within your style sheet and group them accordingly. You can then use one or more Less file; Less will happily compile them into one single style sheet at the end. In our example, we have a number of suitable groups such as posts, sidebar, navigation and the like; we've set our main style sheet to import a single Less file for each of these groups.

Throughout all of the Less files, we've made full use of Less' nesting capability; this is one key skill to master when working with WordPress themes built using Less. Nesting is very much your friend when developing WordPress themes; we can group together all of the relevant styles, which makes it easier to read and manage.

Moving on; anyone notice the presence of two key files, namely `mixins.less` and `variables.less`? These are perfect examples of Less files to be created as part of developing themes for WordPress.

We can store all of our variables within one file and reference them as required. A perfect example is to first create variables for each of our colors:

```
// Colors
@white: #fff;
@vivid-orange: #f95812;
@desaturated-cyan: #335c64;
@gray: #666;
...
```

We can then reference the colors within secondary variables. If there's any need to change, then this is the only file that needs to be updated:

```
// Posts
@entry-title-color: @white;
@entry-title-link: @vivid-orange;
@entry-title-link-hover: @desaturated-cyan;
@border-color: @gray;
```

If we open a copy of `posts.less`, we can see the variables in use as shown in the following code:

```
.entry-header {
  .entry-title {
    .links(@entry-title-link, @entry-title-link-hover);
  }
}

.entry-header, .entry-meta {
  .links(@entry-title-link, @entry-title-link-hover);
```

```
}

.entry-header .entry-title {
  .links(@entry-title-color, @entry-title-link-hover);
}
```

In the same way, we can store all of our mixins in one file, namely `mixins.less`; should any of these change, there is only one file that needs updating, not many!

Taking construction further

At this stage, you're probably thinking, "Great, I've got a theme I can use…" Right? Well, yes, and not quite. (Bet you weren't expecting that…)

Hands up, if you read through each Less file from our new theme? Good. Now, hands up if you really read through the files carefully…ah! not so many of you…

This was done with good reason—the code works perfectly well; as a start point, it will serve the purpose. However, there are some instances where it can be improved; after all, it was never intended to be a Picasso! I thought I should leave you with this little challenge: can you find where it can be improved? *One clue…there are not enough variables, me thinks…up for the challenge?*

Okay, here's a more involved challenge: remember how I said we'll use Crunch! to compile our code? Well, we can do better than this. We've used Grunt elsewhere in this book, so here's another use: we can use it to automate our compilation.

The key to this is compiling only the `style.less` file. While you can try compiling the others, they will no doubt throw errors, as most will not see the variables' file that is a dependency.

The next part is to configure `gruntfile.js`, which will tell Grunt to only compile this file. We can then run Grunt watch in the background to allow it to compile automatically. We will cover this whole process in more detail, later in this chapter.

 If you get stuck, have a look on Google, as there are several examples available; `http://jonathanmh.com/make-grunt-watch-for-lesscss-changes/` contains a useful example by one is the useful blog post by Jonathan Hethey. It contains a number of additional steps, but should be enough to give you an idea of how to use Grunt and watch when compiling Less theme files.

Enough of developing; it's time to change tack and have a breather. Let's delve into using prebuilt Less themes with WordPress.

Using a prebuilt Less theme

If you're not quite up to building a theme from scratch, then you can always use a prebuilt one. There are dozens available online, either for free or at a low cost. It's worth having a look on Google for some examples and then trying them out and deciding whether they match your requirements. Here are some examples to get you started:

- **Less**: This is a minimalistic theme from Jared Erickson, available at `http://jarederickson.com/less-a-free-super-minimal-wordpress-theme/`

- **Starter**: This theme by Roots contains support for Less and is available at http://roots.io/starter-theme/

- **Whiteboard**: This is a theme that uses Less 4 Framework, which can be downloaded from `http://whiteboardframework.com/whiteboard-documentation/`

- **Spare**: This is a paid-for theme, available from Theme Forest, at `http://themeforest.net/item/spare-ultimate-multipurpose-less-theme/7520253`

There are lots of themes available for use and it is worth spending some time on Google to see what is available and trying them out. Hopefully, you will find something that comes close to, or matches your requirements. With luck, you might be able to tweak it a little with skills you've hopefully picked up from reading this book!

Automating WordPress development

If you spend any time developing themes, you will no doubt know that it is a manual process, which takes time. Themes often require careful tweaking and retesting; it can get particularly tedious when recompiling Less files!

Fortunately, there are a number of solutions available to relieve some of the tedium experienced when developing WordPress themes; the most popular option is to use a package we first met back in *Chapter 2, Building a Less Development Toolkit*. It's time to revisit using Grunt!

> For the more experienced, it is worth looking online for `lessphp`, which is a port of Less to PHP. There is code available that allows direct compilation within WordPress, in much the same way as we will cover in this exercise.

Using Grunt in WordPress development

Remember back in *Chapter 2, Building a Less Development Toolkit*, when we met Grunt for the first time?

Well, we're going to meet it again, as it is a perfect tool to help with compiling Less files as part of WordPress development. It makes perfect sense to use it here, as we are compiling style sheets after all! Let's take a look at how we can set up Grunt for use with compiling WordPress style sheets automatically.

 For the purposes of this exercise, I will assume you are using Grunt as installed in the *Watching for changes to Less files* section of *Chapter 2, Building a Less Development Toolkit*. If you've not yet installed it, now's a good time to revert to that chapter and do it.

We'll work with the standard `TwentyFourteen` theme that comes with WordPress 3.8.x and upwards; the process will work perfectly well with other themes too.

1. Start by opening your favorite text editor, then add the following, and save it as `package.json` within the root folder of the `TwentyFourteen` theme:

    ```
    {
      "name": "WordPress_Meets_Grunt",
      "version": "0.0.0",
      "author": "Alex Libby",
      "dependencies": {
        "grunt-cli": "latest",
        "grunt-contrib-concat": "latest",
        "grunt-contrib-uglify": "latest",
        "grunt-contrib-less": "latest",
        "grunt-contrib-watch": "latest"
      }
    }
    ```

2. Next, we need to create a Grunt watch file, which will perform a number of actions, when Grunt's watch facility determines a change has been made. Add the following skeleton to a new file, saving it as `gruntfile.js`, within the root of your theme folder:

    ```
    module.exports = function(grunt) {
        grunt.registerTask('watch', [ 'watch' ]);
        grunt.initConfig({ });

        grunt.loadNpmTasks('grunt-contrib-concat');
    ```

```
     grunt.loadNpmTasks('grunt-contrib-uglify');
     grunt.loadNpmTasks('grunt-contrib-less');
     grunt.loadNpmTasks('grunt-contrib-watch');
   };
```

3. The basic Grunt file contains references to the Node plugins we're going to use—we now need to add the configuration options for each plugin. Let's begin by adding them for `grunt-contrib-concat` to concatenate any JavaScript files into one, as shown:

```
grunt.initConfig({
  concat: {
    js: {
      options: {
        separator: ';'
      },
      src: [
        'javascript/*.js'
      ],
      dest: 'public/js/main.min.js'
    },
  },
```

4. Next comes the options for `UglifyJS`. Go ahead and add the following code immediately below the concat block from the previous step:

```
uglify: {
  options: {
    mangle: false
  },
  js: {
    files: {
      'public/js/main.min.js':
        ['public/js/main.min.js']
    }
  }
},
```

5. Our next plugin we need to add in is the one of most interest—Less. Add this code immediately below the closing } of the previous section:

```
less: {
  style: {
    files: {
      "style.css": "style.less"
    }
  }
},
```

6. Last, but by no means least, is `watch`. This part watches out for any changes to the code and invokes the relevant command:

```
watch: {
  js: {
    files: ['javascript/*.js'],
    tasks: ['concat:js', 'uglify:js'],
    options: {
      livereload: true,
    }
  },
  css: {
    files: ['style.less'],
    tasks: ['less:style'],
    options: {
      livereload: true,
    }
  }
}
```

7. Save the file, and then in a command prompt, change to the location of your theme.

8. We now need to configure Grunt. Although we already have the basic application installed from *Chapter 2*, *Building a Less Development Toolkit*, we still need to tell it what to do when changes to Less files are made. In the command prompt, run this command:

npm install

9. The last step is to activate the `watch` facility. Once Grunt has completed its changes from the previous step, go ahead and run this command at the prompt:

grunt watch

10. Remember the child theme we created earlier in this chapter? Go back to your child theme folder, then open up `style.less`, and make a single change to a character within the style sheet.

11. Save your work as you normally do. If all is well, Grunt watch will have picked up on the change and recompiled the style sheet file:

```
grunt                                                    – □ ×
C:\wamp\www\wordpress\wp-content\themes\twentyfourteen-child>grunt watch
Running "watch" task
Waiting...
>> File "style.less" changed.
Running "less:style" (less) task
File style.css created: 0 B → 2.99 kB

Done, without errors.
Completed in 2.306s at Sun Jun 08 2014 10:15:17 GMT+0100 (GMT Summer Time) - Wai
ting...
```

We can confirm this by checking back in our `theme` folder, where the `style.less` and `style.css` files have the same date and time stamps:

single.php	03/12/2013 17:06	PHP File	2 KB
style.css	08/06/2014 10:15	Cascading Style S...	3 KB
style.less	08/06/2014 10:15	LESSCSS.org file	3 KB
tag.php	05/12/2013 17:55	PHP File	2 KB
taxonomy-post_format.php	05/12/2013 18:31	PHP File	3 KB

Phew! That was a fair bit of code; let's take a moment to recap what we've achieved in this exercise.

If you've spent any time using Grunt as a task manager, then using the `package.json` and `gruntfile` files will be familiar to you; if not, where have you been? Grunt is fast becoming a de facto standard for automating thankless tasks such as compiling Less files; it is well worth getting to know Grunt!

In our exercise, we've configured Grunt to use a number of Node packages such as Less, watch, UglifyJS, and concat. In a nutshell, the Grunt and JSON package files tell Grunt how to compress and concatenate JavaScript or Less files (as set in the configuration); watch is set to run the tasks as soon as any changes are made to our source files.

Provided Grunt watch has kicked in and correctly recompiled our file, we're then free to continue making more changes. We can either use the Less file to dynamically compile our style sheet, as we saw earlier in the *Adding support for Less in WordPress* section, or we can simply use the compiled file as a normal style sheet in our theme.

> There is a completed version of the `gruntfile.js` file on GitHub, at `https://gist.github.com/alibby251/579e3c0308e3cd732b39`.

Summary

Phew! We've covered a lot in this chapter! Let's take a moment to consider what we learned.

We kicked off our foray into using Less with WordPress with a quick recap of the structure of each WordPress theme, where we examined the basic files you will see within the TwentyFourteen core theme and covered the basics of what you need for each exercise in this chapter.

We then started our development work with a look at creating a child theme and the reasons for doing so; we then learned how to add Less support to your function file within the theme.

We took a quick sidestep to see how we can tailor the import for specific users; this will be useful if you are developing as an admin locally, while leaving others to use the compiled CSS style sheet file.

We then moved on and took a look at how to import Less using a plugin. We saw how in most cases, this would be preferred, but that in a plugin-heavy site, it might be wiser to simply import it using the `functions.php` file.

We followed this with a detailed look at some tips on converting existing style sheets to use their Less equivalents. We covered the need to keep the process iterative due to the sheer size of some style sheets. We then took a brief look at creating your own theme using Less; we saw how you can use any prebuilt theme within Less if you are not feeling quite ready for developing your own!

We then finally rounded off our journey through Less and WordPress by taking a detailed look at how to automate the whole compilation process using Node.js and Grunt. While this initially might seem daunting, it will reward your efforts in spades with the time it saves in compiling Less files!

It's at this point we say goodbye to using WordPress. In our next chapter, we'll introduce another well-known product that uses Less: Twitter Bootstrap. Now who hasn't heard of Twitter, I wonder?

10
Using Bootstrap with Less

To Bootstrap or not to Bootstrap, that is the question…

Leaving aside the clear misquote from Shakespeare's Hamlet, many developers might ask themselves whether they want to use a framework for their next project.

Frameworks have one clear advantage in that they can help get your site up and running very quickly—Bootstrap is no different. Developed by Twitter as an internal tool for unifying their own projects, Bootstrap has rapidly become the number one project on GitHub, with a user base that includes NASA and MSNBC.

Why talk about this in a book concerning Less, though? Easy; as you will find out, Bootstrap was built on Less; it is a perfect tool to help get accustomed to working with Less. In this chapter, we will cover the following topics:

- Bootstrap's Less file structure
- Bootstrap's mixins
- Configuring Bootstrap for your site
- Developing a workflow for using Bootstrap

Curious? Let's get started…!

Dissecting Bootstrap's Less file structure

So, you've decided to take the plunge and use Bootstrap; it, like many other frameworks available on the Internet, is a good way to help get a website up and running quickly. However, this chapter is about how Less is used in Bootstrap, right? Absolutely; Less plays a key part in producing the CSS used to style each of the elements that make up the Bootstrap library. To see how, let's take a look at the library in more detail. To begin with, we will download it from the main website.

Downloading the library

We first need to download a copy of the library—for this, visit `http://getbootstrap.com/` and click on **Download Bootstrap**. The Bootstrap library is currently at Version 3.2.0 at the time of writing this and can be obtained in one of several ways, including via CDN or using Bower.

The version that is of interest to us is the source code one, so go ahead and click on **Source Code** and save a copy of the archive to a safe place. Once downloaded, extract a copy of the contents to your hard drive—on opening the archive, we'll see the following contents:

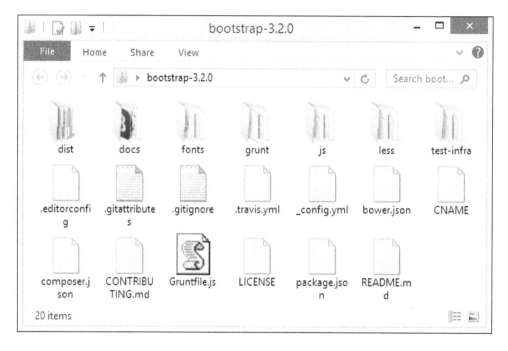

The folder that is of interest to us is naturally the `less` one—if we open this, we can see an array of Less mixin files within the folder.

There are a number of Less files that contain mixins that we can use when building a Bootstrap-enabled site; they can be split into four categories, namely:

- Utilities
- Layouts
- Skins
- Components

We'll cover each of these categories in the *Dissecting Bootstrap's mixins* section later in this chapter. In the meantime, let's move on and familiarize ourselves with installing Bootstrap on your site.

Configuring Bootstrap for your site

Although we've downloaded the source code version of Bootstrap, it's not one you would use by default.

Huh? I hear you ask. You'd be quite right to do so—after all, what's the point of downloading something you aren't going to use, right…? Well, we will make use of this later in the chapter; for now, it is enough to know that this contains all of the mixins that make up Bootstrap styles and that these can easily be customized at a later date.

For now, we will use the compiled version. In the *Building a more realistic site* section later in the chapter, we'll see the effects of what happens when we access the Bootstrap mixin file directly.

Let's change track and take a look at what's required to add Bootstrap to your site:

1. Start by creating a new folder on your hard drive and call it `projects`.

2. Copy the contents of the `bootstrap` folder we downloaded in the previous section into this folder.

3. Crack open the text editor of your choice and add the following code:

```
<!DOCTYPE html>
<html lang="en">
  <head>
    <title>Bootstrap Demo</title>
  </head>
  <body>
    <h1>Hello, world!</h1>
  </body>
</html>
```

4. Next, add the following lines just before the `</head>` tag—these are used by Bootstrap to make the site responsive:

```
<meta charset="utf-8">
<meta http-equiv="X-UA-Compatible" content="IE=edge">
<meta name="viewport"
  content="width=device-width, initial-scale=1">
```

5. We need to add in Bootstrap's base styles, so go ahead and add the following line immediately before the closing `</head>` tag:

```
<link href="css/bootstrap.min.css" rel="stylesheet">
```

6. Save the file as `bootstrap.html` in the `projects` folder—if we preview the results, we will see this:

Granted, it's not going to set the world alight, but it does illustrate how easy it is to install Bootstrap! We will delve into a real-world example later in the chapter in the *Building a more realistic site* section. The key thing to remember is that Bootstrap is an effective collection of CSS style rules—provided we use the appropriate rules at the right points in our code, we can use them to produce anything. Bootstrap is ideal in order to help mock up a basic site; it then gives us the basis for developing it into something more complex at a later date.

Using Internet Explorer 8 or below

Before we look at producing something more detailed, there is something we need to be aware of when using Bootstrap—this concerns our old friend, which is Internet Explorer.

The previous demo will work perfectly in modern browsers—it is worth noting, though, that if you still need to use IE8, then you will need to add the following code in your `<head>` section:

```
<!-- HTML5 Shim and Respond.js IE8 support of HTML5 elements and
    media queries -->
<!-- WARNING: Respond.js doesn't work if you view the page via
    file:// -->
<!--[if lt IE 9]>
    <script src =
    "https://oss.maxcdn.com/libs/html5shiv/3.7.0/html5shiv.js">
</script>
```

```
<script src =
"https://oss.maxcdn.com/libs/respond.js/1.4.2/respond.min.js">
</script>
<![endif]-->
```

Internet Explorer 8 (or lower) does not support HTML5 by default, so we need to use two JavaScript libraries to provide fallback support for both HTML5 and media queries.

Okay; still with me, I hope? Good; let's move on. This is a perfect opportunity to delve into building a more realistic example that uses Bootstrap.

Building a more realistic site

Although we can use Bootstrap to produce any variety of different sites, Bootstrap really comes into its own when used to mock up a site. It doesn't even matter if the colors aren't perfect from the start; it's enough to at least get a feel for what a page or site would look like in terms of layout. This isn't to say that color schemes should be discounted; they can come next, once we have a good idea of how the site will be laid out.

To illustrate how useful Bootstrap can be in order to create a mock-up, we're going to take a look at creating a sample page that would be perfect as a blog post or online article on a website. For the purposes of this example, we will need a copy of the code download that accompanies this book—it contains a copy of the HTML markup required; for reasons of space, we can't reproduce it in full within the text! Okay—now that we have a copy of the code download, let's make a start:

1. From the code download, extract a copy of the `blogpage.html` file, which contains our HTML markup for the sample page. Save the file in the `projects` folder that we created in the previous exercise.

2. Crack open the text editor of your choice, and then add the following lines into the `<head>` tag of the file:

```
<meta charset="utf-8">
<meta http-equiv="X-UA-Compatible" content="IE=edge">
<meta name="viewport" content="width=device-width,
  initial-scale=1">
<title>Bootstrap Theme Demo</title>
<link href="css/bootstrap.min.css" rel="stylesheet">
<link href="css/bootstrap-theme.min.css"
  rel="stylesheet">
```

3. Next, we need to download one small JavaScript file — this is the Holder plugin by Ivan Malopinsky. This plugin isn't essential for running Bootstrap but provides a nice effect for the image placeholder. Holder can be downloaded from `http://github.com/imsky/holder/zipball/v2.3.2`, and `holder.js` extracted from the archive into the `js` folder within our `projects` folder.

There is a minified copy of this plugin in the code download, which is stored as `docs.min.js`.

4. Save `blogpage.html` — if we preview the results in a browser, we can see our mocked-up page in all its glory.

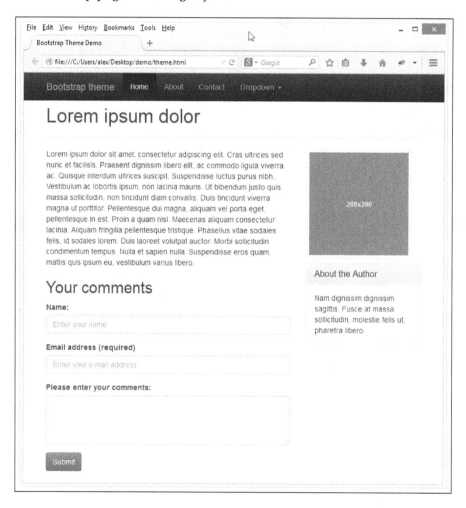

So, what happened here? Although it appears that we have a fair amount of code, in reality, we only have one block of code that is of any importance:

```
<meta charset="utf-8">
<meta http-equiv="X-UA-Compatible" content="IE=edge">
<meta name="viewport" content="width=device-width,
  initial-scale=1">
...
<link href="css/bootstrap.min.css" rel="stylesheet">
```

Why is this so important, I hear you ask? Well, this is simple—Bootstrap is about providing a complete functionality set of styles that can help you get up and running quickly. Bootstrap isn't meant to be a permanent replacement, but it is a good starting point to develop your own styles. Indeed, as we will see in *Chapter 11, Abstracting CSS Frameworks with Less*, relying solely on Bootstrap is not always a good thing!

In this instance, we've set three meta tags—these handle the character set to be used, the version of IE that should be supported when displaying the page, and the display of the site on mobile devices.

> If you would like to learn more about the IE compatibility and viewport tags, then it is worth reading the article by Microsoft at `https://www.modern.ie/en-us/performance/how-to-use-x-ua-compatible`, which describes best practice when setting this tag. Mozilla has a useful article on applying the viewport tag in code, which you can view by visiting `https://developer.mozilla.org/en/docs/Mozilla/Mobile/Viewport_meta_tag`.

The first two can well appear on most sites—the line that is of real interest, though, is the link to the Bootstrap CSS file. This is a precompiled file that contains the Bootstrap styling, which has been generated from the Less mixins that form the library. We've referenced this in our code and used it to apply the styles defined in our HTML markup.

> It is worth noting, though, that if you want to use some of the jQuery plugins that come with Bootstrap, then you will also need to add a link to jQuery itself as well as the Bootstrap plugin:
>
> ```
> <script src="js/jquery-2.1.1.min.js"></script>
> <script src="js/bootstrap.min.js"></script>
> ```
>
> If you still need to support IE8 or lower, then change the reference for jQuery to `jquery-1.11.1.min.js`; Version 2 of jQuery is not supported in these earlier versions of IE.

Compiling the Bootstrap CSS and JavaScript

Now that we've seen how Bootstrap can be used to great effect in getting our site off the ground, we can well decide that we want to move away from simply using the precompiled CSS file and compile the code ourselves.

The main reason for doing this is to update or alter the code to fit our requirements—we should not forget that Bootstrap is intended to be customized in this manner! Fortunately, Bootstrap uses Grunt, which we discussed and installed earlier in the book (in *Chapter 2, Building a Less Development Toolkit*). Bootstrap comes preconfigured with its own `package.json` file, making compilation a cinch. All we have to do is:

1. Fire up a command prompt window, and then navigate to the root of the `/bootstrap` folder and enter the following command:

   npm install

   This will automatically install all of the dependencies required to compile Bootstrap.

2. In the same command window, enter the following:

   grunt

   This will run the JSHint and QUnit tests, and then compile the CSS and JavaScript files into the `/dist` folder within the Bootstrap folder.

That was easy enough, right? Good; let's move on and meet some of the mixins that come with Bootstrap.

Examining Bootstrap's mixins

At the beginning of this chapter, we took a brief look at the file structure of the Bootstrap library download; now is a perfect opportunity to revisit this in more detail.

If we open a copy of the downloaded archive and navigate to the root level of the `less` subfolder, we can see these mixins are spread over 29 mixin files, which can be split into these categories: Utilities, Components, Skins, and Layout.

Most of these mixins are concerned with providing Bootstrap its core styles — the ones that are of particular interest are:

- `bootstrap.less`: This is the master Less file that, when compiled and minified, will form `bootstrap.min.css`

- `theme.less`: This contains some core theme styles

Note that if you download the version of Bootstrap directly from GitHub, then you will notice this additional folder:

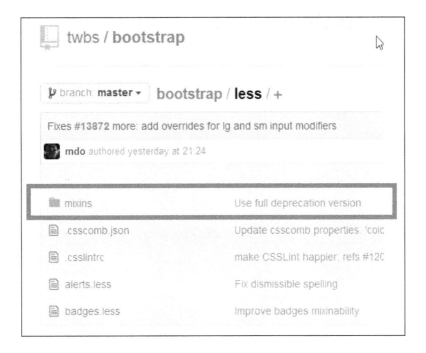

This folder contains the mixins required to control the styling for the theme; if we peek inside the folder, we will see the additional mixins that are used to create what will become `bootstrap-theme.min.css` in the production download file.

If we explore this folder further, we will see that most of the files stored there have the same names as the core mixins, but they have styles that form the basis for the themes within Bootstrap. It is worth noting that these mixins do not form part of the Less download archive that is available at `http://www.getbootstrap.com`; to use them, we need to download them directly from GitHub and compile them using Grunt/Node.js.

> All of the mixins available for use in Bootstrap are stored within the `\less` subfolder—you can also view the original source file versions in GitHub at `https://github.com/twbs/bootstrap/tree/master/less`. The variables are stored within `variables.less`—this is in the aforementioned `\less` folder and is available on GitHub at `https://github.com/twbs/bootstrap/blob/master/less/variables.less`.

Now that we've seen the make-up of the library, let's take a moment to reflect on some of the mixins that are available in the library.

Dissecting Bootstrap's mixins

If we were to take a look at the mixins available for use in Bootstrap, we can see they are broken down into a number of groups. These groups are:

- Core variables and mixins
- Resets and dependencies
- Core CSS
- Component files
- Component files that use JavaScript
- Utility classes

Let's take a brief look at each one in more detail, starting with the core variables and mixins.

Core variables and mixins

Core variables and mixins is probably one of the smallest groups of all of the mixins but is the most crucial—it contains `variables.less`, which lists all of the predefined variables available for use within Bootstrap. The second file contained within this group is `mixins.less`. While it is simpler in design, it plays an equally important role: it contains the `@import` statements that are used to build the `bootstrap-theme.css` file.

Reset and dependencies

Next in the groupings come the reset and dependency mixins—to quote a phrase, these "do as it says on the tin"! `Normalize.less` uses the `normalize.css` project created by Nicolas Gallagher, which is also available from GitHub, and can be downloaded from `https://github.com/necolas/normalize.css`.

If we're setting our site to be printable, then `print.less` is essential; it contains the media queries required to realign a Bootstrap in order to allow it to be printed. `Glyphicons.less` is a useful part of the library—it controls the styles required to display any of the glyph icons that come as part of the Bootstrap library.

Core CSS styles

In this next grouping, we have a number of mixin files that perform different roles:

Name of Mixin file	Used to
`scaffolding.less`	Control elements on a basic site, either directly or indirectly (by referencing styles from other mixin files)
`type.less`	Set the default font sizes for H1 to H6 font sizes, along with some additional styles such as the warning or information text
`code.less`	Determine styles when using markup such as `<code>` and `<pre>`
`grid.less`	Set up the basic styles used to control Bootstrap's responsive grid functionality
`tables.less`	Control styles for any tables we insert into our site
`forms.less`	Apply styles to any forms that we host within our website
`buttons.less`	Set up the base styles that are applied to any buttons on our site

Components

So far, most of our styles that we have looked at cover the structure of the site; let's look at the component files that make up the visual elements we can add to any site:

Name of Mixin file	Used to define styles for
`component-animations.less`	Animating any components with a site
`dropdowns.less`	Drop-down menus
`button-groups.less`	Grouped buttons
`input-groups.less`	Input fields
`navs.less, navbar.less`	Navigation bars and buttons
`forms.less`	Form and non-form elements
`breadcrumbs.less`	Breadcrumb trails
`pagination.less, pager.less`	Pagination in a site
`labels.less`	Various label styles, such as warning or danger
`badges.less`	Badges within buttons or navigation
`jumbotron.less`	Jumbotrons
`thumbnails.less`	Thumbnail images and captions
`alerts.less`	Alert messages and dialogs
`progress-bars.less`	Progress bars
`media.less`	Media objects, such as videos and images
`list-group.less`	Items in a grouped or linked list
`panels.less`	Panels and panel elements, such as titles
`responsive-embed.less`	Embedding items such as iFrames responsively
`wells.less`	Wells
`close.less`	Close icons

Utility classes

The final grouping within the core Bootstrap files contains the utility classes—these are stored within `utilities.less` and `responsive-utilities.less`. These files contain some styles that are not immediately associated with any of the other mixin files but still play a part within a Bootstrap site nevertheless. Examples include the `.clearfix()` mixin and mixins for toggling content.

Let's change gear now and focus our attention on the mixin files that make up Bootstrap's theme styles.

Dissecting Bootstrap's theme mixins

In addition to the core styles and mixins, Bootstrap provides a number of additional mixins that are incorporated into the Bootstrap theme's JavaScript and CSS files.

You can view these in the `mixins` subfolder under the `less` folder within the GitHub repository — it is worth noting that these do not appear in the Source Code option when downloading files from `http://www.getbootstrap.com`. Let's take a look at what lies within this folder — the mixins fall into a number of groups.

Utilities

Name of Mixin file	Used to
`hide-text.less`	Hide images when using CSS image replacement
`opacity.less`	Set opacity levels
`image.less`	Make images responsive.
`labels.less`	Define colors for labels
`reset-filter.less`	Reset filters for IE when gradient backgrounds are removed
`resize.less`	Resize any element if the overflow isn't visible
`responsive-visibility.less`	Provide responsive states for `responsive-utilities.less`
`size.less`	Use a shortcut mixin to set the height and width for objects
`tab-focus.less`	Add the `Webkit-style` focus to tabs
`text-emphasis.less`	Add emphasis to the text
`text-overflow.less`	Handle the text overflow — requires `display: inline` or `display: block` to be set for proper styling

Components

Although we've defined most of the styles required for Bootstrap components by now, there are still some styles that are specific to the theme file; these are handled within this group of mixins:

Name of Mixin file	Used to
alerts.less	Set the background, border, and forecolor values in alerts, along with the `<hr>` element and links within alerts.
buttons.less	Create default styles, along with the `:hover`, `:focus`, `:active`, and `disabled` styles for buttons.
panels.less	Define colors to be used on panel elements.
pagination.less	Handle styles set for page pagination.
list-group.less	Define styles used when selecting or hovering over list elements.
nav-divider.less	Set dividers within dropdowns or navigation lists.
forms.less	Generate form validation styles for use in forms.
progress-bar.less	Set the background color for use with progress bars.
table-row.less	Set additional styles used for controlling the appearance of table rows.

Skins

We've already defined a number of the theme styles at this point; some are added when applying the Bootstrap theme file:

Name of Mixin file	Description
background-variant.less	This mixin sets and then darkens the background color when hovering over it.
border-radius.less	This mixin is not strictly required with the advent of native browser support for `border-radius`, but it is useful in order to set the radius value in pairs.
gradients.less	This mixin sets up the styles for a number of gradient formats, such as striped and radial.

Layout

A key part of any theme is to position elements correctly on a page; this group of mixins handles this for the Bootstrap theme:

Name of Mixin file	Used to
clearfix.less	Implement the micro clearfix hack, as created by Nicholas Gallagher at http://nicolasgallagher.com/micro-clearfix-hack/
center-block.less	Center-align a block-level element in the theme
nav-vertical-align.less	Vertically center elements in a navigation bar
grid-framework.less	Generate the correct number of grid classes from any given value of @grid-columns. by Bootstrap
grid.less	Generate semantic grid columns

Now that we understand the make-up of the library, we might well want to consider using different elements from it rather than just incorporating the library as it stands in our code, which would be wasteful on resources. However, what if we wanted to actually *change some of the default styles and not have to download everything*? Thankfully this is possible — let's take a look at how you can customize your Bootstrap downloads.

Customizing our download

So far, we've used the standard download from Bootstrap — while this has served us well, it can be a little awkward to start introducing our own styles.

Thankfully, the Bootstrap team has provided us with a means to allow us to build a custom download; while it might require a little work to determine what values are to be entered, it will at least allow us to tailor values to our liking! Let's take a look at how this works.

Before doing so, we need to make one small change to our code — load up your copy of blogpage.html and comment out this line:

```
<link href="css/bootstrap-theme.css" rel="stylesheet">
```

Don't worry for now. Why? All will become clear very shortly!

Start by browsing `http://getbootstrap.com/customize/#less-variables-section` — here, we can see a whole array of options that we can choose to include or discard from our download. If you've spent any time using jQuery UI, then the process should be pretty familiar to you — it is a matter of selecting or deselecting the appropriate checkboxes in order to include the components we need in our download.

This is a three-step process — let's begin by choosing the base CSS, components, and utilities that we want to use in our download.

Next, we need to change the values within each component that we are going to include in our download. A great example here is the **Buttons** section — we created a button as part of our comments form, so let's go ahead and change the colors on the image as part of our custom download.

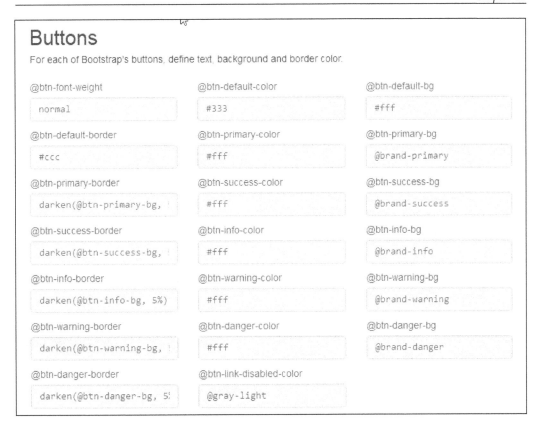

Buttons

For each of Bootstrap's buttons, define text, background and border color.

@btn-font-weight	@btn-default-color	@btn-default-bg
normal	#333	#fff

@btn-default-border	@btn-primary-color	@btn-primary-bg
#ccc	#fff	@brand-primary

@btn-primary-border	@btn-success-color	@btn-success-bg
darken(@btn-primary-bg,	#fff	@brand-success

@btn-success-border	@btn-info-color	@btn-info-bg
darken(@btn-success-bg,	#fff	@brand-info

@btn-info-border	@btn-warning-color	@btn-warning-bg
darken(@btn-info-bg, 5%)	#fff	@brand-warning

@btn-warning-border	@btn-danger-color	@btn-danger-bg
darken(@btn-warning-bg,	#fff	@brand-danger

@btn-danger-border	@btn-link-disabled-color	
darken(@btn-danger-bg, 5	@gray-light	

Let's revert to the `blogpage.html` demo that we delved into earlier—if we view the source code for the button using a DOM Inspector such as Firebug, we can see the classes in use.

```
<form role="form">
    <div class="form-group">
    <div class="form-group">
    <div class="form-group">
        <button class="btn
        btn-primary" type="submit">Submit<
        /button>
</form>
<p> </p>
```

We can clearly see two classes in use—the base `.btn` and `.btn-primary`. Using a DOM Inspector such as Firebug, we can see the compiled styles for `.btn`:

```
.btn {
    -moz-user-select: none;
    background-image: none;
    border: 1px solid transparent;
    border-radius: 4px;
    cursor: pointer;
    display: inline-block;
    font-size: 14px;
    font-weight: normal;
    line-height: 1.42857;
    margin-bottom: 0;
    padding: 6px 12px;
    text-align: center;
    vertical-align: middle;
    white-space: nowrap;
}
```

On its own, this won't show you a great deal—it will really begin to make sense once we take a look at the `.btn-primary` class:

```
.btn-primary {
    background-color: #428bca;
    border-color: #357ebd;
    color: #fff;
}
```

At this point, if we browse `http://getbootstrap.com/customize/#less-variables`, we can see all of the Less variables that can be customized in our download. We can see that the `#428bca` value is being set by the `@btn-primary` value.

What is Less easy to spot, though, is how `#357ebd` is being set—this value is set using the `@btn-primary-border` variable, which is darkened by 5 percent.

To see the effects of lightening or darkening colors, visit the Hex Color tool site at `http://www.hexcolortool.com`, enter your hex value (without the hash), and click on **Lighten** or **Darken** to see a range of colors and their values.

We can also see how the button's colors are being set—it is worth browsing the `buttons.less` mixin file on GitHub at `https://github.com/twbs/bootstrap/blob/master/less/buttons.less`, where we can see the mixin in action on line 60:

```
.btn-primary {
  .button-variant(@btn-primary-color; @btn-primary-bg;
    @btn-primary-border);
}
```

Now that we've seen how the variables link back to the mixins, let's make a change to our download by setting a nice shade of red for our button.

Changing the values in our download

Altering the code download from Bootstrap is a cinch—we simply need to choose our primary colors, alter the ones already shown, and hit **Download** at the bottom of the page to get our customized library. Let's do this now—you'll see how easy it is:

1. Start by browsing `http://getbootstrap.com/customize/#less-variables` and altering the value for `@brand-primary` to `#be0000`, as shown:

2. Next, scroll down to the bottom of the page, and click on **Compile and Download** — save the folder to a safe location, when prompted.

   We now have the library, but need to update our code. Remember how I asked you to comment out the line referencing the `bootstrap-theme.css` file? Well, here's why: the customized downloads only apply to the core styles, and not the theme that has been applied. If we had not commented out this line, then our change would have been redundant — the theme would have overridden it!

3. At this point, go ahead and rename the CSS folder in our project folder — open the archive file we've just downloaded and copy the `css` folder into the project folder.

If we browse a copy of the `blogpage.html` file and refresh the screen, we can see the updated colors in use on the **Submit** button.

If we open up a DOM Inspector such as Firebug, we can see that the code has changed:

```
.btn {
  . . .
  border: 1px solid transparent;
  . . .
}
```

A look at the `.btn-primary` styles, show us the new values as a result of the change in our CSS:

```
.btn-primary {
  background-color: #be0000;
  border-color: #a50000;
  color: #fff;
}
```

```
.btn-primary {
  background-image: linear-gradient(to bottom, #be0000 0px,
    #810000 100%);
  background-repeat: repeat-x;
  border-color: #700;
}
```

There are plenty more styles we can change — the world is our oyster! To help with changing colors, it's easier to change the existing hex color codes rather than swapping out the functions for explicit colors. If we leave the calculation statements alone, then we can be sure that they render the right shades of updated colors correctly, such as `:hover`.

 A modified version of the CSS folder, which incorporates this color change, is included in the code download that accompanies this book. You will need to extract a copy of the REDcss folder and rename it in order to replace the default css folder that comes with Bootstrap.

Let's change track now and move on — one of the key parts of using Bootstrap is developing your own workflow process; while there is no right or wrong answer, we'll look at an example that you can develop for your own projects.

Developing a workflow for using Bootstrap

Now that we've seen something of how Bootstrap can be configured for use when creating a basic site, the final key stage in our journey using Bootstrap is to begin to develop a workflow that helps us be as efficient as possible.

Ultimately, designing our workflow will be a very personal affair — the same method won't suit everyone! The key to this is to find something that works for you; to give you a flavor of how to go about it, it is worth reading an article by Erik Flowers, which is available at `http://www.helloerik.com/bootstrap-3-less-workflow-tutorial`.

In summary, his workflow centers on the following steps:

1. Download a copy of the Bootstrap library from `http://www.getbootstrap.com`.

2. Decide which method you want to use to compile your Less files — will it be in a preprocessor app such as Crunch!, via the command line, or as an add-on package to an editor such as Sublime Text?

3. Create a source folder to hold your Less files — the name is not critical as long as you know what and where it is being stored.

4. Create a folder within the source folder, called `vendor`, and store copies of the Bootstrap Less files within it — this is to help keep yourself from making changes to core files that would be overwritten when upgrading Bootstrap.

5. Inside your source folder, create a file called `styles.less` that imports `bootstrap/bootstrap.less`.

6. Store any other Less files that are required within the top level source folder, and then import them to `styles.less` using the same format.

7. Add your Less style rules into these individual files and not the `styles.less` file.

8. Compile `styles.less` to wherever you want to refer to your `styles.css`; minify or compress the files as desired, either separately, or as part of using a package such as Grunt.

While there are a few steps involved, this should give you a feel for an example workflow — it is worth noting that some of this can, potentially, be automated; the key to this is to ensure that it fits with any existing process that you have in place as part of your development workflow.

Summary

For a project that was originally created for internal use within Twitter, Bootstrap has rapidly become one of the world's most popular projects on GitHub. Let's take a moment to recap what we've covered throughout this chapter.

We kicked off our journey with a look at downloading the library, followed by configuring it for use within our projects. We then created a basic example to illustrate how easy it is to add it to your projects; we then developed this into a more realistic example in order to better show how Bootstrap would look.

We moved on and examined how easy it is to compile Bootstrap's mixins in order to produce valid CSS code; we then covered the make-up of the `less` folder within the code download in order to see what mixins are available and how they make up Bootstrap. We then finished looking at Bootstrap by delving into how we can customize the download in order to tailor it more towards our needs.

Let's move on now — in the next chapter, we'll take a look at abstracting CSS frameworks using Less and why using Bootstrap isn't actually as good as it might first seem!

11
Abstracting CSS Frameworks with Less

Back in late 2011, the popular social networking site, Twitter, released Bootstrap — the framework caused such an impression, it quickly became the most followed project on GitHub!

Anybody who has spent time developing must have at least heard of Bootstrap, even if they haven't yet had a chance to use it. In the previous chapter, we took a brief look at how it uses Less to compile rules into valid CSS and how you can experiment with using one of the many mixins available to create your own styles.

The trouble is that Bootstrap as a framework is not without its own faults — it encourages us to overload HTML with dozens of classes! This goes against the trend that has developed over the last decade, where content should be separate from presentation. In this chapter, we'll see why this is bad practice and how we can fix the problem by being clever about how we use Bootstrap's mixins.

In this chapter, we will cover the following topics:

- Discovering what's wrong with using frameworks
- Keeping your HTML clean
- Simplifying complex styles

Keen to learn more? Let's get started…!

Discovering what's wrong with using frameworks

Think back to the previous chapter, where we introduced Bootstrap and covered how Less is used to create the styles that are compiled into clean, semantic HTML… Bootstrap looks good, is easy to use, and provides a nice, consistent theme to our site, right?

Wrong—it suffers from one particularly nasty problem: Bootstrap embeds CSS classes directly within HTML. We could argue that there is nothing wrong with that, except for the fact that the style names used are not always semantic!

This whole concept of providing semantic code has been at the forefront of developers' minds for years. Some frameworks such as Scaffold (for PHP) or Compass (for Ruby) recognized the problem back as far as 2009, yet Bootstrap still forces us to use nonsemantic CSS styling in our HTML code. To see what this all means, let's delve in deeper, take a look at an example, and understand how we can correct this using Less.

Diagnosing the problem

To see the problem in the flesh, so to speak, we need to view the source code for a Bootstrap-enabled site; ironically, the main Bootstrap website has several examples, which clearly show the issue!

Begin by navigating to `http://getbootstrap.com/examples/blog/`, which is the demo site for Bootstrap's Blog Theme. Right-click anywhere on the page to select the source code as seen in the browser. If you scroll down to on or around line 42, you will see the following:

```
42
43    <div class="container">
44
45      <div class="blog-header">
46        <h1 class="blog-title">The Bootstrap Blog<
47        <p class="lead blog-description">The office
48      </div>
49
50      <div class="row">
51
52        <div class="col-sm-8 blog-main">
53
```

In the screenshot, lines 50 and 52 have been highlighted, which are perfect examples of nonsemantic code; the three styles that have been added all belong to Bootstrap. "Why should we not use them when they are clearly a part of Bootstrap?", I hear you ask.

 For a useful introduction to the benefits of separating markup, then look no further than the book, *Designing with Web Standards*, by Jeffery Zeldman (and Ethan Marcotte, from Version 3 onwards).

The answer is simple—the HTML markup should describe the meaning of the content and nothing else. The problems we have with this code extract are two-fold:

- It makes it difficult to update any code style—if a style needs to be changed, then this must be done in every single page of the website, where it appears. This can be tedious at best for a small site, but a nightmare if the site is huge!

- Hardcoding Bootstrap's style names into your HTML code means that you are now dependent on Bootstrap. If Twitter changes Bootstrap's classes (which has happened), then you've just landed yourself a whole heap of unnecessary work.

 It's always a good idea to keep an eye on versions being used in your code and not simply use the latest version. Following the latter practice leaves you open to trouble!

Fortunately, the answer to our dilemma lies in Bootstrap itself and its array of mixins. Instead of using the Bootstrap class names within our code, we can abstract in a layer by creating more semantic names and applying the Bootstrap classes to these names instead. To see how this would work, let's work through a few simple examples, using Bootstrap's Jumbotron theme demo as a basis for our changes.

Keeping HTML code clean

If we view the source for Bootstrap's Jumbotron example, we can clearly see some nonsemantic examples, similar to those used in the Blog demo; we'll use them as a basis to work through the solution that we can use to fix the issue.

There are three examples of interest to us; the first is on line 67:

```
<div class="row">
```

The next example follows suit immediately on line 68:

```
<div class="col-md-4">
```

The third and final examples we will look at, appear several times, on lines 71, 76, and 81:

```
<p><a class="btn btn-default" href="#" role="button">View details
    &raquo;</a></p>
```

It goes without saying that there are more examples present; you can see where each of our three selected examples are being used:

```
65    <div class="container">
66      <!-- Example row of columns -->
67      <div class="row">
68        <div class="col-md-4">
69          <h2>Heading</h2>
70          <p>Donec id elit non mi porta gravida at eget m
71          <p><a class="btn btn-default" href="#" role="bu
72        </div>
73        <div class="col-md-4">
74          <h2>Heading</h2>
75          <p>Donec id elit non mi porta gravida at eget m
76          <p><a class="btn btn-default" href="#" role="bu
77        </div>
78        <div class="col-md-4">
79          <h2>Heading</h2>
80          <p>Donec sed odio dui. Cras justo odio, dapibus
81          <p><a class="btn btn-default" href="#" role="bu
82        </div>
83      </div>
```

All three examples use names that are too specific to what they do and not to the content they apply to. We can easily change the style names used to something more semantic, using a technique that can be reused elsewhere in your code without difficulty.

Let's take a look at how the technique works; it's based around directly referencing the Less mixins included as part of the Bootstrap library.

Fixing the code

Before we get into editing any code, we first need to download a copy of the code that accompanies this book. Here, we will find an (unadulterated) copy of the Jumbotron theme, which we can use for the purpose of this exercise:

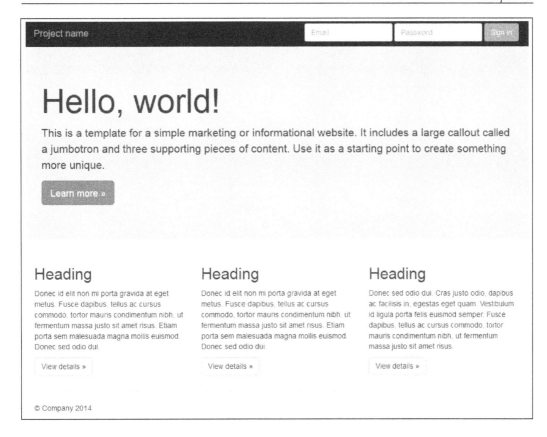

For the purposes of this exercise, I will assume you have extracted a copy of the code that accompanies this chapter and stored it in a folder called `jumbotron`, ready for editing. We also need a copy of the Bootstrap library, which we can get from the main site at `http://getbootstrap.com/getting-started/#download` and then by clicking on **Download source** against the **Source code** option.

Assuming we have everything in place, let's make a start:

1. Open the zip archive file we downloaded from the Bootstrap site, then extract the `less` folder, and copy it to our `jumbotron` folder.

2. In a separate file, add the following code, saving it as `semantic.less` in the `css` subfolder within the `jumbotron` folder:

```
@import "../less/variables.less";
@import "../less/mixins.less";
@import "../less/buttons.less";
@import "../less/grid.less";

.wrapper {
```

```
      .container;
}

.left-content {
  .make-md-column(4);
}

.middle-content {
  .make-md-column(4);
}

.right-content {
  .make-md-column(4);
}

.heading-row {
  .make-row();
  .clearfix;
}
```

3. Now, we need to alter our HTML, so open `jumbotron.html` and add the highlighted line:

```
<!-- Custom styles for this template -->
<link href="css/jumbotron.css" rel="stylesheet">
<link href="css/semantic.css" rel="stylesheet">
</head>
```

4. Next, we're going to rename each of the three columns; move down and look for the first `<div class="col-md-4">` tag, which is on or around line 60. This can be removed and replaced as shown in the following code; you will need to repeat it for two more instances further down the code:

```
<div class="container">
  <!-- Example row of columns -->
  <div class="row">
    <div class="left-content">
      <h2>Heading</h2>
      <p>Donec id elit non mi porta gravida at eget metus.
Fusce dapibus, tellus ac cursus commodo, tortor mauris condimentum
nibh, ut fermentum massa justo sit amet risus. Etiam porta sem
malesuada magna mollis euismod. Donec sed odio dui. </p>
      <p><a class="btn btn-default" href="#"
        role="button">View details &raquo;</a></p>
    </div>
```

5. Our third change concerns the heading row container; `row` isn't sufficiently semantic, so we're going to change it:

```
<!--<div class="container">-->
    <div class="wrapper">
      <!-- Example row of columns -->
      <div class="heading-row">
        <div class="left-content">
          <h2>Heading</h2>
          <p>Donec id elit non mi porta gravida at eget metus.
Fusce dapibus, tellus ac cursus commodo, tortor mauris condimentum
nibh, ut fermentum massa justo sit amet risus. Etiam porta sem
malesuada magna mollis euismod. Donec sed odio dui. </p>
          <p><a class="view-details" href="#"
            role="button">View details &raquo;</a></p>
      </div>
```

6. Our last change concerns the `<div>` tag that is used to wrap the three columns. The container isn't particularly semantic, so we're going to change this to use the wrapper as its replacement. Go ahead and remove the container `DIV` line and then replace it as shown:

```
<div class="wrapper">
  <!-- Example row of columns -->
  <div class="heading-row">
    <div class="left-content">
      <h2>Heading</h2>
```

If we preview the results in a browser, we should not expect to see any change visually, but be safe in knowing that we have started to use more semantic class names within our code.

There is one very valid point here—it would be a perfectly valid question to ask why we use `wrapper`, in place of `container` here? We could equally use either, nothing wrong with that. My preference though is to use the wrapper here, purely because it encompasses all of the code (give or take!).

Exploring our solution

So, now that we have semantic code in our example, what does this mean and how does it work? It's based on two key elements: one of substitution and the other of knowing the available Bootstrap mixins that we can use.

In this instance, we've taken advantage of the group of Less mixins that form the basis for creating columns and rows within Bootstrap. We first import four Less files, which contain the mixins that we need to use, then create four new styles (in the form of `left-content`, `middle-content`, `right-content`, and `heading-row`), and assign the `make-md-column`, `make-row`, or `clearfix` mixins as appropriate. To ensure that our HTML reflects the changes, we then replace the original styles with the new, more semantic style names.

Simplifying complex styles

We can go further in our code to abstract and simplify the presentational classes being used; as an example, we'll edit the code to replace the CSS style names used on the two button types present in the code:

1. Let's start by opening up the `jumbotron.html` file again. Here, we need to remove the line starting with `<p><a class="btn btn-default"`... and replace it as indicated:

    ```
    <!--<div class="container">-->
        <div class="wrapper">
          <!-- Example row of columns -->
          <div class="row">
            <div class="left-content">
              <h2>Heading</h2>
              <p>Donec id elit non mi porta gravida at eget metus.
    Fusce dapibus, tellus ac cursus commodo, tortor mauris condimentum
    nibh, ut fermentum massa justo sit amet risus. Etiam porta sem
    malesuada magna mollis euismod. Donec sed odio dui. </p>
              <p><a class="view-details" href="#"
                role="button">View details &raquo;</a></p>
            </div>
    ```

2. We also need to change the current classes assigned to the **Learn more** button, so go ahead and modify it as shown:

    ```
    Use it as a starting point to create something more unique.</p>
              <p><a class="learn-more" role="button">Learn more
                &raquo;</a></p>
            </div>
    ```

3. Now that our new style names have been assigned, let's rework the Less styling rules listed in `semantic.less` to reflect the changes in our HTML, by assigning the relevant mixins to our style classes:

```less
.learn-more {
  .btn;
  .btn-primary;
  .btn-lg;
}

.view-details {
  .btn;
  .btn-default;
}
```

Save the files. If all is well, our code will look something like this screenshot extract:

```
56        <!--<div class="container">-->
57        <div class="wrapper">
58            <!-- Example row of columns -->
59            <div class="heading-row">
60                <!--<div class="col-md-4">-->
61                <div class="left-content">
62                    <h2>Heading</h2>
63                    <p>Donec id elit non mi porta gravida at eget met
                       . </p>
64                    <!--<p><a class="btn btn-default" href="#" role="
65                    <p><a class="view-details" href="#" role="button"
66                </div>
```

If we preview the results of our work in a browser, we should not expect to see any difference visually, but know that our code is now more semantic. This doesn't mean to say that these changes are the only ones we can do; there is definitely scope to do more, at least in this example! This is something I will leave for you as my readers to work out, but I will give you a hint: check out the navigation…

In the meantime, let's take a moment to explore what we've achieved here — we've used the same solution as outlined in the *Exploring our solution* section we saw earlier in the chapter.

In this instance, we've taken advantage of the group of Less mixins that make up button support within Bootstrap. All we've done is created a new style rule in our Less code, called .learn-more, then assigned to it the three Less mixins that were previously used: .btn, .btn-primary, and .btn-lg, respectively.

> It's important to note that this process will not work for grouped buttons due to what Bootstrap expects to see in terms of CSS classes; have a look at http://stackoverflow.com/questions/24113419/ and http://stackoverflow.com/a/24240819, for some useful discussions on why this doesn't work for grouped buttons and how to work around it.

The key is to get them in the right order so that we maintain the same appearance as before. As long as we do this, there should be no change to the appearance of the page. We've then repeated the same process with the .view-details button, but this time, assigned the .btn and .btn-default styles to it.

> There is a complete version of jumbotron.html along with the changes. You can find it in the code download as jumbotron_updated.html.

Summary

In this modern day of web development, designers are often using frameworks to help get a website off the ground quickly. Bootstrap is often considered to be one of the most popular frameworks in use today.

We kicked off this chapter by examining a key flaw of frameworks such as Bootstrap, where presentational CSS must be included in HTML directly.

We took a look at the problem with using Bootstrap's CSS styles inline in more detail and discussed how to use a method to get around the issues. We then went on further to apply the same technique to help simplify our HTML so that we can still use Bootstrap's styling framework, while removing any dependency on it, which can affect how we develop the site in the future.

In the next chapter, we're going to change tack and take a look at a topic where we can really use the power of Less, in the form of processing colors within your website or online application.

12
Color Processing with Less

Imagine the scene if you will—you're a designer, creating the latest sale adverts for a department store. You've spent hours creating your masterpiece, submitted it for approval… only to find that the Sales Director hates your choice of color. He doesn't think it works properly ("there's not enough contrast…"), so it's a case of back to the drawing board. Only you know that he is… shall we say… very picky about his choice of colors, which you know does not always work that well…

Sound familiar? What if we could pick our main color and have code (yes, code) automatically pick a color for you that not only works technically but also suits your chosen principal color? Sound impossible? Not with Less—welcome to the world of color processing! In this chapter, we will cover the following topics:

- Introducing color management in Less
- Color spaces and formats
- Color functions
- Generating color palettes
- Examples of blending modes and parallels with Photoshop
- Working with W3C and WCAG standards for color management

Intrigued? Let's start…

Introducing color management in Less

Printer profiles ...colorimeters... sRGB... huh? You're probably a developer, thinking, "I know nothing about color management; what the heck does it all mean?"

Well, to put it into context: imagine you've taken a picture of a red flag on a boat (yes, I know, stay with me on this), which appears to take on an orange tone when viewed on screen, but starts to come out purple when printed. Now, I bet you're really confused... let me explain it all.

This is all about color management. In simple words, it's the art of making sure your printer, camera, and computer all display accurate shades of the same color. This sounds perfectly reasonable, right? After all, all devices should display the same color, no matter the device...

Wrong. The key to color management is that every device reproduces color differently. In a sense, they all speak different languages and are not as sophisticated as our own eyes; here's where we need that colorimeter to balance everything...!

Making sense now? However, where's the link with Less? Well, it's exactly the same principle in Less—we need to make sure that colors are correctly balanced; it's no good putting blues against purples, as they are too similar. Thankfully, Less has a range of functions that can help us with this. We can choose a primary color, such as purple, then use functions such as `darken()` or `lighten()` to choose suitable colors that complement our primary one. Less will then compile this function into valid CSS; for example, if we choose `#6600FF` (a shade of purple), we can get Less to lighten it by 10 percent to produce `#801AFF`. This value will then be rendered on screen when Less has compiled your code.

We will delve into the various functions that Less supports, but for a moment, let's turn our attention to a little theory to help us better understand more about the importance of color formats and spaces.

Examining color spaces and formats

When we think of colors, most of us will probably think of red, green, or blue, but do we ever think of color spaces? If the answer is no, then think again; you've just mentioned one of several color spaces we can use.

Color spaces are a means of uniquely specifying color. The most well-known one is **red, green, and blue (RGB)**. However, others are available, such as **Hue, Saturation, Lightness (HSL)**, its cousin, which includes alpha support (HSLa) or **HSV (Hue, Saturation, and Value)**. Less includes support for these and others; we will look at these in more detail shortly, but first, let's take a look at using basic mathematical operators to create new colors.

Working with arithmetic operators

How often have you spent hours fine-tuning a palette for a client, only to find they want to change the whole lot? It will be impossible to simply change one color, you will need to change them all…

We can use Less to help us with this. It contains support for a number of functions that we can use to automate the creation and manipulation of colors. We can pick the red, blue, or green shades from colors, or use HSL to get the hue, lightness, or saturation levels from a color. However, we can also do something that you might not expect to see, but which makes perfect sense: use simple math operators, such as + or – to create our colors.

Try this little experiment. If you have installed Crunch!, then add this to a new file within, and save it:

```
@basecolor: #333;
.container {
  color: @basecolor *2;
  background-color: @basecolor - #111;
}
```

When compiled, we get two colors, generated from one base color:

```
.container { color: #666666; background-color: #222222; }
```

This compiled line of code gives us….a very dark gray, and…another dark gray. Not quite the colors I had in mind, but hey, it shows the principle very well; we can easily create multiple colors from one single base color. The key to it is to ensure that we get the right balance of numbers, in terms of base colors against those we calculate using operators. Let's see whether we can improve on this, and start exploring the world of functions to create some more appealing colors.

Working with color functions

The functions available within Less can be used to provide some interesting colors. It is worth taking the time to familiarize yourself with the options available, particularly as it is possible to produce the same color using different methods!

The functions can be split into four groups – they cover color definition, channels, operations, and blending. Let's take a look at each group of functions in turn, starting with defining color formats.

Defining color formats

Before we can alter colors, we naturally need to define them. We could simply provide a HEX code, but this isn't always sufficient; Less allows us to do more. Less provides a number of methods to obtain colors using different formats, and these are the three that you will likely use the most:

Function	Creates an opaque color from	Example value
rgb	Decimal red, green, and blue (RGB) values	rgb(90, 129, 32)
hsl	Hue, saturation, and lightness (HSL) values	hsl(90, 100%, 50%)
hsv	Hue, saturation, and value (HSV) values	hsv(90, 100%, 50%)

> For more information, refer to the full list of functions in *Appendix, Color Functions in Less*. I've created a CodePen that shows these effects in action. This is available at http://codepen.io/alibby251/pen/horqx.

These methods mean that we're not limited to simply using HEX codes all of the time – after all, could you tell that #8a5c16 is dark orange? I suspect not! A better method of defining colors is to use RGB (or RGBA, if we want to define opacity as well); we can then extract the individual base colors, as shown in our next demo.

Converting colors from HEX to RGBA

This is a very simple exercise, in which we'll take a color, extract the constituent base colors, and display them on screen. We can then use these later to produce new colors. We'll begin, with setting up the markup for our demo:

1. Start by downloading a copy of the code that accompanies this book. From it, extract a copy of hextorgb.html and save this to our project folder. This will act as the basis for our demo.

2. We now need to add our styling, so in a new file add the following, starting with defining some base styles for our page:

```
body { margin-left: 10px; padding: 0; }
h3 { margin-top: 10px; margin-bottom: -5px; font-family: "Open
Sans","Helvetica Neue",Helvetica,Arial,sans-serif; width: 100px;
position: absolute; float: left; }
```

3. Next come the Less styles. We first need to extract the red, blue, and green styles from our base color:

```
@r: red(#8a5c16);
@g: green(#8a5c16);
@b: blue(#8a5c16);
```

4. Once we have the base colors, we set them to mixins that will define the background colors of our boxes:

```
.original() { background-color: rgba(@r,@g,@b, 1); }
.red() { background-color: rgba(@r,0,0, 1); }
.green() { background-color: rgba(0,@g,0, 1); }
.blue() { background-color: rgba(0,0,@b, 1); }
```

> If you need to support IE8, then RGBA() will not
> work. Instead, use something like this:
>
> background:rgb(R,G,B);
>
> filter:alpha(opacity=XX);
>
> Here, R, G, and B are equivalent to red, green, and
> blue values; XX is the figure denoting the level of
> opacity to use.

5. The boxes won't display very nicely on their own, so let's add some font styling:

```
.font-style() {
    font-family: "Open Sans","Helvetica Neue",Helvetica,Arial,sans-
serif; width: 160px; font-size: 12px; text-align: center; padding:
15px; font-size: 14px; line-height: 1.42857; margin-top: 5px;
color: #ffffff; }
```

6. Last but by no means least, we need to tweak the positioning of each box, and set the background colors:

```
.box { margin-left: 120px; .font-style; }
.original-box { .original; }
.red-box { .red; }
.green-box { .green; }
.blue-box { .blue; }
```

7. Save the Less code as `hextorgb.less`. If we preview the results of our work, we should see the four boxes displayed on screen; the first is our selected color, followed by each of its constituent primary colors:

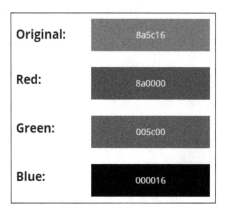

At this point, you might be asking what happened here. It's a good question. Although it looks like a lot of Less code, in reality, it all boils down to the use of three functions, namely `red()`, `green()`, and `blue()`. We first extract the primary colors, then use the `rgba()` function in various mixins to create `background-colors` and assign each to the three boxes displayed on screen.

Let's move on now, and change focus to look at another of the color function groups in Less, which is working with color channels.

Channeling colors using Less

Now that we have established a suitable color space to work with, we might come across a need to extract and potentially alter part of an existing color. Thankfully, Less includes a range of functions that can help in this respect; let's take a look at the three functions you will likely use the most; a full list is available in *Appendix, Color Functions in Less*, at the end of the book:

Function	Extracts	Example value
hue	The hue channel of a color object in the HSL color space. Returns an integer value between 0 to 360.	`hue(hsl(90, 100%, 50%))`
saturation	The saturation channel of a color object in the HSL color space. Returns a percentage value between 0 to 100 percent.	`saturation(hsl(90, 100%, 50%))`

Function	Extracts	Example value
lightness	The lightness channel of a color object in the HSL color space. Returns a percentage value between 0 to 100 percent.	lightness(hsl(90, 100%, 50%))

 For more information, it is worth reading the documentation on the main Less site at http://lesscss.org/functions/#color-channel.

While it is key to understand how these functions work, we can only truly appreciate their power, if used in action. Let's set that right by building a demo that puts at least one of these to work, in the form of some simple alert boxes.

Creating alert boxes

Sebastian Ekström, a Swedish developer, has produced a perfect example of how to use the lightness and darkness functions within Less. I've reproduced it here with some minor changes to use HSL colors in place of standard HEX codes. You can see the original version of this demo at http://codepen.io/sebastianekstrom/pen/uHAtL.

Let's make a start. We first need to download some icons; for the purposes of this demo, I will assume you've used these:

- The confirmation dialog (http://www.iconarchive.com/show/oxygen-icons-by-oxygen-icons.org/Status-dialog-information-icon.html)
- The error dialog (http://www.iconarchive.com/show/nuoveXT-2-icons-by-saki/Status-dialog-error-icon.html)
- The warning dialog (http://www.iconarchive.com/show/oxygen-icons-by-oxygen-icons.org/Status-dialog-warning-icon.html)

If you want to use alternative icons, then adjust the code accordingly.

1. From a copy of the code download, extract a copy of alerts.html. This will act as the basis for our demo.
2. Next, let's create our Less styling. In a new file, add the following color styles, beginning with the principal text color:

```
@text-color: hsl(0,0%,53.3%);
@button_confirm: #008000;
@button_warning: #ffc53a;
@button_error: #ff0000;
body { background: hsl(0,0%,13.3%); }
```

3. Next, add the following two mixins; these determine the background color to use:

```
.text-color(@text-color) when (lightness(@text-color) > 40%) {
    color: #000000;
}
.text-color(@text-color) when (lightness(@text-color) < 40%) {
    color: #ffffff;
}
```

> Notice the use of the when statements? Only one text color will be used; this will be determined if the lightness value of @ text-color is above or below 40%. If it is above, then plain black is used; if below, then white is used instead.

4. Our next two mixins control the font formatting and basic button design:

```
.h3-text() { background-repeat: no-repeat; font-size: 1.5rem;
padding-left: 40px; }
.button(@button_type) { text-decoration: none; padding: 1em 3em;
width: 20%; margin: 1% auto; display: block; text-align: center;
font-family: sans-serif; border-radius: 5px; line-height: 40px;
border: 1px solid #000000; background: @button_type; }
```

5. We can now tie our styles together. We first call the mixin that creates the confirmation dialog, followed by the mixins for the warning and error dialogs, respectively:

```
#confirm { .button(@button_confirm); .text-color(@button_confirm);
  h3 { background-image: url(confirmation.png); .h3-text; }
}
#warning { .button(@button_warning); .text-color(@button_warning);
  h3 { background-image: url(warning.png); .h3-text; }
}
#error { .button(@button_error); .text-color(@button_error);
  h3 { background-image: url(error.png); .h3-text; }
}
```

Save the file as alerts.less in the css subfolder. If all is well, we will see the three dialogs, against an all-over dark background:

Okay, so we can now set our color space and extract a base color of our choice. However, what are we going to do with the colors? It's unlikely that simply extracting a color is going to be sufficient; we will very likely need to do something more with it. Not a problem with Less. We can operate on our chosen color, to produce any color we so desire!

Operating on colors

At this point, you're probably asking yourself, "Why would we need to use operators on colors?" Surely that's what you do with numbers, right…?

Not necessarily. Using simple arithmetic operators, as we saw earlier in the *Working with arithmetic operators* section, will work perfectly well, but what happens if we need to change colors and end up picking colors that look terrible using the fixed calculations we provide? Clearly we need a better method…!

Fortunately for us, there exist a number of functions within Less that we can use, and assuming that we have a suitable color to work from, we can use any of these functions to produce a different shade, or change hue, saturation, or lightness levels for example. Let's take a moment to consider the three you are likely to use most:

Function	Purpose of function	Example value
lighten	This is used to increase the lightness of a color in the HSL color space by an absolute amount.	lighten(#a52a2a, 20%);
darken	This decreases the lightness of a color in the HSL color space by an absolute amount.	darken(#a52a2a, 20%);
fade	This sets the absolute transparency of a color. This can be applied to colors irrespective of whether they already have an opacity value or not.	fade(#a52a2a, 20%);

For more information, refer to the full list of functions given in *Appendix*, *Color Functions in Less*, at the end of this book. I've also created a CodePen that shows these effects in action and is available at `http://codepen.io/alibby251/pen/KGltj`.

This makes perfect sense on any site, but more so on larger sites that use colors throughout and where updating them would be a nightmare. Instead, we can choose our master color, assign it to a variable, and use functions to generate the remaining colors. Let's take a look at how this would work in practice, with a quick and easy example that changes text colors based on the H attribute we use.

Making text darker or lighter in color

The first of our two real-world demos is very simple. Let's say we have a number of text styles on our site, which use different shades of the same color.

We could easily set the colors within our CSS, but this would miss out on a major key part of Less; why set them explicitly, when we can get Less to do this for us? To see what this means, let's knock up a quick demo that creates some different styles for the standard H1 to H6 markup as shown here:

This H6 text color has been darkened by 20%

This H2 text has been saturated by 30%

The red in this H3 text has been faded out by 70%

This H4 color is from mixing the base color with blue, and displayed at a 50% opacity

This H5 text color has been lighted by 20%

This is some sample text at H6 size, using a base color of #893939

Let's start:

1. For this demo, we need to download a copy of the code that accompanies this book. From it, extract a copy of `altercolor.html` and save to our project folder. This will act as the basis for our demo.

2. In a separate file, go ahead and add the following styles, beginning with our base font mixin, to style the text:

```
.font-family() { font-family: Helvetica, arial, times new roman;
font-weight: bold; }
```

3. Next comes the variable that sets our base color:

```
@base_color: #893939;
```

4. We all need to add the all-important mixin calls that create the font styles:

```
h1 { color: @base_color; .font-family; }
h2 { color: saturate(@base_color, 30%); .font-family; }
h3 { color: fadeout(red, 70%); .font-family; }
h4 { color: mix(blue, @base_color, 50%); .font-family; }
h5 { color: lighten(@base_color, 20%); .font-family; }
h6 { color: darken(@base_color, 20%); .font-family; }
```

Save the file as `altercolor.less` in the `css` subfolder. If we preview our work, we should expect to see six statements, styled as shown at the start of this exercise.

Beautifully simple, huh? With a little work and one single color, we've set all of the styles automatically, using Less. Our demo is creating the styles dynamically, but we can easily precompile the Less statements into valid CSS code, and use this instead. All we need to do is just use the right H attribute when designing our pages!

Let's move on now and take a look at some more of the functions of Less that we can use—the blending group. These functions work in a similar fashion to those options available within graphics packages such as Photoshop or GIMP. Let's explore these in more detail.

Color blending

So far, we've seen how we can define a color space, extract one of its constituent elements out of it (such as hue or level of green) and that we can transform the color through fading or spinning the original. There's one more way we can change a color using Less—blending.

The principle works in the same way, in that we require two colors, but the effects are quite different. Let's have a quick look at the three functions you will likely use the most:

Function	Purpose of function	Example value
`multiply`	This function multiplies two colors.	`multiply(#9ec1ef, #091d37);`
`screen`	This does the opposite of multiply. The result is a brighter color.	`screen (#9ec1ef, #091d37);`
`overlay`	Conditionally make light channels lighter and dark channels darker.	`overlay (#9ec1ef, #091d37);`

For more information, refer to the full list of functions given in *Appendix, Color Functions in Less*, at the end of the book. I've also created a CodePen that shows these effects in action, available at `http://codepen.io/alibby251/pen/IKqEk`.

Now that we've seen the various color blending modes available in Less, let's move on and take a look at how these compare with performing similar actions in Photoshop.

Comparing Less with Photoshop

Working with blend modes in CSS is likely to raise a very important point—how does Less stack up against applications such as Photoshop?

Well, the good news is that for those already familiar with blend modes in Photoshop, the same values exist within Less, although the range is not as extensive as Photoshop. We can use values such as lighten, darken, hardlight, and so on, to produce similar effects to creating images in Photoshop.

Two good examples of how we can use blending modes can be found at `http://css-tricks.com/basics-css-blend-modes/`; have a look also at `http://www.dummies.com/how-to/content/photoshop-ccs-blending-modes.html` to get a feel for how these modes fit in with the other blend modes available in the latest version of Photoshop (CC at the time of writing this).

The downside is that support for blend modes is still very new; for example, support for `background-blend-mode` (at the time of writing this) is limited to the latest versions of modern browsers, with the exception of IE.

This limitation aside, it is definitely worth spending time getting familiar with how we can replicate the same effects from Photoshop within Less/CSS. As we've already seen, there are a host of blend values we can use. As a tester of what is possible using CSS, have a look at the excellent gradients produced by Bennett Feely, which use `background-blend-mode`. You can see the gradients at `http://bennettfeely.com/gradients/`.

To really get a feel of how we can use blend modes in Less, it is strongly recommended that you understand at least these three: `screen`, `multiply`, and `overlay`. The others will follow in due course. Let's take a moment to cover these three modes in more detail:

- `screen`: This ignores blacks and makes images appear lighter with light tones appearing washed out.

- `multiply`: This is the direct opposite, with darker tones reinforced, while light will pass through anything that is clear or bright.

- `overlay`: This is a balance between screen and multiply; it ignores midtones, making the blended result lighter and darker at the same time, to increase contrast.

Let's change tack at this point and move on. We can easily use blend modes to help produce new colors, or interesting effects (particularly with images!); this won't be truly effective unless we've worked out what our site's palette will look like.

It's at this point we can really put Less to good use, in calculating suitable values for our palette. Before we do so, let's begin with a primer on creating successful palettes to help set the scene.

Introducing palettes

We all work with colors as part of designing a site. Colors are key to making or breaking our design. The creation of a cohesive and interesting website relies on the right choice of colors that form our palette. Historically, we frequently used either a white or color background; as our tastes have evolved, so has the need to choose the right colors to form our palette.

The key to any successful palette, and that is even before we get into the depths of producing it, is to really understand how color works. The theory of color is a complex subject, where we can get to grips with understanding how different shades and hues interact with each other and the effect this has on the visitor to the site.

To help us through the minefield of choosing the right colors to create our palette, there are a number of tips we can use:

- Try to choose a palette type that creates suitable colors, based on a color of your choice. There are several palette types available, but three of particular note are Analogous, Complementary, and Triadic.

- Instead, choose colors based on current trends. This might, for example, be muted pastel colors, which have become popular in producing soothing, flat designs.

- An alternative is to use bright colors, which are usually heavily saturated, to make elements really stand out. The range of colors is often limited, with lots of white or gray space, to help equalize the stark colors used in this palette.

- We can even go for a monochromatic design, which is often based around shades of black or gray, with specific elements highlighted in reds or blues. Monochrome palettes help convey an emotional or psychological message, whereas we can use an accent color to highlight important elements in the design.

A great tool to use when choosing colors is Adobe's Kuler, which is available at `https://kuler.adobe.com/create/color-wheel/`. It shows some other palettes that you can use, such as Triad or Compound; it is worth trying these once you've become familiar with creating palettes.

Let's take a moment now to look at some of these palette types in more detail.

Analyzing color palette examples

It is surprising how consumers can frequently be guided by the colors used on a website; for example, a study found that between 60-80 percent of customers' purchasing decisions are influenced solely by color! Let's take a moment to consider a couple of examples to show the importance of choosing the right colors.

Trüf, a Los Angeles-based web design company, uses a monochromatic design, with red to highlight critical elements of their site — you can see their design at `http://www.trufcreative.com`.

A similar use of colors, but for a different site, Etch uses various shades in its bold background, with pink elements to make the design really stand out. Their site is at `http://www.etchapps.com`.

To get a feel for the importance of choosing colors well, take a look at the infographic on Column Five Media's site, at `http://www.columnfivemedia.com/work-items/infographic-true-colors-what-your-brand-colors-say-about-your-business`; there are some very revealing facts!

It is worth noting though that accessibility must be considered where practical; this will often be determined by the appeal of the product or service on offer to visually impaired visitors; Geri Coady has produced a useful guide in the form of an e-book, which is available for sale at `http://www.fivesimplesteps.com/products/colour-accessibility`.

Let's move on now and turn our attention to what we've been waiting for — choosing some colors.

Choosing our colors

So far, we've learned about the importance of choosing our colors carefully and the impact this will have on our site's visitors; getting it wrong will be disastrous! In comparison, once we know which colors we want to use, creating our palette is really easy.

The first stage is to choose our primary color. Column Five Media's infographic suggests that only 5 percent of the world's top 100 brands use more than two colors; the key here is to use as many colors as is suitable for your project. A good rule of thumb is to choose at least 2-3 colors to work with, alongside a neutral light or dark color for the background. We can then use Less to produce any shade needed from your choice of principal colors.

Using a photo as our source

How often have you wondered where you will get that inspiration for a design? I'll bet the answer is frequently, and I'm willing to bet that photos will feature somewhere in this list of sources!

Photos are perfect as a source of inspiration. We can pick a principal color from it, then manually choose colors that would work. It can be a little hit and miss though; not every color scheme will work, but the key to using this method is experimenting until you find colors that would provide a good harmony in your design.

We can take a more pragmatic route though. Adobe released Kuler, a brilliant app (and website), to help choose suitable colors according to the type of palette we use.

We can either choose a color, then get Kuler to choose appropriate colors for us, or we can upload a photo of our choice and select suitable colors from it. In the following screenshot, we can see the results of selecting a color from a photo, such as the one used in my first book, *jQuery Tools UI Library*, published by *Packt Publishing*.

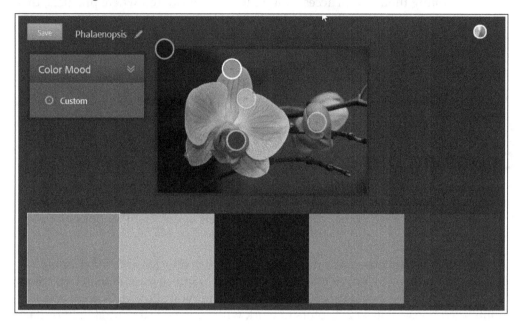

In comparison, if we take the purple from far left (#a67097) and use it in Kuler's color wheel, we get a completely different result, using the Analogous palette:

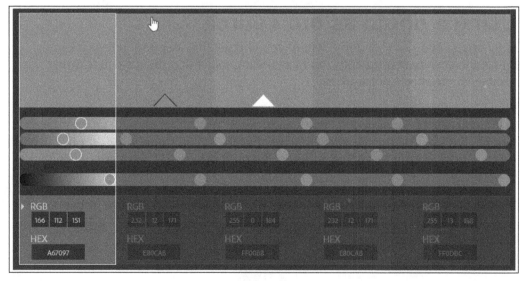

It really comes down to what your project needs in terms of color; to help with this and understand the impact on your visitors, it is worth reading an article by Rachel Shillcock, on Tuts+, at `http://webdesign.tutsplus.com/articles/understanding-the-qualities-and-characteristics-of-color--webdesign-13292`.

 For a good source of inspiration, take a look at the palettes created on Kuler by others; they are at `https://kuler.adobe.com/explore/newest/`.

Choosing a color using a tool, such as Kuler, can be an interesting experience. It opens up a world of possibilities, although one person's idea of harmony might not align with others! Choices, choices...

To help take some of the guesswork out of creating palettes, we can easily use the power of Less to create a suitable palette, based on our choice of color. Let's take a look at how this will work in practice.

Creating a color palette using Less

Now that we've chosen our color scheme, we can get stuck into creating our palette. There are literally hundreds of tools available, but we want Less to do all the heavy lifting for us.

Now, I have a confession to make: while we can absolutely get Less to do the hard work for us, we still have to work out the formulae that generates our colors. Or do we?

Fortunately, one kind soul, Jimmy King (a developer at Meltmedia) has already produced a very simple, yet brilliant tool for this purpose. If we head over to `http://jimmyking.me/colors.less`, not only can we set a color picker to our choice of color, but also get a preview of suitable colors that fit different types of palettes. What's more, we can even get the Less code to generate the colors to boot!

Let's put this into action with a quick demo that uses our #a67097 color from the previous exercise to create a Triadic-based color palette:

1. Download and extract a copy of `colorpalette.html` from the code that accompanies this book; we'll use this as a basis for our markup.

2. In a separate file, add the following Less statements, beginning with creating variables that define our colors:

```
@baseColor: rgba(166,112,151,1);
@distance: 120;
@triad1: @baseColor;
@triad2: spin(@baseColor, (180 - (@distance * 0.5)));
@triad3: spin(@baseColor, (180 + (@distance * 0.5)));
```

We've used the spin function in this step; spin is used to rotate the hue angle of an color in a HSV color wheel. You can learn more about this operation at `http://lesscss.org/functions/#color-operations-spin`.

3. Next, add the following mixins. Note that we can combine these with the color style rules shown further down in the code; I've separated these out for clarity:

```
.triad1() { background-color: @triad1; }
.triad2() { background-color: @triad2; }
.triad3() { background-color: @triad3; }
```

4. We also need some basic font styling; this is not essential, but it helps make it look better! Go ahead and add the following mixin:

```
.font-style() { font-family: "Open Sans","Helvetica Neue",
Helvetica, Arial, sans-serif; width: 160px; font-size: 12px;
text-align: center; padding: 15px; font-size: 14px; line-height:
1.42857; margin-top: 5px; color: #ffffff; }
```

We're almost done. Here come the most important mixins; these create the boxes and style them with the appropriate background colors:

```
.box { margin-left: 250px; .font-style; }
.firstcolor { .triad1; }
.secondcolor { .triad2; }
.thirdcolor { .triad3; }
```

5. We need to make the demo look a little more presentable, so go ahead and add the following styles:

```
body { margin-left: 10px; padding: 0; }
h3 { margin-top: 10px; margin-bottom: -5px; font-family: "Open
Sans", "Helvetica Neue", Helvetica, Arial, sans-serif; width:
300px; position: absolute; float: left; }
```

6. Save the file as `colorpalette.less`. If we preview the results in a browser, we will see something akin to this screenshot:

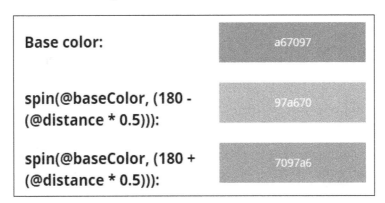

At this point, you're probably thinking, "What's happened here?". Well, if we revert to Jimmy's tool, the keen-eyed among you should spot that I've used the formulae to produce a Triadic color palette. All we've done is packaged up the formulae into a small demo, where we're setting the background color for three boxes, based on the results of each formula.

Jimmy has produced formulae for a number of different palette types, so rather than reinvent the wheel, we can simply choose our principal color, then take a copy of the code automatically produced by the site once we've decided which palette to use! The key point though is that there is absolutely no room for debate as to whether the colors work; they are mathematically chosen to produce a harmonious palette.

 When producing palettes, try to decide on and keep to a suitable naming convention. There are no hard and fast rules on format, but consistency and reuse is very much the order of the day!

So, we've seen how easy it is to produce color palettes and that Jimmy's tool makes it a cinch to get the all-important calculations needed to create each color. This gives me an idea... what if we were to ditch Photoshop and design in the browser instead?

Ditching old habits

What?? No—that would be absolutely impossible, I hear you say! We can't do that...

Or can we...? Well, surprising as it might sound, it is perfectly possible; what's more, Less can help make this a painless process. Let me explain.

Historically, designers and developers have relied on using Photoshop to create mockups of sites. "Nothing wrong in this", I hear you say. However, it doubles the work; clients can't use the design to see how it looks and works, and changes cannot be made on the fly. Also, Photoshop is expensive. We need a high-end PC or Mac just to get the full benefit from using it; can developers working on small sites, where costs are a concern, really justify the cost?

In contrast, designing straight into the browser makes the process more dynamic; we can make changes quickly and easily, particularly if Less has been used! We can even produce several style sheets that can completely alter the appearance of a site with just a few clicks; creating designs in Photoshop means recreating the base view from the ground up for each subsequent design. With the best will in the world, there is always a risk that each design will have some slight differences, despite following the same process in each case!

However, we should not forget that the real key to design is actually not to concentrate on the color, but the content first. If we get that right, then the colors will fall easily into place.

 To help get the feel of the mindset of designing in the browser, Creative Bloq has published an interview with web developer, Sean Fioritto, which is available at http://www.creativebloq. com/css3/why-web-developers-should-sketch-css-not- photoshop-51411711. This makes for an interesting read!

If, however, we really cannot afford to stop using Photoshop, then we can at least make our development workflow smarter. CSS Hat has made a plugin that can convert any design into the equivalent Less code and export them as Less files. It's available at http://www.csshat.com, and versions are available for both Windows and Mac with licenses priced at 35 USD for both versions.

To see it in action, Kezz Bacey has written a two-part tutorial that shows how easy it is to use the plugin to produce Less code; part 1 of the tutorial is available at `http://webdesign.tutsplus.com/tutorials/how-to-improve-your-photoshop-workflow-with-csshat-and-pnghat--cms-20786` and part 2 at `http://webdesign.tutsplus.com/tutorials/how-to-code-a-photoshop-layout-with-csshat-lesshat-and-pnghat--cms-20997`.

We're almost at the end of our mini journey of working with colors in Less. Before we finish and move to look at animation in the next chapter, we need to take a look at some legal requirements that every designer should consider within their designs. This is, of course, the WCAG standards; let's take a look at these in more detail.

Working with W3C and WCAG standards

Throughout this chapter, we've been on a journey of discovery, seeing how various different functions within Less can help simplify the work required to create new colors. There is one important part of creating colors that we have yet to cover and which designers must be aware of: the need to ensure compliance with the WCAG guidelines for accessibility.

Overcoming blocks on access to a site

In this modern age, one would hope that all sites would be accessible to everyone; the truth is that this is not always the case. Access can be blocked for a number of reasons, and in terms of color, they are:

- Visitors who cannot differentiate between particular colors and therefore can't access information that relies on the use of those colors to convey meaning (for example, red/green color blindness)

- Visitors who need to use devices that can't display information that uses color

- Visitors with color deficiencies, who struggle to see sites that have foreground and background colors that are very close in hue

So, how can we get around these issues and ensure we produce a site that is accessible?

Introducing WCAG

WCAG has compiled an extensive list of guidelines to help guide designers through ensuring compliance, which can be viewed at http://www.w3.org/TR/WCAG/. These need to be followed, although designers can opt to choose compliance at either A, Double-A, or Triple-A grade levels.

The WCAG recommendations make for dry reading, and there are, nevertheless, two key factors to consider, which in summary are:

- Colors should not be used as the only means of conveying any information; a green button marked **OK** is preferable to a simple green circle
- Text (and images of text) should have a contrast ratio of at least 4.5:1, except when large-scale text is used, or the text forms part of a decorative image or brand logo

To ensure that information is not likely to fall foul of WCAG compliance, we can use several guidelines:

- Avoid using colored text or strong background colors
- Black text on white background is recommended (avoid using underlined text as your customers might think the text is a hyperlink when it is not)
- Use standard fonts (for example, Arial, Times New Roman)
- Uppercase text should not be used for entire page headings or blocks of text

In addition, we can use a number of tools to help us decide whether we have the right contrast levels. Two such examples are available at http://www.dasplankton.de/ContrastA/ and http://webaim.org/resources/contrastchecker/.

There are plenty of resources available online for further reading, including case examples and guidelines issued for specific companies or government organizations. Some examples include:

- http://www.w3.org/WAI/WCAG20/quickref/
- http://www.w3.org/TR/2008/REC-WCAG20-20081211/
- http://www.w3.org/TR/compositing-1/

It is worth noting that the Less library has been modified to help compliance. Although it is not completely compliant yet, one example of change to help towards compliance is the pull request issued at `https://github.com/less/less.js/pull/1704`; this deals with changes made to color functions within Less, such as multiply or overlay.

Making a site useable

Okay, this might seem like a strange question, given we've just talked about how to make sites compliant, right?

Well, yes and no. While researching for this book, I came across a brilliant discussion on Stack Overflow, which talks about ensuring compliance to the WCAG guidelines and why adhering to them can actually be detrimental to your site.

In a nutshell, the responder to the original question discusses the good work being done by the team behind the guidelines even though they are not perfect. He talks about the need to apply the guidelines with care and that only those that best suit a website should be used. He mentions that many people with disabilities will often find ways around information that is otherwise hidden from view, and that in some respects, they are the perfect individuals to help test the usability of a site!

 You can read the full discussion at `http://stackoverflow.com/questions/21415785/wcag-vs-real-users-opinions`.

Summary

Color management in Less can be seen as something of a paradox; while the tools are relatively simple to use, they can be used to produce complex designs that are only limited by the bounds of your imagination. Throughout this chapter, we've covered a number of tools that you can use to extract, mix, and blend colors. Let's take a moment to review what we have learned throughout this chapter.

We began with a little theory to set the scene and introduce color management; we also learned a little about color spaces and formats. Our delve into using Less began with a look at using simple arithmetic operators such as multiplication or division; this was swiftly followed by an introduction to the various color functions available in Less and how these functions compared to working with Photoshop.

Next up was an introduction to palettes and an analysis of some examples, to illustrate the importance of choosing colors carefully. This included using photos as a potential color source, which we then used to create a color palette using Less.

Next up came something that some might see as controversial, which was a look at ditching old habits and moving to using something like Less to develop straight into the browser. While some may argue this is not sensible, we covered some of the reasons why this practice might turn out to be beneficial; for those who couldn't face the move, we looked at a simple way of getting the Less styles created automatically from Photoshop. To close out the chapter, we took a look at how developers must adhere to the WCAG guidelines on the use of color, why they were devised, and how we need to be careful in applying them to our sites.

Phew! We certainly covered a lot! Let's move onto our next chapter, which will take a look at how we can use Less to simplify development of animation within our projects.

13
Animation with Less

How many times have you seen animated sites using Flash? OK, a fair few. I'll also bet that you wanted to skip the animation as soon as you could, right?

Yep, I thought so; not many hands going down now…

We cannot forget the bad old days of sites that used Flash, where we frequently wanted to skip badly designed animations, which often didn't provide any useful content but instead made sites slow. Sounds familiar?

Thankfully, things have moved on; over the next few pages, we'll see how you can use CSS3 animations instead to achieve the same effects that otherwise would have required Flash. The use of CSS3 animations eliminates the need for a heavy Flash plugin (for modern browsers), and provided they are done properly, can make a site faster, more enjoyable to browse, and engaging to the end user. We'll delve into the use of Less to simplify the process of coding some real-world examples in order to make our development workflow much easier.

In this chapter, we will cover the following topics:

- How a CSS animation works
- Transitions and transformations
- Animated menus
- Simplifying the animation markup with Less

Intrigued? Let's make a start…

Introducing animations

Back in the early days of the Internet, it was common to see animated GIFs that were often liberally plastered over a website — the excuse often being that they "look cool," even if they didn't really serve any purpose!

Nowadays, animation is being used more and more on the Internet — this is often in the form of SVG images, background videos, sounds, and so on. This increasingly used technologies such as Flash, but with the advent of HTML5, designers have found ways to recreate many effects natively in the browser without the use of Flash.

Today, browser vendors are adding more and more functionalities to each version of their product; this means that CSS3 animation is gaining ground to the likes of Flash, such that Adobe has stopped developing Flash for the mobile platform, preferring to concentrate on HTML5.

Over the next few pages, we'll be taking a tour of CSS3 animations, looking at various elements such as transitions and transforms, and how we can use Less to help simplify the process of developing animations. You might be surprised to learn that there aren't a lot of new techniques to master when using Less to produce an animation — in fact, all of the techniques we've covered so far can be used to help make development easier.

Let's start though with a quick look at what makes a good animation — after all, there is no point in creating them if they aren't successful!

Creating a good animation

How often have you looked at a site only to find that it looks like the inside of someone's brain in the middle of a migraine? Too many sites fall victim to the temptation to animate everything — animation is a secret ingredient that can make the most impact when care has been taken over its use.

So, what makes a good animation? This will depend on the context of the site, but there are some good tips that every designer should follow:

- Don't overdo the attention grabbers — visitors want to feel in control of their browsing experience, so plastering a subscription dialog just when they reach the information they need is a big no-no! Use it to highlight something they might have missed, not to distract them.

- Animation works well when it is used to highlight context and navigation features; a good example is an animated sidebar that provides useful local information. The contents of the sidebar will change frequently, so the use of animation will help to point out new information to users.

- On some sites, telling a story is one way to use animation. While this might be an overkill for some sites, the popular full-page scroll effect works well, as it suggests that there is more to be read, which helps to keep the user interested.

- If an animation is used, then make it physical and believable. You can use any effect on the elements, such as bouncing or shaking, but if they aren't believable, then users will find them a distraction and a big turn-off!

Let's move on now and turn the focus of our attention to something more in-depth: how do animations work? This is the key to creating successful animations. As we are about to see, the different types of animation appear similar, but they have some key differences; this can affect how we use them to develop effects on our site.

How a CSS animation works

We've talked about animations in general, but the term covers no fewer than four different types that we can use within Less. They are animations, transitions, 2D transforms, and 3D transforms.

There are two out of these four properties where particular attention should be paid to how they work: animations and transitions. This doesn't mean that transforms are any less important—that's not the case. They merely work in a different way to transitions and are easier to understand and use.

Animations and transitions can appear to provide the same result but work in different ways. The two crucial differences are:

- Transitions work on a two-state basis—they change an element from the starting position to the finishing position if we switch CSS states or if a pseudo-class has been triggered, such as :hover or :focus

- Animations can use multiple @keyframes or positions set between the starting and finishing state

The remaining two animation properties, 2D and 3D transforms, don't work in the same way—they can manipulate the size and appearance of an element, but usually in situ (although they can be used while the element is moving).

Now that we've seen how animations work, it's an opportune moment to get to know each type of animation property in more detail.

Introducing animation types

When we talk about creating animations, this could be taken to mean that we're moving content; while this is perfectly true, we're not limited to simply moving elements. We could equally transition elements from one state to another or bend and manipulate their appearance on the screen. Let's take a look at each animation type in more detail, beginning with animations.

Animating content

Animating content is used to move objects and can be used as an alternative to using Flash. They define what happens to a set of element's properties — we can control how these properties behave when defining our animation, including their frequency.

The key difference between animations and transitions is that animations can be fired without any user interaction, as soon as a page loads. Transitions can only be fired when an element becomes active, such as a `button` element or a `div` element.

A simple animation will follow this format:

```
animation: <name of animation> <duration of the animation>
```

Let's test this by creating a simple animation that changes the color of a box. For this, we will need a copy of the code download that accompanies this book; from this, extract a copy of `animatebox.html` and `animatebox.css`.

If we run the demo, we can expect to see the box go through several shades of purple before reverting to the original color, as shown in the following screenshot:

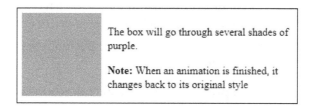

The box will go through several shades of purple.

Note: When an animation is finished, it changes back to its original style

The key to this is `@keyframes animbox` in our CSS; this contains the changes that should be made in each keyframe within our animation. We've had to include it twice in order to allow support for Chrome, Safari, and Opera:

```
/* Chrome, Safari, Opera */
@-webkit-keyframes animbox {
   0% { background: #85486d; }
  25% { background: #9F6287; }
  50% { background: #B87BA0; }
```

```
   100% { background: #D295BA; }
}

/* Standard syntax */
@keyframes animbox {
   0% { background: #85486d; }
   25% { background: #9F6287; }
   50% { background: #B87BA0; }
   100% { background: #D295BA; }
}
```

The animation is a little jittery—this will be due to the large gaps within each keyframe; we could use smaller gaps for a smoother experience.

 You can learn more about the different attributes for CSS3 animations at http://www.w3schools.com/css/css3_animations.asp.

Let's continue and take a look at how transitions work.

Transitioning elements

Transitions are effectively animations that change the state of an element from its original state to a new state; the key difference in animations is that transitions can only take place when they are explicitly triggered—for example, if a mouse hovers over a DIV or button.

A simple transition will follow this format:

```
transition: <the css property you want to add the effect to> <the
effect duration>
```

Let's test this by creating a simple transition that increases the size of a box. For this, we will need a copy of the code download that accompanies this book; from this, extract a copy of `transitionbox.html` and `transitionbox.css`. If we run the demo, we can expect to see the box increase in size before reverting to the original size:

Hover over the div element above, to see the transition effect.

Note: When this animation is finished, it changes back to its original size.

The key to this is the transition code for the `#transitionbox` DIV in our CSS—this contains the changes that should be made in each keyframe within our animation. We've had to include it twice to allow support for WebKit browsers:

```
-webkit-transition: width 2s; transition: width 2s;
```

We can always adjust the time taken for the animation to perform, should 2 seconds not be sufficient.

 You can learn more about the different attributes for CSS3 animations at http://www.w3schools.com/css/css3_transitions.asp.

Let's move on now and take a look at the remaining two options, which are 2D and 3D transforms.

Transforming elements

At first glance, you'd be forgiven for thinking that transforms are identical to transitions; after all, you can easily use `translate()` to move an object, whereas you can use an animation otherwise.

However, there are two key differences: transitions can be applied as part of animating an element, whereas transforms are completely independent. Transitions allow you to apply changes to just about any CSS property, whereas transforms will be used to move, scale, turn, spin, or stretch any element on the page:

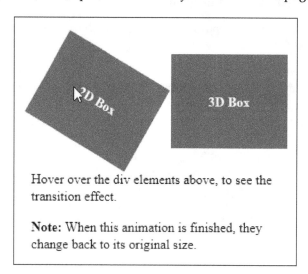

Hover over the div elements above, to see the transition effect.

Note: When this animation is finished, they change back to its original size.

A simple transform will follow this format:

```
transform: <the transform action you want to use>(<the value to apply
to the transform>)
```

Let's test this by creating two simple transforms: the first transform performs a 2D rotation on a box, and the second performs a 3D rotation along the *x* axis of the second box.

For this, we will need a copy of the code download that accompanies this book; from it, extract a copy of `transformbox.html` and `transformbox.css`. If we run the demo, we can expect to see both the boxes rotate when hovering over either of these; the box on the left-hand side is rotated by 30 degrees, and the box on the right-hand side is rotated on its *x* axis by 130 degrees, as shown in the screenshot at the start of this section.

The key to this is the transform code in our CSS—for the first box, we're rotating it by 30 degrees; the second is being rotated on its *x* axis by 130 degrees. Note how the support for 2D transforms is much better than that for 3D transforms; we still need to use the `webkit` prefix for most desktop browsers:

```
#transform2dbox:hover {
  transform: rotate(30deg);
}

#transform3dbox:hover {
  -webkit-transform: rotateX(130deg); /* Chrome, Safari, Opera */
  transform: rotateX(130deg);
}
```

Once support for browsers has improved on the 3D transform, we can then remove the first line in the second demo.

You can learn more about the different attributes for CSS3 transforms at http://www.w3schools.com/css/css3_2dtransforms.asp and http://www.w3schools.com/css/css3_3dtransforms.asp.

We've talked a little about support for CSS3 animations as part of exploring these mini demos; now is an opportune moment to cover support in more detail.

Supporting animations in browsers

One small point that we need to cover before moving on is browser support. Here you should have no trouble while working with animations; all the key elements of CSS3 animations have been supported by the major browsers for some time:

IE	Firefox	Chrome	Safari	Opera
10+	5+	5+	4+	12+

Do check out the site **Can I Use** (`http://www.caniuse.com`), as some of the newer elements of animation might still require vendor prefixes at the time of writing.

Mobile support is equally well-supported; the only exception to this is Opera Mini, which lacks support for animations. Chrome for Android was a little buggy at the start, but this issue has since been resolved, so support will not be an issue. It is important to remember though that mobile devices don't have fast processors, so complex animations will run slowly and should be kept to a minimum on this platform.

Right, enough of the theory! Let's move on to what you all have been waiting for: writing some code.

Simplifying the animation markup with Less

Okay, we're finally at the point where I am sure you're itching to get to: writing some code! Don't worry, we're almost there. I just want to cover a small but key point, about how we can use Less to make coding animations simpler. To illustrate this, we're going to rework the critical parts of the animation demo we created earlier in this chapter.

If we take a look back at the key parts of the animation demo, we have this:

```
/* Chrome, Safari, Opera */
@-webkit-keyframes animbox {
  0% { background: #85486d; }
  25% { background: #9F6287; }
  50% { background: #B87BA0; }
  100% { background: #D295BA; }
}

/* Standard syntax */
@keyframes animbox {
```

```
    0% { background: #85486d; }
    25% { background: #9F6287; }
    50% { background: #B87BA0; }
    100% { background: #D295BA; }
}
```

Seems pretty reasonable, right? Well, as always, we can do better! Let's see how:

1. The first change that we can make is save `animatebox.css` as `animatebox. less` — we'll introduce some mixins, so saving it as a Less file will allow us to compile it into valid CSS later in this exercise.

2. We need to modify the HTML markup to include a reference to our new Less file and the Less library; so, go ahead and add the following in between the `<head>` markup:

    ```
    <link rel="stylesheet/less" href="css/animatebox-
        updated.less">
    <script src="js/less.min.js"></script>
    ```

3. Next, let's turn the `@keyframes` code into a generic animation mixin — remove the existing two blocks at the end of the code (lines 15-29) and then replace it with the following code:

    ```
    .keyframes (@name, @color0, @color25, @color50, @color100) {
        @-webkit-keyframes @name {
            0% {background: @color0}
            25%  {background: @color25;}
            50%  {background: @color50;}
            100% {background: @color100;}
        }

        @keyframes @name {
            0% {background: @color0}
            25%  {background: @color25;}
            50%  {background: @color50;}
            100% {background: @color100;}
        }
    }
    ```

4. Next, we add a new mixin that references the `@keyframes` code we've just created:

    ```
    .keyframes(animbox, #85486d, #9F6287, #B87BA0, #B87BA0);
    ```

If we rerun the demo, we should see no change in the effect. So what's different and why have we done what we've done here? Well, there are several benefits of what we've done.

We moved the @keyframes code into its own mixin—while the code might not seem shorter here, the benefits will really show when we create larger, more complex animations that have to be repeated to allow vendor prefixing.

The .keyframes mixin can now go into our own mixin library; this means that we can import the library into future projects:

```
@import "animations.less";
```

Reference the mixin in our code:

```
.some-animation {
  .keyframes(...);

  ...
}
```

Using Less to simplify our code isn't necessarily about making it shorter; it's also about making it reusable and easier to add to future projects!

 There's an updated demo available in the code—extract and run animatebox-updated.html to view the results.

Let's move on and work on a practical use of Less. How many times have you designed a menu for a site, only to think that it is becoming very code repetitive and needs animating? Okay, probably a little bit of a contrived question, but it could be possible...

Creating animated menus

Menus are the doyen of many a site; we all need some form of navigation, but styling the navigation menus is very much left to the imagination of the site's designer.

We can even go further and add some useful effects to menus; we can at least animate the drop-down motion so that they glide in a little more gracefully. To do this, we're going to revisit an exercise from an earlier instance in the book— remember, back in *Chapter 4, Working with Variables, Mixins, and Functions*, where we created a simple web page using some Less functions? Well, we're going to add a menu to that page and when we're done, it will look something similar to this:

Okay, let's make a start:

1. For this exercise, we need a copy of the code download that accompanies this book; from it, extract a copy of menus.html. This contains a copy of the code from *Chapter 4, Working with Variables, Mixins, and Functions*, with the additional markup for our menus and some cosmetic changes to import Less files.

2. Next, crack open a text editor of your choice and add the following code to a new file—we'll break it down and go through it section by section, beginning with the main container for our menu:

```
#navigation {
  width: 788px; height: 35px; font-family: 'Kite One', sans-serif;
font-weight: normal; font-size: 14px;
  ul { position: relative; z-index: 1000; list-style: none;
margin: 0; padding: 0; }
}
```

3. Next come the top-level menu entries:

```
#navigation > ul > li {
  position: relative; float: left; margin-right: 10px;
  &:hover ul ul { height: 0; }
  &:hover ul { height: 220px; }
  & > a:hover ul { height: 220px; }
}
```

4. These entries need to be turned into links; so, go ahead and add in this style rule:

```less
#navigation > ul > li > a {
  background-color: #2c2c2c; color: #aaaaaa; display: block;
padding: 8px 14px; text-decoration: none; transition: background-
color 0.3s ease 0s;
  &:hover {
    background-color: #666666; color: #eeeeee;
    ul ul { height: 0; }
  }
}
```

5. Some of our submenus have second-level submenus, so we need to cater to these submenus in our styling:

```less
#navigation ul ul {
  width: 340px; position: absolute; z-index: 100; height: 0;
overflow: hidden; transition: height 0.3s ease-in;
  li {
    background-color: #eaeaea; width: 170px;
    transition: background-color 0.3s ease;
    &:hover {
      background-color: #999;
      & > a { color: #ffffff; }
          & > ul { height: 220px; }
    }
  }
}
```

6. This style caters to our first-level submenus:

```less
#navigation ul ul li a {
  display: block; text-decoration: none; margin: 0 12px;
padding: 5px 0; color: #4c4c4c;
  &:hover {
    color: #ffffff;
    & > ul { height: 220px; }
  }
}
```

7. Last, but by no means least — this provides the container for our second-level submenus:

```less
#navigation ul ul ul {
  left: 170px; width: 170px;
  li a { border: 0 !important; }
}
```

8. We need an arrow to tell the users of our submenus, so let's add an arrow now:

```
.arrow { background: url(arrow.png) right center no-repeat;
}
```

9. Save the file as `menus.less`. Our `menus.html` file already has a link to it, along with a link to `base.less`; the latter contains the original code from *Chapter 4*, *Working with Variables, Mixins, and Functions*, but in a suitably renamed file.

At this point, if we preview the results, we can see the new menu, as shown in the screenshot at the start of this exercise.

So, what have we done here? In this instance, we've kept it very simple; most of the styles in `menus.less` are there to provide the basic styles to render our menu.

We've added three transition statements in though to add a subtle touch to our menu so that they each glide in more smoothly and then suddenly appear. Remember, animating elements can provide that extra sense of dynamism to a site; in this instance, if the transform styles were not understood, then the menus will still work but will not render so gracefully on the screen.

Libraries using Less

Over the last few pages, we've created some great demos of varying complexity — they show off something of what can be done with animations and how we can use Less.

The trouble is, there's one small but crucial problem here. How many of you have noticed that we've created each demo from scratch, with all the mixins included? I thought so, one of the precepts of Less is DRY or Don't Repeat Yourself.

If we take a look back at *Chapter 4*, *Working with Variables, Mixins, and Functions*, one of the subjects we covered was the use of external libraries within our code. Doing this means that we can avoid the need to write lots of mixins — while our examples here might have been a little too simple to warrant the use of an external library, we will definitely need to use at least one external library in a more complex site.

Thankfully, we can continue the same precept of DRY when working with animations; there are a number of Less-based libraries available that handle animation properties (and this includes both transitions and transforms):

- LESS Prefixer (`http://lessprefixer.com/`)
- More-or-less (`http://more-or-less.org/`)
- Animate.less (`https://github.com/machito/animate.less`)
- LESS Hat (`https://github.com/madebysource/lesshat`)
- Bootstrap's LESS (`https://github.com/twbs/bootstrap/`)
- LESS Elements (`http://www.lesselements.com/`)

We can even go one step further — if there isn't a library available in Less that is to your liking, then we can always use a plain CSS library.

The trick here is to resave it as a Less file and incorporate it in the usual manner. Over time, we can then convert it piecemeal as our skills improve. The beauty of this is that Less will still compile the original version as normal — don't forget, Less is after all a superset of CSS. With this in mind, let's take a look at a few examples of pure CSS animation libraries:

- Magic CSS (`https://github.com/miniMAC/magic`)
- Animate.css (`https://github.com/daneden/animate.css`)
- Effeckt.css (`https://github.com/h5bp/Effeckt.css`)

Now that we've seen the details of some of the libraries we could use, let's take a moment to try converting one of them to Less. I hear you ask, "Why should I do it?" Simple, while there are some good Less libraries available, you might as well find a CSS animation library that is more to your liking but that doesn't have a Less version available. If you do, then we need to convert it to use Less!

Converting from other libraries

The beauty about Less is that it is a superset of CSS — this means that the conversion of an existing CSS library to its Less equivalent is easier than it might first seem. The trick behind it is all in the planning — to prove this, let's work through a simple example using the Magic CSS animation library.

Let's begin by downloading a copy of the library — we can do this by browsing to `https://raw.githubusercontent.com/miniMAC/magic/master/magic.css` and then saving a copy locally. Open a copy of `magic.css` in the text editor of your choice and then resave it as `magic.less` — that's it!

Sorry to disappoint you if you were expecting more; technically though, this is the minimum requirement to convert a library to its Less equivalent. We can then compile this using Crunch!, or if you have configured Sublime Text as detailed in *Chapter 2, Building a Less Development Toolkit*, then the compilation will have taken place to the point of saving your work.

Now, we could stay with this, but…there's a fair amount of repetition in our code, which isn't ideal; we can definitely do better. Let's fix the repetition now:

1. Create a new file and save it as `keyframes.less` in the same folder as the original `magic.less` file.

2. Look for `@-moz-keyframes magic {` on or around line 468 — select from this line down to the end, which will be on or around line 4595.

3. Cut and paste this in the `keyframes.less` file you've just created and then save the file.

4. Revert to `magic.less`. You need to import the new file you've just created; so, go ahead and add this line at the top:

   ```
   @import "keyframes.less";
   ```

5. You can also improve the animation classes by adding the following lines immediately below the `@import` statement:

   ```
   .vendor(@property, @value) {
     -webkit-@{property}: @value;
     -moz-@{property}: @value;
     -ms-@{property}: @value;
     -o-@{property}: @value;
     @{property}: @value;
   }
   ```

6. Now comes the tedious part: you need to convert each of your animation classes to use the new mixin. Let's take the first, which is `.magictime`:

   ```
   .magictime {
     -webkit-animation-duration: 1s;
     -moz-animation-duration: 1s;
     -ms-animation-duration: 1s;
     -o-animation-duration: 1s;
     animation-duration: 1s;
     -webkit-animation-fill-mode: both;
     -moz-animation-fill-mode: both;
     -ms-animation-fill-mode: both;
     -o-animation-fill-mode: both;
     animation-fill-mode: both;
   }
   ```

7. We can easily convert the animation classes — the trick behind this is to use **Search and Replace** within a tool such as Sublime Text. We can update both the `animation-duration` and `animation-fill-mode` lines to use the Less mixin and then remove the remaining lines.

8. Once the search and replace work has been completed, the remaining lines can be removed completely. We will end up with this as the first example:

```
.magictime {
  .vendor(animation-duration, 1s);
  .vendor(animation-fill-mode, both);
}
```

9. We can then use the same process until we've converted all the animation classes within `magic.less`.

At this point, we will have a half-converted CSS file — this will work perfectly well. However, we can use the same principles to convert the `keyframes.less` file at the same time — this is something that I will leave for you to work out! Hint: there's an example in the code download, if you really get stuck…

Using vendor prefixes – a warning

Having said this, there is one important point we must visit: we've spent all this time converting the files, yet we're potentially following a bad practice! Huh — how does this work, I hear you ask?

Well, some of you will argue that this process is an antipattern — a practice that should not be followed, as it can make the CSS more verbose than it really needs to be.

 For more information on anti-patterns, you can refer to Mark Daggett's useful article that is worth a read and is available at `http://markdaggett.com/blog/2011/12/04/css-anti-patterns/`.

We can add to this, as vendor prefixes will come and go; moving them into one file may help reduce the amount of code we need to write, but it will assume that vendor prefixes remain the same for all the properties. This won't be the case — the trouble is, we can't remove any one of them until such time that none of the animation properties need it, and that is not likely to be for some time!

I've used the process here purely to illustrate how it can be done—it doesn't mean that it should be done. A better process is to use an Autoprefixer, such as Alejandro Beltrán's Autoprefixer, which is available at `https://github.com/ai/autoprefixer`. There is a plugin available for Autoprefixer to allow it to work in Sublime Text—this can be downloaded from `https://github.com/sindresorhus/sublime-autoprefixer`.

Okay, let's take a break from coding for a moment and move on. We've spent some time using Less to create our animations and converting some from CSS. There is one nagging question though, which I am sure you will be asking too: is using CSS really any better than using JavaScript, or is there more to it than what it first seems?

Using CSS or JavaScript

If you've spent time using JavaScript (and more likely, jQuery), then you will know that we can use it to produce some complex animations. Achieving the same results in CSS might be a little bit of an eye-opener for some, but they may ask: which is better? If you thought CSS, then you'd be right...and wrong! Let me explain.

Conventional wisdom has always said that CSS is better—after all, JavaScript and jQuery use custom animation handlers that will repeat code between 30 and 60 times a second. This puts more pressure on a browser than a browser just running pure CSS.

However, lots of people have argued in favor of either; there are clear arguments for or against using either technology in a site. For example, in a post for the CSS-Tricks site, Jack Doyle (the creator of the professional animation library GSAP), puts forth a detailed case on why using CSS3 animations isn't always the right way forward; CSS3 still has a long way to go to match the likes of Flash.

The developer, David Walsh, has written an equally useful article that also explains why there might be cases where we should use CSS or JavaScript and that limitations in the former might require use of the latter. However, to really turn the tables, head over to `http://css3.bradshawenterprises.com/blog/jquery-vs-css3-transitions/`; you can see a great demo that proves JavaScript libraries, such as jQuery, actually perform worse than CSS when they are used to animate lots of elements!

David's article is available at `http://davidwalsh.name/css-js-animation`; it is definitely worth a read!

There is no right or wrong answer; the only way to be sure is to test your animations using tools such as Chrome's Developer toolbar to gauge the impact on the browser. A good rule of thumb though is to use vanilla CSS for animations and 2D transformations. If, however, your animation involves complicated timeline-based effects or you are moving a lot of elements, then JavaScript will be a better choice (animations frequently need to use more code than JavaScript to create the same effects).

Only testing will tell whether you've made the right choice; start with seeing how much you can achieve in CSS, and fallback to using JavaScript if CSS can't handle your requirements or places too much demand on the browser to manage the effect efficiently.

 You can read the posting in full at `http://css-tricks.com/myth-busting-css-animations-vs-javascript/`.

Okay, let's move on; we've seen now why it is important to choose whether we need to use jQuery instead of using Less/CSS. Assuming that you are still using Less/CSS to provide some form of animation, there are some tips we can use to help improve the performance of these animations; so, let's take a look at those now.

Improving the animation's performance

Working with CSS animations can be very rewarding, but we must be careful of the performance—if not done with care, animations can lead to unnecessary demands on the browser or can drain the battery power if you are working on a mobile device!

Unfortunately, a number of factors exist, which can affect performance and over which we may not have any control:

- **Browser performance**: All browsers behave differently with CSS3 and JavaScript.

- **GPU performance**: Some browsers now offload animation and transition operations to the GPU, in which case, the speed/performance is limited by the GPU. If you're on an integrated Intel GPU, it's not likely to be very smooth compared with a discrete NVIDIA or AMD graphics card.

- **CPU performance**: The main CPU will be used if the browser doesn't offload to the GPU (and therefore, become the bottleneck).

- **The number of other tabs/windows opened in a browser**: Browsers often share processes across tabs, so other animations or CPU-consuming operations occurring in other tabs or browsers could create performance degradation.
- **The use of gradients or box-shadow properties in our CSS code**: This can cause big performance hits, so avoid using these when animating elements.

Currently, the best way to improve performance is to limit the number of things that are being animated or transitioned at the same time.

Forcing hardware acceleration for a CSS animation

All is not lost though—we can force browsers to trigger hardware acceleration in the desktop or mobile browser by the addition of a simple property, `transform: translateZ(0);`, in our code. This will hand over the rendering to the GPU, not the CPU.

As an example, if we have a class called `.animate`, it would look similar to this:

```
.accelarate {
  -webkit-transform: translateZ(0);
  -moz-transform: translateZ(0);
  -ms-transform: translateZ(0);
  -o-transform: translateZ(0);
  transform: translateZ(0);

  //Add other properties below this line...
  ...
}
```

Notice how we need to add the vendor prefixes for each browser? The `translateZ(0)` property is still experimental, so all the vendor prefixes are required to ensure full support. Browser support is good, but care needs to be taken, as overusing it can cause performance issues and battery draining.

A good test to see whether performance is being impacted is to use Chrome's **Timeline** and **Profiles** option in the **Developer tools** option. Do check out the article by Addy Osmani at `http://addyosmani.com/blog/performance-optimisation-with-timeline-profiles/`, where he talks about how to use development tools to gauge performance. It is 2-3 years old, and there have been some changes in how development tools work, but the principles are still valid.

Summary

Animating elements on a web page or a site is like crossing a fine line — one wrong foot can turn a site that looks stunning into a real dog's dinner of a mess that will turn off everyone who visits it! Throughout this chapter, we covered the basics of animation and saw how we can use Less to simplify the process. Before we move on to the next chapter, let's take a moment to recap what we learned.

We kicked off with a simple introduction to what makes a good animation before moving on to examine how a CSS animation works. We then explored the different types of animations before covering off the all-important browser support for the technology.

Next, we took a look at how we can simplify the creation of animation styles by reworking a simple animation demo to use Less. We then moved on to create a more real-world example in the form of a simple menu demo, which uses transitions to animate the drop-down elements. With the demo completed, we moved on to examine how we can use Less libraries to help with our animation styling, and saw that the principles from *Chapter 4, Working with Variables, Mixins, and Functions*, could easily be applied when developing animation styles. We covered a few examples of CSS animation libraries before taking a look at how we could convert one of them to its Less equivalent.

Before continuing, we discussed the importance of monitoring vendor prefixes and how some see the use of vendor mixins as an antipractice that should be discouraged. We then discussed how performance can be impacted by some factors that are outside our control, before taking a look at how we can enable hardware acceleration to improve performance.

Phew! What a tour! However, it's not over yet: in the final chapter of this book, we'll take a look at how you can contribute to and help extend the Less library. After all, it wouldn't be where it is today without our help…!

14
Extending and Contributing to Less

Throughout this book, we've covered an array of topics, from getting started with Less to using it in CMS systems or creating colors.

It's at this point we can say that the world is your oyster. Hopefully, this book has whetted your appetite sufficiently to go out and produce the next killer web application. However, I suspect some of you will say, "What if I want to alter Less itself?"

It's a valid question. After all, the ethos of many open source applications (of which Less is no exception) is to try to give back something to the project if it has been of help to you in your own. Thankfully, there are a number of ways in which you can contribute, from reporting issues and bugs to submitting patches and feature requests for future versions of Less.

Throughout this chapter, we'll go on a whirlwind tour of some of the information you need to know, in order to be able to contribute to the project. In this chapter, we will cover the following topics:

- Where to find Less repositories
- How to report bugs
- How to contribute code
- Testing
- Documentation

Want to know more? Let's get started...!

Locating the Less repositories

By now, we've spent a fair amount of time learning about Less and how it works. There will come a point when we might find that we have an issue with our code and need help.

With most open source applications or projects, access to the original source code will be available in some form; Less is no different. The source files for both the library and documentation are stored on GitHub in two different repositories; they are accessible from the top-right corner of the main Less website:

We can either access the GitHub repositories through these links, or directly via a URL:

- For the main documentation repository, go to `https://github.com/less/less-docs`.

- To log any issues with the Less documentation, go to `https://github.com/less/less-docs/issues`; you can also see any existing issues listed.

- You can find the main repository of interest at `https://github.com/less/less.js`. This is the Less.js repository for the source code for Less and to which any changes or updates will be merged into core as part of each release.

- If you have any issues you need to log, visit `https://github.com/less/less.js/issues`; there's a thriving community who will be able to offer advice and assistance in fixing the issues.

Now that we've seen where we can go for more assistance, let's turn the focus of our attention to what is arguably the most important step: logging our requests for help.

Finding and reporting issues in Less

Once you've started using Less, there will no doubt be occasions where you need some assistance. The Less team advises the best place to log such requests for help is on the popular Stack Overflow site, which is `http://www.stackoverflow.com`. If, however, you have an issue that relates to the documentation on the site, then this should be logged on the Less documentation area in GitHub at `https://github.com/less/less-docs`.

Any requests for assistance shouldn't be logged in the GitHub areas for Less; these should be kept for the purpose of logging and fixing bugs within the code. The Less Core team has released a set of guidelines to help with raising issues to ensure they stand the best chance of successful resolution:

- **Search for existing issues**: The team gets a lot of duplicate issues, so it is worth checking first to see if anyone has already reported the same issue and whether a fix has been posted for it.

- **Create an isolated and reproducible test case**: This helps to ensure that the issue is within the Less library; have a look at `http://css-tricks.com/reduced-test-cases/` for some tips on how to create such a test case.

- **Test with the latest version**: It is surprising, but a lot of issues are resolved by updating to the latest version of Less.

- **Include a live example**: You can use `http://www.less2css.org` to help create and share your isolated test cases.

- **Share information**: Share as much information as possible about the nature of your issue. There are some useful snippets of information that will help:

    ° Mention the operating system and version

    ° Describe how you use Less

    ° If you use it in the browser, include the browser and version and the version of Less.js you're using

    ° Include whether you are using the command line (`lessc`) or an external tool

    ° Try to include steps to reproduce the bug

If you have a solution or suggestion on how to fix the bug you're reporting, include it, or make a pull request—don't assume the maintainers know how to fix it just because you do!

If, however, you find that the problem is more than just an issue with how to do something and that there is clearly a fault in the library itself, then you might find a bug report needs to be filed. Let's take a look at how to achieve this within GitHub.

Reporting bugs in the library

No, this isn't an excuse to go swatting every insect you find (pardon the pun), but an opportunity to ask for help if you come across an issue or bug that you find in Less.

The Less team welcome any reports of bugs, which once fixed can help improve the code; the following guidelines are worth noting:

- **Use the GitHub issue search facility**: Check whether the issue has already been reported by others; it is not worth duplicating the effort, but you might like to add your voice to the existing issue log to help prioritize the issue.

- **Check whether the issue has been fixed**: Try to reproduce it using the latest master or development branch downloads, which are usually available in the repository.

- **Isolate the problem**: Create a reduced test case and a live example; Chris Coyier has a useful article at `http://css-tricks.com/reduced-test-cases/` on how to produce such a test case.

The key to a good report is providing enough information for others to work on, without going overboard. It's not easy to get the right balance. This will come with more experience over time. However, you can help others by providing key details, such as:

- What is your environment? Is the problem limited to one browser, or does it surface in different browsers?

- What are the steps to reproduce the issue, and are they consistent?

- What do you expect to see as the outcome?

All of these details (and more) will help people to fix any bugs you find; to help with presenting the right information, there is a useful format you can follow:

Short and descriptive example bug report title

Please provide a summary of the issue and the browser/OS environment in which it occurs. If suitable, include the steps required to reproduce the bug.

- This is the first step.
- This is the second step.
- Further steps and so on.

The `<url>` is a link pointing to a reduced test case, showing the issue.

Any other information you want to share that is relevant to the issue being reported. This might include the lines of code that you have identified as causing the bug and potential solutions (and your opinions on their merits).

If, however, you want to help fix some bugs, then there is a process you need to follow. Let's change tack and have a look at how you can help contribute to the library.

Contributing to the Less source

Once you've become more accustomed to working with Less, you might feel a desire to contribute something back to the project. After all, the project owners spent countless hours developing the library, so any help is always welcome.

There are two ways you can help with contributing to the project: submitting feature requests and creating pull requests. Before we look at them, there is a small bit of work that is worth completing first, that is, install Node.js and Grunt.

Getting prepared

If you spend any time in developing code submissions for Less, then it is essential to install two tools; these are key to the whole development process for Less:

- **Node.js**: This can be downloaded from `http://www.nodejs.org` for your platform. At the time of writing this, the latest Version is 0.10.28.
- **Grunt**: This is available from `http://www.gruntjs.com`; at the time of writing this, it is at Version 0.4.5.

Next, we need to install Grunt. In a command prompt, enter the following and press *Enter*:

```
npm install -g grunt-cli
```

Now that we have our base environment set up, let's look at each method of contributing in turn, beginning with feature requests.

Submitting feature requests

Feature requests are always welcome. It is recommended that you take a moment to find out whether your idea is something that fits in with the vision of the project.

It's down to you to provide a sufficiently strong case for a new feature, based on as much detail as you can provide. Bear in mind that as projects are open source, you might find it preferable to simply fork the existing project before adding your new feature.

It is worth checking to see whether someone hasn't already suggested it. The team is always receptive to new ideas, but won't add functionality unless there is a good reason to do so. It might be preferable to implement your new feature in a third-party build system such as assemble-less, rather than implementing it within the core library itself.

Creating pull requests

If you've submitted a feature request that has gained traction and is likely to be committed to source, the team always encourages submission of a pull request where possible.

The team asks that if you create a pull request, it should stay within scope and avoid containing unrelated commits. I always try to follow the principle of one change per commit, which makes it easier to remove if there is a need to do so at a later date. If your pull request is set to implement significant changes, such as porting to a new language, then it is worth asking the developers first; it otherwise means that you could spend a lot of time developing new functionality that the developers might not want to merge into the main library.

If your pull request solves an existing issue but using a different (or better) solution, then it should be raised as a new issue, not as a replacement for an existing pull request. Any pull request that is submitted should be accompanied with a set of tests. We will cover this in more detail later in this chapter.

No matter what the reason is for developing a pull request though, you should follow some simple standards that have been set to ensure consistency within the submitted code:

- Always use spaces, never tabs
- End lines with semicolons
- Loosely aim towards jsHint standards

Any patch that is submitted will be licensed by the Less team under the Apache License.

 To help guide you through a consistent process to submit via Git, it is worth taking a look at the process outlined by Nicolas Gallagher, which is available at `https://github.com/necolas/issue-guidelines/blob/master/CONTRIBUTING.md`.

Using GUIs with Git

It's worth noting that using Git requires a certain level of skill. It is often easier using a GUI-based client, instead of working with the command line; there is a list of some of the popular clients available at `http://git-scm.com/downloads/guis`. My personal favorite is GitHub for Windows, available at `http://windows.github.com`.

 If you're interested in learning more about Git, then it's worth taking a look at *Git: Version Control for Everyone*, *Ravishankar Somasundaram*, published by *Packt Publishing*, or go to the website at `http://git-scm.com/book`.

Testing your submissions

A key part of submitting any changes to a functionality is to ensure that your code has been through a linting process, to analyze it for any potential errors. There are a number of ways to do this, but the preferred one is to use Grunt; packages have been produced to help with this process.

A good example of this is the Less Lint Grunt plugin, by Jacob Gable, which is available at `https://github.com/jgable/grunt-lesslint`. For a more in-depth option, you can check out the article by Tom Loudon of Axisto Media, at `https://coderwall.com/p/g1kqzg`, which details a process to add pre-Git commit linting with Grunt.

Once your code has been linted, then it needs to be tested. To do this, we need to do the following (assuming you have installed Node and Grunt as detailed in the *Getting prepared* section earlier in this chapter):

1. Clone the Less repository. This can either be done via the command line, or using a GUI such as GitHub for Windows.

2. Open a command prompt and then change the folder to the location where you've stored your local copy of the Less repository.

3. At the command prompt, enter `npm install` to install Less' npm dependencies.

4. When completed, enter the following command at the prompt:

```
grunt browsertest-server
```

You can now visit `http://localhost:8088/tmp/browser/` to view the test runner pages. You should also be able to enter `lessc <name of file>.less` at the prompt; this will be compiled by Less and rendered on screen; this will allow you to compare it with your local copy of compiled CSS to see if it produces the same results.

Contributing to the Less documentation

So far, we've seen how you can make a contribution to the Less library, either as reporting issues or bugs, or by contributing suggestions and code for new features. What happens if your issue lies with the documentation?

The Less team maintains the source documentation within GitHub; it's here that you can find the source for all documentation published at `http://www.lesscss.org`, along with options to raise issues if you find any, or submit pull requests to help maintain the documentation. All of the documentation content can be found in the `./content` directory:

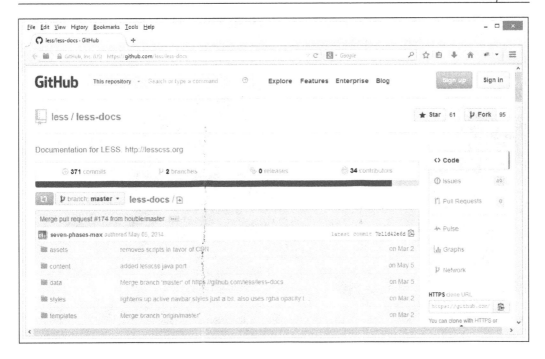

 To get a feel for how Less works, it's worth taking a look at the Less schematic diagram, which is available at `http://www.gliffy.com/go/publish/4784259`.

Installing the documentation locally

To get started with updating the documentation, we need to build a local copy on our own PC. This requires installing Assemble (`http://assemble.io/`), by performing the following steps:

1. Browse to the GitHub area for the Less documentation, which is at `https://github.com/less/less-docs`, and then click on **Download ZIP** to get the latest version of the Less documentation.

2. Create a folder on your PC. We will assume it has been called `lessdocs` for the purpose of this exercise; extract the contents of the archive file into this folder.

3. Bring up a command prompt, and change the current location to the `lessdocs` folder.

4. At the prompt, enter `npm install` to install Assemble and then wait for it to complete its process:

```
npm http GET  https://registry.npmjs.org/matchdep/-/matchdep-0.1.2.tgz
npm http 200  https://registry.npmjs.org/matchdep/-/matchdep-0.1.2.tgz
npm http GET  https://registry.npmjs.org/isarray/0.0.1
npm http GET  https://registry.npmjs.org/string_decoder
npm http GET  https://registry.npmjs.org/argparse
npm http GET  https://registry.npmjs.org/esprima
npm http 200  https://registry.npmjs.org/string_decoder
npm http GET  https://registry.npmjs.org/string_decoder/-/string_decoder-0.10.25-
1.tgz
npm http 304  https://registry.npmjs.org/argparse
npm http 304  https://registry.npmjs.org/esprima
npm http 200  https://registry.npmjs.org/isarray/0.0.1
npm http GET  https://registry.npmjs.org/isarray/-/isarray-0.0.1.tgz
npm http 200  https://registry.npmjs.org/string_decoder/-/string_decoder-0.10.25-
1.tgz
npm http 200  https://registry.npmjs.org/isarray/-/isarray-0.0.1.tgz
npm http GET  https://registry.npmjs.org/handlebars-helpers
npm http 200  https://registry.npmjs.org/handlebars-helpers
npm http GET  https://registry.npmjs.org/handlebars-helpers/-/handlebars-helpers-
0.5.5.tgz
npm http 200  https://registry.npmjs.org/handlebars-helpers/-/handlebars-helpers-
0.5.5.tgz
npm http GET  https://registry.npmjs.org/underscore
npm http 200  https://registry.npmjs.org/underscore
```

5. Once completed, enter this command to build the documentation:

```
node data/utils/pkg && grunt
```

When this has finished, you will be able to view the documentation offline and use it to submit pull requests into GitHub for consideration by the Less team.

Working to coding guidelines

Now that we have a copy of the documentation installed locally, we're ready to start contributing! However, before we do so, there are some guidelines that are worth noting and it will help make the documentation consistent, readable, and maintainable. Let's take a brief look at these standards in more detail, beginning with markdown standards:

- Use # for titles, not underlines. Underlines are not semantic, aren't as flexible, and aren't always highlighted properly in code highlighters.
- Always add a space between # and the heading.
- Wrap the inline code with a single backtick, or blocks of code with three backticks (code fences).

- With code blocks, always use the correct language after the first code fence. Although GitHub does not highlight Less, our documentation is more likely to show up in GitHub's and Google's search results when the correct language is used. For example, use ```less for Less and ```css for CSS.

A similar set of guidelines exist for maintaining standards in Less code; they are reproduced in full by browsing to the CONTRIBUTING.md page, which is listed in the main index at https://github.com/less/less-docs; the main points of note relate to proper spacing, use of multiple line formatting, and correct use of quotes.

 It is worth taking a look at the guidelines for reporting issues, bugs, and feature requests, which are based on a generic set created by Nicolas Gallagher, for any GitHub project; you can view the original set at https://github.com/necolas/issue-guidelines/blob/master/CONTRIBUTING.md.

If you follow these guidelines, it will help maintain a consistent, manageable set of documentation relating to Less.

Summary

We covered a lot of content throughout our journey in learning Less, finishing with a look at how you can give back to the project in the form of reporting issues and bugs, or submitting code to help fix or improve the existing functionality within the library.

We kicked off this chapter with a look at how to access the two source repositories for Less. We also covered where you can log issues and bugs within the GitHub issue logs for the source code and documentation.

We moved onto looking at the guidelines that should be followed when submitting feature or pull requests and took a quick look at how any code that is submitted should be tested against the Less tests and linted to ensure quality of code is maintained and any errors have been fixed.

We then examined how you can contribute to the documentation by reporting issues or suggestions for improvements. We covered the need to download and install a local copy of the documentation, before looking at the standards that need to be followed to ensure that the quality of document is maintained for the Less project.

It's at this point that we've come to the end of the book. I sincerely hope you've enjoyed our journey through learning how to use Less as much as I have and that it is of some help to you in your future projects.

Color Functions in Less

The Less library includes a number of color functions that we can use to manipulate colors within our site—this appendix lists the details of each function, within the four groups of defining color formats, channeling colors, performing color operations, and blending colors.

Defining color formats

The following is a list of the color functions that handle the color formats within Less:

Function	Purpose of the function	Example value
rgb	Creates an opaque color object from the decimal red, green, and blue (RGB) values	rgb(90, 129, 32)
rgba	Creates a transparent color object from the decimal red, green, blue, and alpha (RGBA) values	rgba(90, 129, 32, 0.5)
argb	Creates a hex representation of a color in the #AARRGGBB format (not #RRGGBBAA!)	argb(rgba(90, 23, 148, 0.5));
hsl	Creates an opaque color object from the hue, saturation, and lightness (HSL) values	hsl(90, 100%, 50%)
hsla	Creates a transparent color object from the hue, saturation, lightness, and alpha (HSLA) values	hsl(90, 100%, 50%, 0.5)
hsv	Creates an opaque color object from the hue, saturation, and value (HSV) values	hsv(90, 100%, 50%)

For more information, read the documentation on the main Less site at `http://lesscss.org/functions/#color-definition`. I've also created a CodePen that shows these effects in action — this is available at `http://codepen.io/alibby251/pen/horqx`.

Channeling colors using Less

The following is a list of the functions that allow us to channel colors when using Less:

Function	Purpose of the function	Example value
hue	Extracts the hue channel of a color object in the HSL color space	hue(hsl(90, 100%, 50%))
saturation	Extracts the saturation channel of a color object in the HSL color space	saturation(hsl(90, 100%, 50%))
lightness	Extracts the lightness channel of a color object in the HSL color space	lightness(hsl(90, 100%, 50%))
hsvhue	Extracts the hue channel of a color object in the HSV color space	hsvhue(hsv(90, 100%, 50%))
hsvsaturation	Extracts the saturation channel of a color object in the HSV color space	hsvsaturation(hsv(90, 100%, 50%))
hsvvalue	Extracts the value channel of a color object in the HSV color space	hsvvalue(hsv(90, 100%, 50%))
red	Extracts the red channel of a color object	red(rgb(10, 20, 30))
green	Extracts the green channel of a color object	green(rgb(10, 20, 30))
blue	Extracts the blue channel of a color object	blue(rgb(10, 20, 30))
alpha	Extracts the alpha channel of a color object	alpha(rgba(10, 20, 30, 0.5))
luma	Calculates the luma (perceptual brightness) of a color object	luma(rgb(100, 200, 30))
luminance	Calculates the value of the luma without gamma correction	luminance(rgb(100, 200, 30))

For more information, read the documentation on the main Less site at `http://lesscss.org/functions/#color-channel`.

Operating on colors

The following is a list of the operation functions that can be applied to the Less code:

Function	Purpose of the function	Example value
saturate	Increases the saturation of a color in the HSL color space by an absolute amount.	saturate(hsl(0, 59.4%, 40.6%), 20%);
desaturate	Decreases the saturation of a color in the HSL color space by an absolute amount.	desaturate(hsl(0, 59.4%, 40.6%), 20%);
lighten	Increases the lightness of a color in the HSL color space by an absolute amount.	lighten(hsl(0, 59.4%, 40.6%), 20%);
darken	Decreases the lightness of a color in the HSL color space by an absolute amount.	darken(hsl(0, 59.4%, 40.6%), 20%);
fadein	Decreases the transparency (or increases the opacity) of a color, making it more opaque.	fadein(hsl(0, 59.4%, 40.6%), 20%);
fadeout	Increases the transparency (or decreases the opacity) of a color, making it less opaque.	fadeout(hsl(0, 59.4%, 40.6%), 20%);
fade	Sets the absolute transparency of a color. It can be applied to colors irrespective of whether they already have an opacity value or not.	fade(hsl(0, 59.4%, 40.6%), 20%);

For more information, read the documentation on the main Less site at `http://lesscss.org/functions/#color-operations`. I've also created a CodePen that shows these effects in action—this is available at `http://codepen.io/alibby251/pen/KGltj`.

Color blending

Our final group of functions handle the blending of colors within Less:

Function	Purpose of the function	Example value
`multiply`	Multiplies two colors.	`multiply(#9ec1ef, #091d37);`
`screen`	Does the opposite of `multiply`. The result is a brighter color.	`screen (#9ec1ef, #091d37);`
`overlay`	Combines the effects of both `multiply` and `screen`. Conditionally makes light channels lighter and dark channels darker.	`overlay (#9ec1ef, #091d37);`
`softlight`	Similar to `overlay` but avoids pure black resulting in pure black, and pure white resulting in pure white.	`softlight (#9ec1ef, #091d37);`
`hardlight`	The same as `overlay` but with the color roles reversed.	`hardlight (#9ec1ef, #091d37);`
`difference`	Subtracts the second color from the first color on a channel-by-channel basis.	`difference (#9ec1ef, #091d37);`
`exclusion`	A similar effect to `difference` but with lower contrast.	`exclusion (#9ec1ef, #091d37);`
`average`	Computes the average of two colors on a per-channel (RGB) basis.	`average (#9ec1ef, #091d37);`
`negation`	Does the opposite of `difference`.	`negation (#9ec1ef, #091d37);`

For more information, read the documentation on the main Less site at `http://lesscss.org/functions/#color-blending`. I've also created a CodePen that shows these effects in action—this is available at `http://codepen.io/alibby251/pen/IKqEk`.

Index

Symbols

3L
URL 96, 133
@basewidth variable 99
@font-face
font, embedding into demo 151, 152
font files, downloading 150
using 150
!important keyword
URL 88
using 87
.keyframes mixin 282
@mainwidth variable 99
@media keyword, Less
Less file, examining 160, 161
media query, creating 160
working with 159

A

accessibility 10
Adobe AIR
URL 34
Adobe Kuler
about 51
URL 51
alert boxes
creating 255-257
all keyword
used, for extending styles 112-115
alpha function 306
Animate.css
URL 286

animated menus
creating 282-285
Animate.less
URL 286
animation markup
simplifying, with Less 280-282
animations
about 274
and transitions, differences 275
creating 20, 21
supporting, in browsers 280
animation types
about 276
animations, supporting in browsers 280
content, animating 276, 277
elements, transforming 278, 279
elements, transitioning 277, 278
anti-patterns
URL 288
argb function 305
arithmetic operators
working with 251
Assemble
URL 301
attributes, CSS3 animations
URL 277, 278
attributes, CSS3 transforms
URL 279
Autoprefixer
URL 289
autotext function 12
average function 308

B

basic page
building 181-183
Bitbucket
URL 134
bitmap media types
aspect-ratio 171
device-aspect-ratio 171
orientation 171
resolution 171
blending modes
URL 260
blocks
overcoming, on site access 269
blue function 306
Bootstrap
configuring, for site 219, 220
Internet Explorer 8, using 220, 221
used, for building realistic site 221-223
Bootstrap CSS
compiling, with JavaScript 224
Bootstrap library
downloading 218, 219
URL 243
URL, for downloading 218, 237
Bootstrap's Blog Theme
URL 240
Bootstrap's Less file structure
dissecting 217
Bootstrap's mixins
about 224-226
components 228
core CSS styles 227
core variables and mixins 227
dissecting 226
reset and dependencies 227
URL 226
utility classes 228
Bootstrap's theme mixins
components 230
dissecting 229
layout 231
skins 230
utilities 229
Bootstrap usage
workflow, developing for 237, 238

Bower
URL 57
used, for installing Less 57-59
Bower package
using 60
Brad Frost
URL 180
browser performance 290
browsers
animations, supporting in 280
bugs
reporting, in library 296, 297
business card
creating 106
buttons.less mixin file
URL 235

C

calculations
moving, to mixin 99, 100
CDN
URL 56
used, for installing Less on client side 56
changes
identifying 137-139
making 139
child theme
creating 195, 196
features 205
Chrome
Less, debugging in 46
ClearLess
URL 96, 133
client criteria
setting 168, 169
Coda
about 28
URL 28
code
compiling 68
fixing 242-245
reusing, across multiple projects 21, 22
solution, exploring 245
standalone compiler, using 68-70
code bloat
avoiding 123-125

---

development process, Less
  about 297, 298
  Grunt 297
  Node.js 297
device-pixel-ratio
  URL 189
difference function 308
different weights
  handling 157, 158
div tag 67
documentation repository
  URL 294
download
  customizing 231-235
  values, modifying 235-237

E

editor
  Coda 28
  Codekit 28
  Less syntax support, adding 29-31
  Notepad++ 28
  selecting 28
  Sublime Text 28
  Sublime Text 2, installing 28, 29
  URL 28
Effeckt.css
  URL 286
elements
  transforming 278, 279
  transitioning 277, 278
em value 156
environment
  preparing 195
EOT, font format 152
Eric
  URL 159
error dialog
  URL 255
Etch
  URL 262
example, media queries
  creating 173-177
examples, contrast levels
  URL 270
exclusion function 308

expand attribute 40
extend
  all keyword, using 112
  URL 110
  used, for creating information
      alerts 110, 111
  used, for inheriting styles 109
  used, for overriding styles 109
extend keyword
  highlights 114, 115
external libraries
  using 96

F

factors, animation performance
  browser performance 290
  CPU performance 290
  GPU performance 290
  number of other tabs/windows opened,
      in browser 291
  use of gradients or box-shadow properties,
      in CSS code 291
fade function 257, 307
fadein function 307
fadeout function 307
feature requests
  submitting 298
features, media types
  all 170
  braille 170
  embossed 170
  handheld 170
  print 170
  projection 170
  screen 170
  speech 170
  tty 170
  tv 170
finished article
  viewing 145
Firebug
  URL 45
Firefox
  used, for debugging Less 45, 46
FireLESS
  URL 46

Prefixr 51
SpritePad 51
WinLess Online 51
transitions
and animations, differences 275
Trüf
URL 262
TTF, font format 152

U

utilities, Bootstrap's theme mixins
about 229
hide-text.less mixin file 229
image.less mixin file 229
labels.less mixin file 229
opacity.less mixin file 229
reset-filter.less mixin file 229
resize.less mixin file 229
responsive-visibility.less mixin file 229
size.less mixin file 229
tab-focus.less mixin file 229
text-emphasis.less mixin file 229
text-overflow.less mixin file 229
utility classes, Bootstrap's mixins 228

V

validation 10
values
calculating, operations used 66
generating 18
variables
changing 63, 64
creating, for colors 141
creating, for fonts 140
discovering, in Less 78
lazy loading, in Less 118-121
redundancy, reducing with 16
reusable blocks of code, creating 17
syntax 16
used, for calculating sizes 155-157
working with 62
variables.less
URL 226

variables, Less
loading 81, 82
Polaroid images, creating 79-81
scope, setting 81, 82
vendor prefixes
about 19
using 288, 289
ViewPort Resizer
URL 180
viewport tag
reference link 223
visual and tactile media
color 171
color-index 171
device-height 171
device-width 171
grid 171
height 171
monochrome 171
width 171

W

W3C CSS Validator
URL 128
W3C standard
working with 269
WAMP
URL 188, 195
WampServer
installing 47-50
URL 47
warning dialog
URL 255
Watch mode 39, 71-74
WCAG
about 270
key factors 270
URL 270
WCAG standard
working with 269
web form
creating 83, 84

Thank you for buying
Learning Less.js

About Packt Publishing

Packt, pronounced 'packed', published its first book "*Mastering phpMyAdmin for Effective MySQL Management*" in April 2004 and subsequently continued to specialize in publishing highly focused books on specific technologies and solutions.

Our books and publications share the experiences of your fellow IT professionals in adapting and customizing today's systems, applications, and frameworks. Our solution based books give you the knowledge and power to customize the software and technologies you're using to get the job done. Packt books are more specific and less general than the IT books you have seen in the past. Our unique business model allows us to bring you more focused information, giving you more of what you need to know, and less of what you don't.

Packt is a modern, yet unique publishing company, which focuses on producing quality, cutting-edge books for communities of developers, administrators, and newbies alike. For more information, please visit our website: www.packtpub.com.

About Packt Open Source

In 2010, Packt launched two new brands, Packt Open Source and Packt Enterprise, in order to continue its focus on specialization. This book is part of the Packt Open Source brand, home to books published on software built around Open Source licenses, and offering information to anybody from advanced developers to budding web designers. The Open Source brand also runs Packt's Open Source Royalty Scheme, by which Packt gives a royalty to each Open Source project about whose software a book is sold.

Writing for Packt

We welcome all inquiries from people who are interested in authoring. Book proposals should be sent to author@packtpub.com. If your book idea is still at an early stage and you would like to discuss it first before writing a formal book proposal, contact us; one of our commissioning editors will get in touch with you.

We're not just looking for published authors; if you have strong technical skills but no writing experience, our experienced editors can help you develop a writing career, or simply get some additional reward for your expertise.

Less Web Development Essentials

ISBN: 978-1-78398-146-5   Paperback: 202 pages

Use CSS preprocessing to streamline the development and maintenance of your web applications

1. Produce clear, concise, and well-constructed code that compiles into standard compliant CSS.

2. Explore the core attributes of Less and learn how to integrate them into your site.

3. Optimize Twitter's Bootstrap to efficiently develop web apps and sites.

Bootstrap Site Blueprints

ISBN: 978-1-78216-452-4   Paperback: 304 pages

Design mobile-first responsive websites with Bootstrap 3

1. Learn the inner workings of Bootstrap 3 and create web applications with ease.

2. Quickly customize your designs working directly with Bootstrap's LESS files.

3. Leverage Bootstrap's excellent JavaScript plugins.

Please check **www.PacktPub.com** for information on our titles

Extending Bootstrap

ISBN: 978-1-78216-841-6   Paperback: 88 pages

Understand Bootstrap and unlock its secrets to build a truly customized project!

1. Learn to use themes to improve your user experience.

2. Improve your workflow with Less and Grunt.js.

3. Get to know the most useful third-party Bootstrap plugins.

RESS Essentials

ISBN: 978-1-84969-694-4   Paperback: 134 pages

A practical introduction to programming responsive websites using an innovative methodology in web design and development

1. Easy-to-follow tutorials on implementing RESS application patterns.

2. Information flow diagrams which will help you understand various RESS architectures with ease.

3. Perform browser feature detection and store this information on server side.

Please check **www.PacktPub.com** for information on our titles

www.ingramcontent.com/pod-product-compliance
Lightning Source LLC
Chambersburg PA
CBHW062058050326
40690CB00016B/3131